The Thinking Revolutionary

ALSO BY RALPH LERNER

Medieval Political Philosophy: A Sourcebook
  (editor, with Muhsin Mahdi)

Averroes on Plato's "Republic" (translator)

The Founders' Constitution
  (editor, with Philip B. Kurland)

RALPH LERNER

The Thinking Revolutionary

PRINCIPLE AND PRACTICE
IN THE NEW REPUBLIC

Cornell University Press | Ithaca and London

First published 1987 by Cornell University Press.
Second printing 1988.
First published, Cornell Paperbacks, 1988.

International Standard Book Number 0-8014-2007-5 (cloth)
International Standard Book Number 0-8014-9532-6 (paper)
Library of Congress Catalog Card Number 87-5287
Printed in the United States of America
Librarians: Library of Congress cataloging information
appears on the last page of the book.

The paper in this book is acid-free and meets the guidelines for
permanence and durability of the Committee on Production Guidelines
for Book Longevity of the Council on Library Resources.

TO CAROL

CONTENTS

Contents

PREFACE

THESE STUDIES of early American political thought and practice could, with equal accuracy and fewer words, be titled "Essays Out of Tocqueville," for they all spring from my long reflection on Alexis de Tocqueville's analysis of our modern democratic age. But where he thought he detected in the America of the 1830s the very face of the future, I have been prompted to find in his analysis the features of an earlier revolutionary design. Recovering that now often slighted intention is the unifying theme and purpose of this book.

This project might appear, at first glance, to be the least needful task imaginable. After all, no one contests that there was an American Revolution or indeed that its leading actors were informed by a high degree of self-consciousness. Yet a case can be made for looking again—and deeper—into the matter. The efforts of successive generations of historians in this century to make sense of the Revolutionary epoch have met not even their own expectations, let alone those of others not sharing their enthusiasms or convictions. For in the course of accounting for the words and deeds of that age, those scholars have left its most prominent speakers and actors strangely bereft of revolutionary intent, or conviction, or clarity, or significance. The truth, that words and deeds may entail consequences beyond the agent's imagining, has been converted into an untruth, that actual consequences owe little to the studied intentions of the thoughtful. As a result, the events of the age and the stances of its leading figures now are commonly viewed through the refracting medium of everyday life, in which confusion, ignorance, shortsightedness, mean calculation, and downright foolishness are more conspicuous than informed and weighty deliberation. One might say that such efforts to explain high human actions by recurring to the acts and beliefs of the many (for the thoughtful, as distinguished from the influential, are always few) tell more about the explainer than about the events themselves.

This volume's argument proceeds otherwise. It attempts to show that ideas matter because certain individuals act on them. My contention is that the founding fathers (the individuals in question) thought for themselves and then deployed the results of that thinking coolly to reason with the reasonable, to persuade the persuadable, and to impress the impressionable.

Demonstrative proof, it must be confessed, is hard to come by. Although I have striven to marshal the evidence for my hypothesis, I am under no illusion that there is a syllogism in the lot. These are essays in persuasion, attempts to offer a better way of looking at the American founding. They seek to reopen a question in the reader's mind: How might we best understand the extraordinary efforts that attended the creation of the American republics—by deflating high public discourse and reducing it to the common coinage of ordinary political dealings, or by taking at face value (to begin with at least) the lofty claims and aspirations of those who sought to reshape and mold social thought and action?

Put in these terms, the dichotomy seems simplistic. Few would deny that hard political dealing and in-fighting marked the times and the actors. Nor have most scholars brushed aside the significance of a powerful rhetoric in enlisting allegiance and energizing efforts. But in acknowledging this much, recent students of the American past still have not faced up to what, from our present-day point of view, is perhaps the most incredible assumption of that Revolutionary generation: that their highest and deepest motives derived from their reasoned understanding. It seemed to those founders a matter of course that their moral imperatives and political programs would emerge from their reasoning.

Needless to say, some were more resourceful, better reasoners, or freer by circumstance from passion and necessity than others. As a result, conclusions differed and controversy was rife—as can especially be the case among people who share some premises but cannot get their fellows to draw the obvious and proper inferences (or cannot get them to act on those inferences *at once*). Most of the divisions of mind and policy that beset the founding generation were over different interpretations of what was held in common. This is manifestly the case in the controversies over the proper place of the states in a large union and over the correct way of securing a representative government responsive to majority will yet respectful of minority rights. Or take the question of Negro chattel slavery; the pathos of it for most of the southern founders is simply inconceivable were they not also dedicated to the premises of 1776.

If we feel pressed to look again at these revolutionary premises, it may be because three distinct considerations lead to the same conclusion. First, they are the conscious articulations of extraordinarily thoughtful men and, as such, deserve attention. Second, they are our own; popularly accepted (and hence also rendered humdrum and commonplace), these premises have shaped all succeeding generations of Americans, the present one emphatically included. In studying and trying thus to detrivialize, to recapture and be recaptured by, the premises of the founders, we acquire not only understanding but self-understanding. Third, the founders themselves attached such weight to these premises. Here was no parochial catechism addressed to some small band of sectarians; rather, to use Abraham Lincoln's later characterization, these were the very definitions and axioms of free society. Reaching beyond the necessities of the moment, the author of the Declaration of Independence had improved on the revolutionary moment by fixing, once and for all, "an abstract truth, applicable to all men and all times." That sense of universal relevance and hope invites, even demands, scrutiny.

In the seven studies that make up this book, I look at the thinking revolutionary and his legacy from differing points of view, yet in each I focus on the themes of historical judgment and political rhetoric. My concern with judgment encompasses alike the way the revolutionary viewed his past, his preoccupation with how his own actions would be viewed in time, and finally, our contemporary efforts to assess the intentions and behavior of that receding age. Political rhetoric, too, has more than one face in these essays. It refers not only to the rhetoric of the hustings and the broadside but to those master practitioners' understanding of the place and limits of reasoned and persuasive speech. In this last connection, the accounts by which later historians hope to persuade their contemporaries of the meaning of earlier people's thoughts and deeds may themselves be considered as examples of political rhetoric.

This book takes as its point of departure the present state of scholarship, the stance adopted by many of today's most knowing and influential historians when they come to assess the significance of thought and thoughtfulness in political discourse and political action. It begins by inspecting that regiment of scholars who for the past quarter-century have traversed the historical landscape seeking to ferret out and account for the concerns of an earlier generation of American revolutionaries. Although these historians are a diverse lot, marching indeed to different drummers, they share some beliefs— sharply at odds with earlier modes—that make it useful to treat them *as* a group. In marshaling them here under one banner I mean neither to trick them out in one uniform nor to enlist them under false colors. And yet, just as a common staging area testifies to a unity behind diverse forces going their several ways, so too do these historians' shared assumptions bespeak a deeper level of agreement.

The Prologue, "Recovering the Revolution," reconnoiters that common ground. It tacitly questions the way interpretations original- ly intended to provoke thought (while overcoming earlier simplistic accounts) have themselves been reduced by rote to only another set of one-dimensional answers. It openly challenges these prevailing modes of scholarly analysis by examining anew how the principles and acts of the founding generation ought to be studied. Faulting the modern historians' reliance on ideology as an explanatory device, it holds, rather, that that concept makes us less eager and able to take the indispensable first step toward understanding historical figures, namely, viewing others as they saw themselves. To support that con- tention, it looks again at one of the most consistently misunderstood among the founders, John Adams, and then suggests a mode of analy- sis more respectful of the data and of their complexity.

Part One, "Securing the Republic," examines in detail some of the differing ways thinking revolutionaries sought to shape their public and render it fit for the new society they had in view. It was obvious to them that simply claiming a separate and equal station for an American "people" would not suffice. It would take more than a protracted war and adroit diplomacy at the treaty table to make that claim stick and to make that people one. Similarly, it was not enough to proclaim a republic; one had also to keep it. Although this high political task seemed clear enough, the same could not be said of the means. To be formed, a public must first be reached. The variety of ways the founders tried to reach their public bespeaks the intensity of their common concern and the distinctiveness of their several situa- tions and casts of mind. Three modes are examined here in turn.

In "Franklin, Spectator," I try to read the not-so-bared soul of America's clear-eyed master of reticence. Here I follow the lead suggested by Benjamin Vaughan's acute appraisal of Benjamin Franklin's *Autobiography* as a means of personal and political self-education. In detailing his life story, this founder was both mirroring and shaping "the manners and situation of *a rising* people." Here were lessons that all people everywhere might take to heart and in so doing promote both their domestic and their public happiness. Through his seductive narrative Franklin sought to redefine the field of ambition and thereby render a commercial republic safer and surer.

The reformation of opinion and character was no less an object of legislation. "Jefferson's Pulse of Republican Reformation" considers in detail the revision of revolutionary Virginia's laws that absorbed so much of the thought and energy of Thomas Jefferson, Edmund Pendleton, George Wythe, and, later, James Madison. Although this elaborate project was only partially and imperfectly adopted by the Virginia legislature, the plan as such discloses the coherence and anomalies attending efforts to translate a revolutionary design into the law of the land. Of special interest here is Jefferson's preoccupation with fostering those habits of thinking and acting which he held to be foundations of a self-governing polity.

A corresponding emphasis on basic beliefs and habits informs the discussion of "The Supreme Court as Republican Schoolmaster." The emancipation of mind and body, so earnestly desired by the revolutionaries, was not seen by the thinking ones among them as guaranteeing good results. Highly self-conscious opinion shaping seemed the order of the day. But where Franklin hoped to charm his readers into emulating the model of harnessed passion *he* projected, and where Jefferson looked to a structure of institutions and public encounters that would accustom individuals to acts of common effort and concern, the early national judiciary proceeded less artfully. In the early years, under the Judiciary Act of 1789, federal judges riding circuit felt themselves called upon to mold a public opinion supportive of the nationalizing aims of the new constitutional order (in some instances even going on to defend particular policies of the then-current administration). Looking beyond the imprudence and polemics that undid this practice, the essay considers the place and utility of a nonelective branch in a government wholly popular.

No reader of these early chapters can help noting the gap between the founders' high expectations and their often unyielding circumstances. In the next part, "The Burden of Color," that gap takes on the dimensions of a chasm. "Reds and Whites: Rights and Wrongs" considers early national Indian policy from the viewpoint of the white political leaders. Their hopes and principles, intricately intertwined and by no means simply harmonious, were repeatedly and sorely tried in ways that gratified only those who had few principles at all. If the result was that red and black Americans felt the full force of that policy's failure, it was by no means a burden limited to them. In "The Complexion of Tocqueville's American" I look at the shadow cast by color on the entire American regime and at the strengths and short-comings of the founders' brave experiment in self-governance.

The book closes with an attempt at giving a coherent account of the revolutionary design. Although I concede at the very outset of the chapter the hypothetical character of the collectivity being depicted, that admission is in no sense to be taken as a plea of nolo contendere. Few of the interesting questions in the interpretation of political intentions turn on unequivocal evidence; there is a reason why the "smoking gun" is most often found in fiction. Thus the assemblage of international thinkers in "Commerce and Character" ought to be seen as an invitation to ponder some evidence of a singular movement within modern enlightened thought. That peculiar brand of thought was at once radical in its eagerness to trace out the consequences of its premises and yet markedly politic in converting its theoretical insights into institutional arrangements.

This rare blend of boldness and caution marks the thinking revolutionary as noteworthy in his own right. Daring to reach for a universal truth, but content to let others be persuaded by the power of example, the thinking revolutionary blazed a narrow path between mindless self-absorption and quixotic futility. His ideals, he hoped, might help raise his followers' field of vision beyond the calculus of interest and appetite. At the same time, he accorded a new dignity to a broad range of ways in which individuals might pursue happiness. In so doing, he hoped to arm ordinary citizens against the pretensions of would-be tyrants. The highest claims to rule—wisdom or holiness or virtue—would no longer be the preserve of a monopolizing few or serve so readily to cloak the designs of the overbearing. In striking out on his new course, the thinking revolutionary was content to guard against the worst and to make room for the best. More than that he dared not claim. If his descendants aspired to more, he had at least left them well placed.

Three chapters in this book which first appeared elsewhere are reprinted here in somewhat different versions by permission of their original publishers.

Prologue: Published under the title "The Constitution of the Thinking Revolutionary," in *Beyond Confederation: Origins of the Constitution and American National Identity,* ed. Richard Beeman, Stephen Botein, and Edward C. Carter II, pp. 38–68. Copyright 1987 by The University of North Carolina Press. Published for the Institute of Early American History and Culture, Williamsburg.

Chapter 3: "The Supreme Court as Republican Schoolmaster," in 1967 *The Supreme Court Review,* ed. Philip B. Kurland, pp. 127–180. © 1967 by The University of Chicago. All rights reserved.

Chapter 4: "Reds and Whites: Rights and Wrongs," in *1971 The Supreme Court Review,* ed. Philip B. Kurland, pp. 201–240. © 1971 by The University of Chicago. All rights reserved.

Also, a version of Chapter 6 appeared as "Commerce and Character: The Anglo-American as New-Model Man," in the *William and Mary Quarterly* in 1979.

I am happy to acknowledge the help I have received from others in clarifying my thoughts and in reshaping my text the better to convey those thoughts. While he lived, Herbert J. Storing read drafts of all I was then writing on American themes and offered keen analysis, at once generous and unsparing, that helped me find my way. Two other former colleagues at the University of Chicago have continued to perform the offices of friendship with grace, honesty, and patience. Thomas S. Schrock has saved me and the reader from a greater number of insufficient arguments than I can own up to with propriety. Thanks to Marvin Meyers I have been, for close to thirty years, the beneficiary of an extended and felicitous postgraduate education in what it means to enter into the mind of the founders. By exemplifying through his quiet learning, style, and wit the kind of scholar-teacher Madison wished for Jefferson's new university, he has set the standard for the field of fellow inquirers.

Then there are debts of yet another kind, less readily tallied and already fully known to the two whose business they are. Where so much argues for silence, the simplest dedication may pass for eloquent tribute.

RALPH LERNER

Chicago, Illinois

The Thinking Revolutionary

Prologue:
Recovering the Revolution

An abstract word is like a box with a false bottom; you may put in what ideas you please and take them out again unobserved.
Alexis de Tocqueville

OUR RECURRENT urge to look again at our past—to pose new questions to it, to try making sense of what we have been and what we have become—is especially strong in this season of national anniversary. Yet, wanting more than ever to see into the past, more than ever our vision is obscured. We are assured and reassured by modern historians that our simpleminded desire to recover our past suffers from simplemindedness. Our efforts at self-understanding falter before barriers that seem quite beyond our powers to overcome.

Perhaps the greatest barrier to understanding consists not in the remoteness or intractability of the data but in the presuppositions and points of view we bring to our examination of the past or of the world. If the Progressive generation's historians "could scarcely have avoided the general intellectual climate of the first part of the twentieth century which regarded ideas as suspect," is it to be expected that we in our turn will be more successful in avoiding or overcoming our peculiar intellectual climate? (Wood).[1] Perhaps the most that can

---

1. Gordon S. Wood, "Rhetoric and Reality in the American Revolution," *William and Mary Quarterly*, 3d ser., 23 (1966):7; and "Conspiracy and the Paranoid Style: Causality and Deceit in the Eighteenth Century," *William and Mary Quarterly*, 3d ser., 39 (1982):402, 411.

be hoped for is an acute suspicion that we too are enmeshed in a net of meanings, intentions, and significations largely not of our making and largely beyond our control. This presumably holds at least as much for ourselves as for those whose "acts of thought and speech" we study. Realizing this, modern students will not deny that in their case, too, "there are (if that matters) ideological reasons" for adopting a particular approach to their subject. That hidden agenda "can be accepted and allowed for" without further ado (Pocock).[2]

The hard fundamental questions raised by this line of argument cannot all be dealt with here. To the extent that the argument presses us to become more properly modest in our assertions about the past and more interestedly open to its nuances and ambiguities, that is all to the good. But the proposition itself, that all thinking takes place within horizons beyond our ken and power, may be a peculiar manifestation of our late twentieth-century Western historical situation and intellectual climate. At the least, its standing as a universal principle of interpretation is uncertain. Convinced though we be of its applicability to us in our times and vis-à-vis our past, we cannot know that every eighteenth-century historical actor and thinker was comparably enmeshed in the patterns of the age. With as much reason as we have for denying it, a Benjamin Franklin may have held that there is a recoverable past, that the motives underlying public policies can be discerned and judged, and that the complexity of human affairs can yield to reasoned analysis and can even to some significant extent be altered by it. Knowing or believing that, such an individual would act on that premise and expect both his contemporaries and successors to understand him accordingly. Hence our premise of predetermined disbelief (however modestly phrased) may close rather than open the gate to understanding such historical actors.

Another barrier to understanding the past, less fundamental but equally formidable, is said to be the likelihood that the meanings of important concepts were hardly clear to the very people voicing them. This is a difficulty that may not be entirely solved by the injunction that a text or argument must be considered as "a meaningful item within a wider context of conventions and assumptions" (Skinner). The point here is that those who at any moment are using a language

2. J. G. A. Pocock, "Political Ideas as Historical Events: Political Philosophers as Historical Actors," in *Political Theory and Political Education,* ed. Melvin Richter, 155; and *"The Machiavellian Moment* Revisited: A Study in History and Ideology," *Journal of Modern History* 53 (1981):72.

according to those conventions and assumptions, whether as inheritors, transmitters, or innovators, are far from having perfect knowledge or perfect control of that language. Recognizing that "the historical agent is sometimes the language or thought-pattern which the author used, sometimes the author as modifier of the thought-pattern," contemporary interpreters deny themselves the complacent satisfactions of their predecessors (Pocock).[3] Lacking present-day insight into language, earlier historians failed to appreciate how the reshaping of "words and concepts . . . in the colonists' minds in the course of a decade of pounding controversy" propelled them "toward conclusions they could not themselves clearly perceive" (Bailyn). Accordingly, those earlier historians, like the people they studied, overestimated the power of proclaimed motives, exaggerated the importance of assigning individual responsibility, and altogether overlooked the realm "where the ideas operate, as it were, over the heads of the participants" rather than (one is tempted to add) in them. To put it bluntly, we can now see how "men become more the victims than the manipulators of their ideas." Recognizing this, we can appreciate that individuals are not as free as they (and earlier historians) assumed. "They no longer use ideas but are used by them, and they are forced to deal with their inherited collective culture on its terms." For today's "sophisticated historians" seeking to recover and understand that past, the task has become vastly extended and complicated (Wood).[4]

Driven by this new awareness, we are denied the pleasure of simple answers. To the questions, what happened? and why? we are compelled to confess from the outset either that we *cannot* know or that they *did not* know. On either premise we are no longer bound and fettered by that earlier generation's record. Insofar as previous historians did so confine themselves, they were voluntary prisoners to the simplicities in that record, and their attempts at narrative and explanation accordingly tended toward the simplistic. To do better we must look farther and deeper than that earlier generation possibly

3. Quentin Skinner, "Hermeneutics and the Role of History," *New Literary History* 7 (1975):216–221; Pocock, "Political Ideas as Historical Events," 147–148; "*Machiavellian Moment* Revisited," 51.

4. Bernard Bailyn, *The Ideological Origins of the American Revolution*, 161; Gordon S. Wood, "Rhetoric and Reality," 23; and "Intellectual History and the Social Sciences," in *New Directions in American Intellectual History*, ed. John Higham and Paul K. Conkin, 36; and "Conspiracy and the Paranoid Style," 408–409, 411, 441.

could. Happily, our higher and more distant vantage point enables us to penetrate a scene bewildering or opaque to all contemporaries. Our awareness of their "historicity" and ours frees us from their blinders (Pocock).⁵ To be sure, their verbal legacy remains a prime datum. But while those words must be quoted and used, the modern researcher is compelled to override the lines of argument they trace if there is to be any advance in understanding. Analysis must take an altogether new tack.

Putting Thought in Its Place

We are urged to become very careful listeners, attuned to an ideology that pervades any given historical situation even while or especially while escaping that generation's notice. To begin with, then, we must see that world as its inhabitants saw it. Because their specific situation in all its perplexing particularity filled their minds (Skinner), we must let it fill ours; we must try to immerse ourselves in that world, even naively, if we are to have any prospect of comprehending what happened there and why (Wood). But having done this, we dare not remain at rest. Only by reawakening our awareness of their entanglement in a place and time and way of thinking can we hope to transcend it. For "in tracing history in terms of contemporary self-understanding—which is what the history of ideology really amounts to—one is not playing a barren game of pitting one cause against another cause, or one factor against another factor; one is exploring the contemporary perception of possibilities and impossibilities, and the limitations of that perception" (Pocock).⁶

Thanks to the researches of anthropologists, sociologists, and others, we can now see that the explanations historical actors give for their actions and recommendations are but a part of the story, although worthy of becoming "objects for analysis in and for themselves, historical events in their own right" (Wood). All the more is such analysis called for if people act on their beliefs and on the

5. Pocock, "Political Ideas as Historical Events," 155; see also Quentin Skinner, "Meaning and Understanding in the History of Ideas," *History and Theory* 8 (1969):52–53.
6. Skinner, "Meaning and Understanding," 50; Wood, "Conspiracy and the Paranoid Style," 409, 441; J. G. A. Pocock, "1776: The Revolution against Parliament," in *Three British Revolutions: 1641, 1688, 1776*, ed. J. G. A. Pocock, 267–268.

meaning with which those beliefs invest the world about them. Studies emphasizing the unconscious origins of ideologies and their unreflective or mindless acceptance by a people in search of "a social-psychological crutch" have proved enormously persuasive to modern historians (Shalhope). With new conviction they see that "beliefs must be understood and taken seriously if men's behavior is to be fully explained" (Wood).7 We can know that those actors' ideas are important without inquiring too closely into their validity or even plausibility; it is enough that those actors believed in them.

This new regard for ideas or beliefs or ideologies (terms often used interchangeably) does not, however, carry over to the individuals voicing them. Singly, such figures count for little. Cumulatively, their sundry efforts "to mold and manipulate their inherited language, thoughts, and values in order to explain and justify new circumstances or behavior" may make a great difference. At a certain point conventions crack under "the manipulative pressures of many individuals," leading to a transformation of "the larger aggregate and deterministic world of cultural conventions and collective mentalities where ideas control men." Here, on this large and impersonal scale, ideas matter—but thoughts and thinkers hardly at all. For "the 'great thinkers' we honor" are only manipulators and clarifiers of those moments of transformation; their creations are quickly swallowed up in a process "that always transcends their particular intentions" (Wood).8 Perhaps one might say of such " 'great thinkers' " what Thoreau said in purporting to characterize the Constitution and governments of the Americans from the highest point of view: "Who shall say what they are, or that they are worth looking at or thinking of at all?"

We are adjured to remember that "writers will have been limited, in their intentions in writing, by the range of intentions they could have expected to be able to communicate, and thus by whatever stock of concepts, and whatever criteria for applying them, were generally available." It might even be possible to show that a thinker "could not in principle have held" a particular belief. Thinkers must be put in their place lest we end up attributing to them intentions altogether at

7. Wood, "Rhetoric and Reality," 21, 19; Robert E. Shalhope, "Thomas Jefferson's Republicanism and Antebellum Southern Thought," *Journal of Southern History* 42 (1976):533–535.

8. Wood, "Intellectual History," 37–38; see also his "Conspiracy and the Paranoid Style," 431 n. 75.

odds with "our knowledge of their empirical beliefs" (Skinner).[9] This rule of reading does more than remind us that a writer in the eighteenth-century Virginia piedmont would not address the question of the political use and effects of religion in the accents of Abu Nasr al-Farabi from tenth-century Baghdad. It suggests further, and more problematically, that the range of considerations present in the mind of either thinker could not have been available to the other—and this, notwithstanding the possibility that it might "form a deliberate part of the author's aim to comment on the prevailing handling of certain ideas or events," even "to challenge some of the basic moral assumptions of his age" (Skinner).[10] For ultimately, we are told, the matter under investigation is not thought but ideology.

Accordingly, the vast outpouring of argument that attended the struggle over independence and the formation of a national government has been reviewed and scrutinized with the new eyes and in accord with the new purposes of our new historians. To be sure, this labor has not always been easy to sustain. It is hard to keep one's mind on, let alone take seriously, language and argument that seem so overwrought, fantastical, and "extravagant." Just as the eighteenth-century British "country" writers exhibited "obsessive concern" in harping on their favorite theme of corruption in government, so too did the American colonists dwell "endlessly, almost compulsively," on the theme of containing power, fascinated perhaps by its "sado-masochistic flavor" (Bailyn).[11] Our natural impulse is to want to look no further into a literature said to be rife with "irrational and hysterical beliefs," "patent absurdity and implausibility," "exaggerated and fanatical rhetoric," "hysterical and emotional ideas," "violent seemingly absurd distortions and falsifications of what we now believe to be true," and "frenzied rhetoric." Nor are our spirits lifted to hear that "there is simply too much fanatical and millennial thinking even by the best minds," that even John Adams and Thomas Jefferson were victims of "the enthusiastic extravagance—the paranoiac obsession," the "grandiose and feverish language" of their age (Wood).[12]

---

9. Quentin Skinner, "Motives, Intentions and the Interpretation of Texts," *New Literary History* 3 (1972):406–407. See also his "Meaning and Understanding," 8–10; and Wood, "Intellectual History," 35–36.

10. Skinner, "Hermeneutics and the Role of History," 221–222.

11. Bernard Bailyn, *The Origins of American Politics,* 10–11; *Ideological Origins,* 48, 56, see also 62 n. 7.

12. Wood, "Rhetoric and Reality," 20–21, 25–27.

We are more likely to pity Jefferson than to be fascinated by him on learning that his view of Saxon England, expressed in a pamphlet meant to propel people toward revolution and independence, was "a romantic diversion rather than a meaningful historical appeal" and, in any event, "too obscure to have ideological power" (Henderson). That pity may turn to contempt on learning how, in the last decade of his life, Jefferson's use of language provides "a classic example of symbolic action," growing ever more extreme, rigid, and inflexible (Shalhope).[13] The corpus of early American political writings begins to take on the character of a psychopathologist's cabinet of curiosa.

Yet it would, of course, be wrong to jump to conclude thus about Jefferson and, accordingly, about the new historians; for as these very historians would be the first to assert, our distaste or dismay or disbelief in the face of such language needs to be overcome. We must "listen with care" precisely because that language reflects how the world seemed to those eighteenth-century folk; they sincerely believed and acted on that appearance (Bailyn).[14] Thus "any idea or symbol . . . however irrational or silly" (Wood), however "archaic" or "anachronistic"—even, or especially, if it prevented contemporaries from reaching a realistic understanding of their situation (Berthoff)—holds special significance for the historian. Make-believe is as much part of the real world as tubs and taxes. In analyzing these peculiar notions, the historian makes the incredible intelligible and helps us to see "the inescapable limits circumscribing [one's] ability to think and to act" (Shalhope).[15]

Nor should one misunderstand the new historians' disinclination to ask—and answer—the question, Was there anything to those fears? Were they solely or principally matters of subjective perception? No one maintains that they were merely neurotic fantasies. The solidity and appositeness of this anxious analysis were vindicated for eigh-

---

13. H. James Henderson, *Party Politics and the Continental Congress*, 89; Shalhope, "Jefferson's Republicanism," 538–539.

14. Bailyn, *Origins of American Politics*, 10–11, 148, 159–160; and *Ideological Origins*, 94–95; Lance Banning, "Republican Ideology and the Triumph of the Constitution, 1789 to 1793," *William and Mary Quarterly*, 3d ser., 31 (1974):184; Wood, "Conspiracy and the Paranoid Style," 420–429; but see Wood, "Intellectual History," 33.

15. Wood, "Intellectual History," 34; Rowland Berthoff, "Independence and Attachment, Virtue and Interest: From Republican Citizen to Free Enterpriser, 1787–1837," in *Uprooted Americans: Essays to Honor Oscar Handlin*, ed. Richard L. Bushman et al., 101–105; Shalhope, "Jefferson's Republicanism," 556.

teenth-century folk in a number of ways: by newspaper dispatches, by recent history, by the accounts of ancient historians—and also, let it be said, by the testimony of direct experience. Here in 1768 was "in bold, stark actuality a standing army" (Bailyn). Here in 1791 was a permanently funded debt with its corrupt and corruptible swarm of Treasury dependents (Banning).[16]

Yet these particulars are not the most significant facts. Or, rather, their significance—for contemporaries then and for historians now—rests on the added credibility they gave to already cherished beliefs and on the heightened effect those beliefs accorded the events of the day. Beneath the legalistic polemics and the news dispatches, beneath the extreme intellectualism of the age, lay deep social strains aching for expression and relief. From this perspective, the things debated and bruited about, however much or little they were literally true, were at least "always psychologically true." Caught up by social and economic changes they understood little and could control less, the Americans, like others before and since them, fell into "a revolutionary syndrome." Indeed, it may be enough for us to know that people in the eighteenth century were especially distressed by the "discrepancy between the professed motives of an actor and the contrary effects of his actions," a distress intensified by their lack of "our modern repertory of explanations" (Wood).[17] Thus, if Richard Henry Lee seems to have been "mesmerized" by the notion that Grenville's ministry was trying to reduce the American colonists to slavery, that is to be understood as "an example of the alienation and distrust of established political institutions associated with ideological commitment." And if John Adams appears "excessive" in his "puritanical compulsions," that might better be seen as the expression of a desire "typical of the radical psychology" (Henderson). Once one recognizes the hyperbole of the founding generation as part of an effort by individuals or groups to escape strain, the importance of ideology as a key to understanding becomes evident. Words and arguments and reasons can then best be seen as parts of "highly selective, oversimplified, symbol systems which function primarily to integrate so-

16. Bailyn, *Ideological Origins,* 87, 113; Banning, "Republican Ideology," 182–183.
17. Wood, "Rhetoric and Reality," 25–27, 31; "Conspiracy and the Paranoid Style," 411, 425.

cial systems," "to alleviate the strains engendered by . . . social and economic changes" (Shalhope).[18]

Propelled by an aversion to earlier historians' preoccupation with elitist discourse and drawn by a hope of enlarging historical understanding, scholars of the ideological school have pushed away from eighteenth-century writing desks and gone outdoors. In that bright light, they promise to show us sights and truths undreamt of. At last we can see "how facile and how unreal were our predecessors' unexamined assumptions" about the relation of formal discourse to political life (Bailyn). We can then, with clear understanding and an even clearer conscience, descend from "the high-blown philosophy of life embodied in what are commonly called Natural Rights ideas" to the concerns of actual men and women in the real world. Indeed, why stop with the "elaborate, highly-abstracted, intellectualized" commonwealth ideology? "Were there no 'mentalities' . . . that achieved their expression on a lower level of historical abstraction?" (Ernst). Why stop even there? Progressively, we can detect the fulminations of distressed planters, merchants, and artisans, and finally even "the mob's effigy" (Wood) as a continuing social process of relieving strain and reconstituting social behavior. Similarly, we may come to see gesture, dress, play, and civic ritual as parts of a panorama wherein all segments of society act out their hopes and fears. We will then perhaps have come a long way from "the folly of projecting ideas in the heads of crowds from ideas in the heads of elites" (Lemisch).[19]

Of course, one may wonder at a certain asymmetry in the historians' treatment of those thoughts, ideas, symbols, and expressions after reducing them all to forms of public rhetoric (Wood). It may seem at times that the discount rate applied to the language of learned pamphlets could at least as properly be applied to the symbol making of a crowd burning down a royal official's house. "Looking at broken windowpanes is hanging a lot on a little" (Lemisch).[20] Why should

18. Henderson, *Party Politics,* 80, 82; Shalhope, "Jefferson's Republicanism," 533–535, 556.

19. Bernard Bailyn, "The Central Themes of the American Revolution: An Interpretation," in *Essays on the American Revolution,* ed. Stephen G. Kurtz and James H. Hutson, 10–11; Joseph Ernst, "Ideology and the Political Economy of Revolution," *Canadian Review of American Studies* 4 (1973):143; Wood, "Intellectual History," 34; Jesse Lemisch, "Bailyn Besieged in His Bunker," *Radical History Review* 3 (1976):74.

20. Wood, "Intellectual History," 35; Lemisch, "Bailyn Besieged," 75.

extravagance in the inarticulate masses be treated as a reflection of their true beliefs (about a moral economy, for example) when the same presumption is denied to the productions of the better educated or more literate? Why indeed?

The new historians' reasons have to be divined from their premises. Any historical account that does not mislead must give the real concerns and activities of the age their deserved weight and emphasis. Although those who fancy that "the history of an idea or event can ever be adequately written in terms of its leading actors" may gratify themselves with that conceit, they in fact mistake the actual historical situation. For those very "qualities of intelligence and presentation" that make a John Locke (or an Alexander Hamilton) so arresting and fascinating to a scholar are precisely the features that disqualify such characters from figuring large in the world of "real entities and activities." To assess properly the role of political thinking in political life *as lived,* one must circumvent the canon of great names and great works lest one fall victim to their "distorting perspective." Only by locating those actors, writings, ideas, arguments, and activities within the broader social, economic, and linguistic context, only by reconceiving the past as "the history of ideologies" can we hope to reach some approximation of that past (Skinner).21 In this sense the nuanced sophistications of the few stand in greater need of deflation than the jeers and cries of the many.

Those atypical great works and great thinkers are cast aside, or transcended, in favor of the study of emerging symbolization. Not the ideas, but their formation or emergence, is what matters. As turmoil in social life becomes more evident to people living in a revolutionary age, as words fail, individuals struggle to voice "an idea, which in turn must symbolize or grasp a complex of ineffable feelings" (Shalhope). A revolutionary struggle should perhaps be seen as a linguistic or "mental revolution," the revolutionary moment to be marked at the point when a people "suddenly blinked" and saw their familiar world in a new perspective (Wood).22

It is in this context of seeking what really matters that thought and the thinking human actor are relegated to their newly assigned place.

---

21. Quentin Skinner, "The Limits of Historical Explanations," *Philosophy* 41 (1966):212–213, 215; and "Some Problems in the Analysis of Political Thought and Action," *Political Theory* 2 (1974):280. See also Joyce Appleby, "Republicanism in Old and New Contexts," *William and Mary Quarterly,* 3d ser., 43 (1986):28.

22. Shalhope, "Jefferson's Republicanism," 538; Wood, "Rhetoric and Reality," 13.

For if "human thought is necessarily rhetorical" and public, "and not, or at least not fundamentally, a private activity," we may properly subsume all that under the heading of communication. And if we are concerned to identify the communications that really stirred that generation to action, we would do well to cast our eyes and nets beyond "just the literary terms expressed by a few supposedly representative thinkers." If we do, "mental worlds" beyond our imagining await discovery. The full range of symbolic actions or meanings, from a wink to an effigy, are thus fodder for our historians. This is only proper, for in "this postpsychological age" no one with the dimmest awareness of "how people really behave" could accept the notion that "individuals acted as they did because they believed, 'sincerely' believed, in the ideas or principles they expressed" (Wood)[23]—least of all if those beliefs are expressed in stately Augustan prose.

Yet the very acceptance of "ideology" as the key term carries with it a train of assumptions and implications that effectively bar our ever recognizing the power of thought and of thoughtfulness. However one understands the term—whether as the pleasant-sounding non-sense with which devious folk deck out their darker purposes, or as the unintended energizing and symbolization of the hopes and anxieties of a faceless age—at bottom lies a common understanding, so common that it no longer needs assertion: ideas may be important at a given moment or place, but they are not and can never be the central reality or the independent variable. An underlying reality—strain, anxiety, interest, whatever—*uses* thought and shapes it to its ends. Ideas, then, in the modern researcher's eyes, become "important for what they do rather than for what they are." Accordingly, the resort to explanation "in terms of the intentions and designs of particular individuals" becomes only a recurrence to the crude modes of eighteenth-century figures obsessed with motives (Wood).[24]

The relative insignificance of individual thought and individual actors is amply illustrated by the work of the new historians. When they turn, for example, to inspect the use eighteenth-century authors made of others' thoughts and writings, they are quick to dip beneath the appearance of things. They are not inclined to be overwhelmed by the show of learning—classical, secular, legal, or religious—with

23. Wood, "Intellectual History," 29–30, 32–35.
24. Ibid., 34; and "Rhetoric and Reality," 16–17. Contrast the noncrude examples in Bailyn, *Ideological Origins*, 150; and in Wood, "Conspiracy and the Paranoid Style," 421.

which those eighteenth-century controversialists adorned their speeches, letters, and pamphlets. They focus instead on what they take to be those authors' superficiality or tendentious selectivity. In fact, what appears, "at first glance, [as] a massive, seemingly random eclecticism" turns out to be just about that: "clusters of ideas" marked by "striking incongruities and contradictions." We do not see men and women thinking hard about things they have heard or read; we see them citing what they have found useful for "illustrative, not determinative," purposes. Thus although Bernard Bailyn grants that not all learning was superficial, that not all recurrence to learned citations was offhand or in order "to score points" against an adversary, he shows no instance in which a powerful searching mind engages with another such mind. Notwithstanding that he judges some earlier authors to have contributed substantially or to have been in certain ways powerfully influential or even (in the exceptional case of John Locke) "authoritative" in some respect, those authors and their distinctive ideas remain strangely evanescent in his account (Bailyn).[25]

Even when an element of "the Revolutionary ideology" is described in some detail, its bearing on people's actions appears both obscure and negligible. Our confidence that the revolutionaries of '76 made good use of the "Puritan value system" gains little from the assurance that Sukarno manipulated "ancient Indic tradition to frame the 'sacred' ideological base for a newly independent" Indonesia. At issue is not whether the incorporation of Puritan values would fit in with "this nationalist revolutionary paradigm"; rather, the question is whether the changes effected by American independence and the establishment of the new state and federal governments were in fact "greatly facilitated by endowing the new form with cultural attributes of older institutions." Clearly, one cannot leave it at the observation that, "being many things to many men, . . . [the Puritan value system] was a superb instrument of Revolutionary ideology." For whatever made that old New England tradition "many things to many men" also made it unequally assimilable by all and unequally welcome to all (Henderson).[26]

The gist of the ideological interpretation is, of course, not that classical or Enlightenment or legal or religious sources mattered little, but that the country or classical republican or English opposition

25. Bailyn, *Ideological Origins*, 23–34, 36.
26. Henderson, *Party Politics*, 84–85.

writers mattered more. This group was "unique in its determinative power"; its writings were "central to American political expression" (Bailyn). In its "complete and consistent Americanization," this "structured universe of classical thought continued to serve as the intellectual medium through which Americans perceived the political world." The political language the Americans inherited shaped their hopes, discontents, and the way they saw the world. As in the case of any intellectual universe, people find that "some ideas are native and others are difficult to conceive." Paradoxically, but perhaps not surprisingly, the truth that would liberate individuals' bodies and minds from arbitrary and overbearing authority rendered people incapable of thinking differently. "The heritage of classical republicanism and English opposition thought, shaped and hardened in the furnace of a great Revolution, left few men free" (Banning).[27]

Not all historians have been happy with this characterization, but their reservations have more to do with the monolithic quality ascribed to opposition ideology than to the adequacy of the concept of ideology as an explanatory device. Thus Joyce Appleby argues that there were competing ideologies, that of an opposition at once reactionary and legalistic and that of a secular liberalism advocating a natural order of undifferentiated competitors. Another reading finds two country parties and two court parties at work in eighteenth-century Britain and thus a still more complex tradition to which Americans could refer. Another finds the options in Jeffersonian America ranging from "Burkeanism and the court party on the right through the country party and Smithian liberalism to Christian and secular radicalisms on the left," all drawing on the heady brew of "Scottish ideas" (Howe). At this stage of the inquiry, the only consensus among these historians is that ideology is a prime explanation; there is none about which ideology was decisive.[28]

Fundamental to the concept of ideology is the premise that, however things happen and change, those outcomes are not properly at-

---

27. Bailyn, *Ideological Origins*, 34, 43; Banning, "Republican Ideology," 172–173, 178–179.

28. Joyce Appleby, "The Social Origins of American Revolutionary Ideology," *Journal of American History* 64 (1977–1978):937, 953–954; Daniel Walker Howe, "European Sources of Political Ideas in Jeffersonian America," *Reviews in American History* 10, no. 4 (December 1982):34, 40–41; Robert E. Shalhope, "Republicanism and Early American Historiography," *William and Mary Quarterly*, 3d ser., 39 (1982):334–356.

tributable to deliberating individuals. This is not the same as asserting that "formal discourse and articulated belief" are merely weapons in a battle to manipulate men's minds, but then neither is it to assert that formal discourse "in some simple sense . . . constitutes motives" (Bailyn).29 Rather, all that talk and writing should be viewed within the broader context of a "political culture" (or a "popular culture," depending on the historian's political leanings). Within that broader culture, and as shaped by it, transformations take place "indeliberately, half-knowingly," the workings of "in effect an intellectual switchboard" wired by no one in particular and to all appearances fully automatic. Changes in feeling, belief, and attitude occur somehow, but as far as we are told not as a result of anyone's deliberate intention (Bailyn).30 It may even turn out to be the case that the actors are "the languages rather than (or on an equal footing with) the human individuals who have used them" (Pocock). Nor, finally, do we need to distinguish between those expressing a "visceral reaction" and those acting in response to considered convictions. At the energizing level of ideology, it does not matter that some "*feel* Country ideology," thereby "giving voice to socio-economic grudges," while others syllogize their way to similar conclusions (Hutson).31

Such differences do not matter all that much for the same reason that ideas count in only limited ways. When historians realize that thinkers and actors are mistaken in believing that they have direct access to ideas unmediated by ideology, when historians explode the illusion of autonomous thought conversing with autonomous ideas, when they realize that all mental activity and mental objects take place in or are given by ideology, they are thereby freed from the blinders of the past. Neither the eighteenth-century "obsession with motives," nor the "simple nineteenth-century intellectualist assumption," nor a "stifling judicial-like preoccupation with motivation and responsibility" need any longer impede the modern student from perceiving the more fundamental sociological, psychological, or economic determinants (Wood).32 If some historical behavior perversely

29. Bailyn, "Central Themes," 10–11.

30. Bailyn, *Ideological Origins*, ix, 22, 160, 190, 302; and "Political Experience and Enlightenment Ideas in Eighteenth-Century America," *American Historical Review* 67 (1961–1962):349.

31. Pocock, "*Machiavellian Moment* Revisited," 52; James H. Hutson, "Country, Court, and Constitution: Antifederalism and the Historians," *William and Mary Quarterly*, 3d ser., 38 (1981):366–367.

32. Wood, "Rhetoric and Reality," 16–17, 19–20, 22–23.

argues that deliberating individuals matter, if a Jefferson continues "to rely extensively on private correspondence for the dissemination of his views" and a Madison continues "to write learned pieces . . . for a restricted audience of educated gentlemen" (Wood),[33] that behavior is best understood as the fixed habits of old fogies, the intellectual equivalent of persisting in wearing breeches and wigs long out of fashion. Whether the botanizing founders of the Republican societies and the moving spirits behind Philip Freneau's *National Gazette* and the Virginia and Kentucky Resolutions were oblivious of the democratization of mind in the early national period is not at issue. What is at issue is the historians' persistence in looking for ideology, a preoccupation that literally obscures the significance of those moments when "the best minds" are "compelled to ask . . . serious questions" (Wood).[34]

Such moments are neither reducible to, nor explicable in terms of, some "elaborate pattern of middle-level beliefs and ideas." Nor can one leave it at an ideology that reshapes and promotes "moods, attitudes, ideas, and aspirations that in some form, however crude or incomplete, already exist." For that only pushes the search for causes back in time, not out of mind. Do those moods and ideas have ideological origins as well? Did "the complex and integrated set of values, beliefs, attitudes, and responses that had evolved through a century and a half of Anglo-American history" (Bailyn) owe anything, at any point, to the abstractions and formal arguments of thoughtful, even purposefully thoughtful, individuals? Not, it would seem, if there is no such thing as thought trying to achieve knowledge, if we have only opinion growing out of an age's "conspiratorial fears and imagined intrigues" (Wood).[35] If that is the case, then what purports to be thought is in fact fundamentally derivative, little better than a patchwork of miscellaneous remnants, like the stuff quilts and dreams are made of.

In that event, the subject of an intellectual historian's study ought to be the *invokers* of ideas, not some presumed great theoretical originators. Those invokers might differ little from casual marketers,

33. Gordon S. Wood, "The Democratization of Mind in the American Revolution," in *The Moral Foundations of the American Republic,* ed. Robert H. Horwitz, 122.
34. Wood, "Rhetoric and Reality," 24, 25.
35. Bailyn, "Central Themes," 10–11; Wood, "Conspiracy and the Paranoid Style," 407.

people afflicted with the myopia of short-range concerns. Of course one might still wonder where those middlemen get their stock in trade or, for that matter, whether they are after all and in every case mindless factors of other people's goods. Although it is worth examining how the historical accretion and evolution of a people's values, beliefs, attitudes, and responses may shape that people's view of themselves and of the world, that inquiry need not preclude the possibly significant part played by some purposive and maybe magisterial thinker in the history of those values, beliefs, and attitudes—unless, of course, we know that such singular figures *cannot* matter decisively.[36] But if we doubt that certainty or if we eschew that convenience,[37] then we are left with the need to come to terms with a first-class (or even second-class) mind in the act of thinking clearly, forcefully, and deliberately.

A Mind of One's Own: The Case for John Adams

Coming to terms with an independent mind will not and cannot take place as long as we look and act on the premise of the new historians. Given their point of departure, it is no surprise, however striking, that these historians largely ignore, when they are not misconstruing, how their historical subjects viewed their principles and acts. The very gravity, even high-mindedness, with which the generations of 1776 and 1787 (and beyond) debated alternative principles and policies remains fundamentally alien to practitioners of the ideological approach. To be intelligible within the terms of that analysis, political thought and speech must be transmuted into something else. Thus, for example, the debate over ratification of the Constitution turns out to be a court-country dispute that gave vent to "the social resentment and antagonism of the agrarian interests that were preponderant in the Country, in both England and America" (Hutson); or it is at bottom a social conflict between those who would preserve a community of equals and those who would reinstitute hierarchical distinctions—in short, a debate on "an essential point of political sociology" (Wood).[38] Even the conversion of Anti-Federalists into

36. Wood, "Conspiracy and the Paranoid Style," 408–409.
37. Alexis de Tocqueville, *Democracy in America*, 463 (II, pt. i, chap. 20).
38. Hutson, "Country, Court, and Constitution," 368; Gordon S. Wood, *The Creation of the American Republic, 1776–1787*, 484–485. See Gary J. Schmitt and

strict constructionists is reduced to a "reflexive literalism," an instinctive inclination "that seems inevitable" given the Americans' upbringing on "a diet of opposition writings." Indeed, that heritage
"left few men free" to think otherwise. But where that ideology
required an "ancient constitution" as a bench mark by which to
gauge political corruption and constitutional decay, those Americans,
having only the newly minted Constitution to fall back on, "instinc-
tively settled for the next best thing. Symbolically speaking, they
made the Constitution old" (Banning).[39] By this account a sharp
division over the character of the Union and the requirements of free
government is transformed into an ideologically prescribed obsession
with corruption. Of course it was common doctrine that, over time,
good constitutions would become worse and bad ones insufferable.
But those former Anti-Federalists most apt to cry alarm at deviations
from the constitutional text did not need classical republicanism or
country ideology to prompt them. The most thoughtful and the most
radical of the opponents of the Constitution could hardly have taken
the amendments of 1789 through 1791 as meeting their major objections of 1787 and 1788. If they sought to hold the Constitution to its
word, it was not out of some instinctive or reflexive impulse. Rather,
they tried with great deliberateness to prevent what they believed the
Constitution invited. This was Anti-Federalism in its postratification
garb. Strict construction could not alone remedy what they had found
most objectionable in the Constitution as proposed, but it was the
best they had—short of resistance grounded in the right of self-
preservation.

With such a stance toward authors and arguments, texts and thinking, it is altogether understandable that the necessary discriminations
should often be gross or even lacking. By subsuming a broad range of
intelligence under the heading of ideology, the ideological interpretation in effect disarms us for the task at hand. In order to discriminate
those who merely absorbed what was useful, with little regard for
coherence and consistency, from those who sought to trace the premises of their preferences and the consequences of their principles, a

---

Robert H. Webking, "Revolutionaries, Antifederalists, and Federalists: Comments on
Gordon Wood's Understanding of the American Founding," *Political Science Reviewer* 9 (1979):215–229; and Herbert J. Storing, "What the Anti-Federalists Were
For," in *The Complete Anti-Federalist* I:4.
  39. Banning, "Republican Ideology," 178–179, 182, 187.

historian today must first recover the possibility of rank among thinkers and then listen carefully for intimations of such rank. Especially and above all must the historian learn to attend to those historical actors who seem most to have considered what they were about and who, far from being the unconscious puppets of the presuppositions of their age, were most intent on reshaping those presuppositions—on replacing old intellectual precepts and societal purposes with new precepts and purposes of *their* design. Then, and only then, will the constitution of the thinking revolutionary finally hover into sight.

A closer look at an ideological interpretation of a major American thinker affords a singular opportunity to weigh alternative approaches. By abstracting from details in order to sketch the main features of the ideological mode of interpretation, I have, of course, hardly established the adequacy or shortcomings of that mode. Ultimately, any interpretation must be judged by its ability to illumine or account for things said and done, or for things left unsaid and undone. Specific cases are thus indispensable for testing plausibility and estimating relative superiority. But at the same time, such particular instances can be only illustrative, not conclusive; the choice of test cases is always open to cavil. Yet in Gordon Wood's impressive analysis of the republicanism of John Adams we have a coherent, extended reading of America's "political scientist par excellence" (Wood), a reading that invites scrutiny and comparison. Eschewing for once the "encyclopedic historical method" by which big fish and small fry are netted into one swirling school (Schmitt and Webking),[40] Wood turns his attentive eye and ear to a political actor who knows his own mind and addresses ours. It is an instructive encounter.

The John Adams that emerges from Wood's presentation exudes complication and contradiction, invites pity and admiration, and altogether leaves us almost as bewildered as he himself is alleged to have been. True to the premises of the ideological school, Wood early on in *The Creation of the American Republic* insists on the need to look beyond "the nicely reasoned constitutional arguments" of an Adams or a Jefferson lest we miss "the enthusiastic and visionary extravagance" in those men's thinking (Wood).[41] Adams is presented

40. Wood, *Creation of the American Republic,* 568; Schmitt and Webking, "Revolutionaries, Antifederalists, and Federalists," 224 n. 53.
41. Wood, *Creation of the American Republic,* 121. All further parenthetical references in this section are to this work.

as one who moved from hopeful enthusiasm to a redoubled anxiety and loss of republican faith (571, 575). But since neither Adams nor Wood's Adams was a simple fellow, those contrasting moods and casts of mind are themselves fairly complex. The title of Wood's thematic treatment puts the ambiguity plainly enough: "The Relevance and Irrelevance of John Adams" depicts the "bewilderment of a man whom ideas had passed by," one whose "unfortunate fate" it was "to have missed the intellectual significance of the most important event since the Revolution" (48, 567). Further discussion shows Adams's plight to have been less a matter of bad luck than of poor thinking. "Adams never really comprehended what was happening to the fundamentals of political thought in the years after 1776"; "he remained unaware" of its originality (568, 580). His "inability to understand" left him outside the mainstream, ensconced with his "superannuated idea" of mixed government, "thinking in old-fashioned terms," and rendered "seemingly immune" to new thought while "carrying on in a timeworn manner" (581, 583, 586, 587, 591). Far from being contemptuous of so perversely obsolete a thinker, Wood can barely conceal his admiration. He praises Adams for his clarity and insight, for his honest and correct social analysis, for his unflinching readiness "to tell his fellow Americans some truths about themselves that American values and American ideology would not admit" (568, 569, 592). The "obsolescence of Adams's political theory" in no way diminishes for Wood the truth of his observations (587). If he was irrelevant in the America of 1787 and after, it was for all the wrong reasons.

It would be a grave injustice—to Adams and to Wood's complex account—to conclude that Adams suffered the common plight of those who do not change with the times. In fact, the linchpin of Wood's analysis is the belief that Adams did indeed change. Depicting the character of that change compels Wood to bring to bear upon his vast knowledge of primary sources the analytical skills of a parser of texts. For the moment Wood is concerned less with detecting how Adams's beliefs may have reflected the contending passions of "his own tormented soul" (577, also 571) than with establishing the depth and quality of that change. On the one hand, we have the sketch of a young Adams, fired with revolutionary enthusiasm, convinced of the redemptive and regenerative powers of republican institutions and republican education, and ready to see in aristocracy a useful ally of the people in their struggle against executive aggrandizement (570, 579). On the other hand, there is a detailed portrait of an older

Adams, one who had outgrown his illusions and somewhat naive enthusiasms. Though Wood deals at length with the changed Adams, the Adams that became irrelevant, the force of his analysis depends on the adequacy of his account of Adams the revolutionary. Without the contrast, both "the relevance and irrelevance of John Adams" would have to be reconsidered.[42]

The bulk of what we learn in this chapter about the early views of Adams comes less from a direct examination of early writings (569–571, 579) than from an implied contrast with later writings. Hence, the reader who wants to know *whether* Adams changed his political thinking is hard put to discover Wood's grounds for asserting it. A sentence such as this—"Within a few years after Independence, . . . whatever optimism Adams had had for the refinement of the American character was gone"—tells us both that the Adams of 1787 was no optimist *and* that he might have been taken for one in 1776. To be told that he "now saw" the futility of relying simply on popular virtue to sustain popular government implies that he once thought otherwise. Asserting that it was "now clear that there was 'no special providence for Americans, and their nature is the same with that of others'" is tantamount to saying that the earlier Adams had held Americans as a breed apart (571). By repeated recourse to this mode, what Alexander Hamilton in *Federalist,* No. 32, called a "negative pregnant," Wood leaves us with a John Adams who once had "faith in the inspirational and ameliorating qualities of republicanism" (575), who once thought education capable of "compelling the people to submerge their individual desires into a love for the whole" (575), and who once thought of an aristocracy as "different from the people but by no means opposed to the people's welfare" (579).

Almost every one of these assertions can be seconded by citations

42. In focusing on Wood's broad theme of the revolutionary Adams's dramatic reversal, I run the risk of appearing to ignore the other ways Adams figures in this work. Wood portrays as well a more equivocal Adams, one who persistently combined high hopes with deep doubts (121, 569–570). Indeed, Wood's last word on Adams—quoting his lament that he had lived in enemy country for fifty years (592)—at the very least leaves the thesis of a changing Adams up in the air. It also raises the possibility that Wood's larger purpose may lie in a different direction: showing the character of Adams's blind (if half-truthful) resistance to the compelling (if largely deceptive) message of the new, post-Revolutionary politics, both Federalist and Republican. Yet I am reluctant to dismiss as insubstantial or inconsequential the dozen closely worked pages that Wood devotes to detailing this purported change. Not one of the three hundred other political figures mentioned in this book is held by Wood to so steady and prolonged a scrutiny; that judgment deserves consideration.

to chapter and verse in Adams's writings, and yet, strange to say, this account of the earlier Adams is fundamentally awry. It can be shown to be so, not "in order to prove the moderation of the Revolution" (121), but in order to show the thoughtfulness of the revolutionary— as a young lawyer no less than as a mature diplomat or a retired president. It can be seen to be so by recurring to the young Adams's own coherent accounts of his political views.

In one of his earliest published newspaper essays, Adams reflected on the ingredients of public discourse. He held self-deceit, "the spurious offspring of *self-love*," to be the root cause of the ease and glee with which men impugn one another, all the while mistaking the impulses of their own "swarms of passions" for the dictates of conscience. Given this fundamental fact of human nature, it is futile to expect that even the purest or most needful reform will ever pass current in the world without being waylaid by opposition and slander. From this Adams drew a republican moral. Alluding to the antimonarchical parable of Jotham ben Jerubbaal (Judges 9:7–21), he concluded that "we can never be secure in a resignation of our understandings, or in confiding *enormous power,* either to the *Bramble* or the *Cedar;* no, nor to *any mortal,* however great or good." By the same token, predetermined hostility and discredit are equally unjust and unwise. "Let us not be bubbled then out of our reverence and obedience to Government, on one hand; nor out of our right to think and act *for ourselves,* in our own departments, on the other." It was a foregone conclusion for Adams that "ignorance, vanity, excessive *ambition* and venality, will in spight of all human precautions creep into government." This calls not for a politics of righteousness and indignation, but for a politics of attentive thoughtfulness. Like Hamilton in *Federalist,* No. 1, Adams was here loath to cast political antagonists as the children of light against the children of darkness. Hence he was as wary of quick judgments as he was of indifference. Considering that "every step in the public administration of government, concerns us *nearly,*" it behooves all to inspect all rulers strictly and, if need be, to oppose them soberly. "It becomes necessary to every subject then, to be in some degree a *statesman:* and to examine and judge for *himself* of the *tendency* of political *principles* and *measures.*"[43]

43. John Adams, "U" to the *Boston Gazette,* 29 August 1763, in Robert J. Taylor et al., eds., *Papers of John Adams* I:78–81.

This essay's sequel (for some reason unpublished) bears special relevance for any consideration of the supposed changing political thought of John Adams. Taking as his text "All Men would be Tyrants if they could," Adams inquired into that old maxim's meaning and implications. The notion is, not that "all the sons of Adam, are so many abandond Knaves regardless of all Morality and Right," but simply that man cannot be "left to the natural Emotions of his own Mind, unrestrained and uncheckd by other Power extrinsic to himself." Far from being a new discovery, this has been the view of "thinking Men" for many millennia. Heedful of the danger posed by power unchecked, "our Constitution" has wisely provided against all such, whether military, "casuistical," or civil. Its wisdom, Adams concluded, clearly lies in its recognition that "no simple Form of Government, can possibly secure Men against the Violences of Power." Some forty-four years later, the old republican warrior rummaging among his papers saw fit to append: "This last Paragraph has been the Creed of my whole Life and is now March 27 1807 as much approved as it was when it was written by John Adams."[44] What others might take to be obstinacy, Adams thought consistency.

This adherence to considered views is especially evident in the "Dissertation on the Canon and the Feudal Law." Written and published serially over a period of several months in 1765, it affords a close look at Adams's thoughts about knowledge and power, education and liberty. Its somber tone, heightened in all likelihood by news of the recently passed Stamp Act, smacks little of the enthusiastic extravagance we have been led to expect in the young Adams. And yet it is for all that a pronouncedly revolutionary statement.

One of the most striking features of the "Dissertation" is its quiet assumption that the love of power, the spirit of liberty, and even knowledge itself are neutral forces capable of great good or great evil. "The desire of dominion," the very principle that "has always prompted the princes and nobles of the earth, by every species of fraud and violence, to shake off, all the *limitations* of their power," has also impelled the common people to try to confine them. As the people become "more *intelligent* in general," as they find ways of overcoming their ignorance and isolation, their own love of power may make it more difficult for "the great" to lord it over those whom

44. Adams, "An Essay on Man's Lust for Power . . . " [post 29 August 1763], ibid., 81–83.

they contemptuously call "the populace."[45] The spirit of liberty may be no less ambiguous. The "Dissertation" is, among other things, a paean to that spirit, seeking to rouse Americans out of their "habits of reserve, and a cautious diffidence of asserting their opinions publickly." But in urging "a manly assertion" of American rights, Adams was far from proclaiming the spirit of liberty an unqualified good. "This spirit . . . without knowledge, would be little better than a brutal rage." Brutish activity is not preferable to brutish indolence.[46]

Though knowledge may be indispensable for self-governance, it too was no simple good in the eyes of John Adams. An ignorant people is a vulnerable people, one easily seduced into projects leading to ruin or oppression. Yet the knowledge that would make them free is the other side of the science that holds them in thrall. Of all the "systems of iniquity" devised for tyrannizing the people, none had been more "successful," "sublime," "astonishing," and "calamitous to human liberty" than the union of those two vast products of human art and intelligence, the canon and the feudal law. Here was the amplest proof that the intellectual and moral virtues were quite distinct. The young lawyer of 1765 knew full well how knowledge— and the monopolization of knowledge—might be used by self-serving men to further their purposes.[47] It was no new disenchanting revelation that led a wary vice president of 1789 to confess his misgivings about the regenerative "Influence of general Science." For where the political system itself was flawed (because "unballanced"), the heightened ability of partisans promised exacerbation rather than relief. Greater knowledge, an improved science, "would only increase and inflame" the defects of the political system by adding to the number of "able and ambitious Men, who would only understand the better, how to worry one another with greater Art and dexterity."[48]

With these important reservations in mind, one may then consider John Adams's early thoughts on education and republicanism. There is no denying that he held the struggle for liberty to be inseparable from the struggle against ignorance. The "wicked confederacy" that saw temporal and spiritual grandees reinforcing each other's domin-

---

45. Adams, "A Dissertation on the Canon and the Feudal Law," no. 1, 12 August 1765, ibid., 111–112.

46. Adams, "Dissertation," no. 4, 21 October 1765, ibid., 123, 125–126.

47. Adams, "Dissertation," no. 1, ibid., 111–113.

48. Adams to Benjamin Rush, 19 June 1789, in Alexander Biddle, ed., *Old Family Letters: Copied from the Originals . . .* , ser. A, 39.

ion also left them vulnerable to the liberating forces unleashed by the Reformation. Whatever events made the people "more and more sensible of the wrong that was done them, by these systems," to that extent contributed to the cause of liberty. The Puritans' prominent part in that struggle was emphatically connected by Adams to that "sensible" people's intelligence, learning, knowledge, and dedication to inquiry and examination.[49] He made light of the charge that the Puritans were guilty of enthusiasm, but not by denying it. Most of Christendom, he asserted, had that trait in those earlier days; and, besides, "no great enterprize, for the honour or happiness of mankind, was ever achieved, without a large mixture of that noble infirmity." It was, then, no canting zealot out of a Ben Jonson comedy that Adams held up as a model; rather, it was a people praiseworthy for knowing "that government was a plain, simple, intelligible thing founded in nature and reason and quite comprehensible by common sense."[50]

To promote and secure that truth, and thereby to "preserve their posterity from the encroachments of the two systems of tyranny," the Puritans had doubled their efforts on behalf of popular education. It is hard to resist the conclusion that Adams regarded this dedication as his ancestors' finest legacy. The Puritans made "knowledge diffused generally thro' the whole body of the people" into a commitment not only cherished by public opinion but supported by legislative enactment and public funds. In reducing principles to practice, they showed their republican descendants the road to follow.[51]

In what are Adams's people to be educated? If "every order and degree among the people" are to be roused to study and inquiry, it is clearly so that they might absorb "the ideas of right and the sensations of freedom." Some few, the "learned men," would come to concentrate their thoughts on "matters of power and of right." The many, instructed by the men of learning, would come in turn to see that "they have a right, an indisputable, unalienable, indefeasible divine right to that most dreaded, and envied kind of knowledge, I mean of the characters and conduct of their rulers."[52] The result

49. Adams, "Dissertation," no. 1, Taylor et al., eds., *Papers of John Adams* I:113–114.
50. Adams, "Dissertation," no. 2, 19 August 1765, ibid., 115–117.
51. Adams, "Dissertation," no. 3, 30 September 1765, ibid., 118, 120.
52. Adams, "Dissertation," no. 4, ibid., 126–127; "Dissertation," no. 3, ibid., 121.

would be a citizenry—alert, assertive, and mindful of its honor, interest, and happiness. Only with such a people could those mixed forms of government so needful for preserving liberty be sustained. King, lords, commons, and people—none could be dispensed with; each had its contribution to make to prevent government from degenerating into an absolute monarchy, or an oligarchy or aristocracy, or a mixture of monarchy and aristocracy.[53]

Very much depended on "the temper and character of the people." No small part of the case for an independent judiciary, for example, turned on its role in molding "the morals of the people." Similarly, sumptuary legislation and laws providing public support for "the liberal education of youth, especially of the lower class of people," were alike viewed by Adams as means of forming a certain kind of citizenry. But overarching these as a shaping and educative force was the constitution itself. If founded on the right principles, it would as a matter of course work toward making the people more knowing and more conscious of their worth as "Freemen." The prospect Adams held forth evokes positive feelings but promises no miraculous transfiguration: "A general emulation takes place, which causes good humour, sociability, good manners, and good morals to be general. That elevation of sentiment, inspired by such a government, makes the common people brave and enterprizing. That ambition which is inspired by it makes them sober, industrious and frugal. You will find among them some elegance, perhaps, but more solidity; a little pleasure, but a great deal of business—some politeness, but more civility." That would be a happy, a very happy outcome, but it is no Eden under a new dispensation of grace. Only in comparison with "the regions of domination, whether Monarchial or Aristocratical," would one fancy it an "Arcadia or Elisium."[54]

Adams has here depicted a people with the usual passions, but in a setting that tames or channels those passions in socially useful ways. This echoes the system of James Harrington, much admired by Adams, which sought to secure "the Liberty, Virtue, and Interest of the Multitude in all Acts of Government" by balancing the ownership of land and thereby balancing power in a society. If the hope and cautious expectation are that all will be happier as a result, it is not

53. Adams, "The Earl of Clarendon to William Pym," no. 3, 27 January 1766, ibid., 167–169.
54. Ibid., 165; "Thoughts on Government," April 1776, ibid. IV:91–92.

because people in the real world will have forgotten their self-interested projects or have become heedless of the arbitrariness and inequities of the general rules embodied in law: "So fruitfull a Source of Controversy and Altercation" remains just that as long as human nature retains its general character.[55]

None of this is to forget that John Adams was the author of the famous provision of the Massachusetts Constitution of 1780 proclaiming it "the duty of legislators and magistrates, in all future periods of this commonwealth, to cherish the interests of literature and the sciences, and all seminaries of them."[56] Nor is it to discount his expectation that the state constitution's arrangements and commitments might help make the body of the people more humane and sociable, even more generous, than they otherwise would be. John Adams surely had expectations, even revolutionary expectations, but they were grounded in a sober analysis of human character. Precisely because he did not give his fancies free rein, Adams's hopes and disappointments in these matters are to be distinguished sharply from those of a Mercy or James Warren.

His ardor for the revolutionary cause typically expressed itself in a discussion of particulars, concrete proposals and policies, not in a general effusion of sentiment. Thus he could assure Richard Henry Lee that in their adopting a plan of government along the lines Adams was proposing, "human Nature would appear in its proper Glory asserting its own real Dignity." Similarly, a hurried account of prospective European financing and of the present availability of gunpowder led Adams to conclude that "Patience and Perseverance, will carry Us through this mighty Enterprize—an Enterprize that is and will be an Astonishment to vulgar Minds all over the World, in this and in future Generations." Whatever this is, it is not a case, as Wood asserts, of "enthusiastic and visionary extravagance" brought on by Adams's "extraordinary reliance . . . on the eventual ameliorating influence of republican laws and government on men's behavior" (121). For the dignity that the people might ultimately come to display—to the astonishment of vulgar minds—would be of a whole people having learned "to reverence themselves." The people needed to be taught to admire, not heroes, but the nation that produces heroes. Yet the people could raise their estimation of themselves only

55. Adams to James Sullivan, 26 May 1776, ibid. IV:210–212.
56. Charles Francis Adams, ed., *The Works of John Adams* IV:259.

if they had just cause for thinking better of themselves. Imagine a whole people taking "upon themselves the education of the whole people"—and being willing to bear the expenses of it. Imagine a people with "too high a sense of their own dignity ever to suffer any man to serve them for nothing."[57] It is on their *willingness* to think better of themselves and to act on it that Adams placed his hopes.

From this perspective, the story of the twists and turns of a man who insists on perfection and yet despairs of it comes closer to being an account of a Javanese puppet show than of the historical John Adams. No less than Mercy Warren, he believed that a well-regulated commonwealth promoted virtue even as it required it. But unlike Mrs. Warren, the young Adams knew that such perfection was neither to be expected nor mourned after. One might wish to counteract certain vices, most especially "Servility and Flattery," but the means for totally remaking the character of the people were simply not at hand.[58] Thus, too, Adams could admire along with Mrs. Warren the virtuous republic where "a possitive Passion for the public good, the public Interest, Honour, Power, and Glory" overrode all "private Pleasures, Passions, and Interests." But speaking as plainly as a gentleman disagreeing with a lady could, the young Adams asked, "Is there in the World a Nation, which deserves this Character?" Mrs. Warren's cause could not be faulted in principle, but then again, neither could it be reduced to practice. Young Adams's litany of inconvenient facts drives that point home: "I have seen all along my Life, Such Selfishness, and Littleness even in New England"; the corrupting "Spirit of Commerce is as rampant in New England as in any Part of the World," even to the point that "Property is generally the standard of Respect there as much as any where."[59]

This clearly was a people who could stand some improvement. There is no reason to discount Adams's concern expressed to his reverend cousin that, if virtue could not "be inspired into our People, in a greater Measure, than they have it now, They may change their

57. Adams to Richard Henry Lee, 15 November 1775, in Taylor et al., eds., *Papers of John Adams* III:308; Adams to James Warren, 31 March 1777, in Worthington Chauncey Ford, ed., *Warren–Adams Letters: Being Chiefly a Correspondence among John Adams, Samuel Adams, and James Warren* I:308; Adams to John Jebb, 10 September 1785, in C. F. Adams, ed., *Works of John Adams* IX:538–542.

58. Adams to Mercy Warren, 8 January 1776, in Taylor et al., eds., *Papers of John Adams* III:398.

59. Adams to Mercy Warren, 16 April 1776, ibid. IV:123–125.

Rulers, and the forms of Government, but they will not obtain a lasting Liberty.—They will only exchange Tyrants and Tyrannies." Adams reiterated this apprehension in a letter written to Abigail on the very eve of Congress's declaration of independence. The new status of the American governments—and the consequent "un- bounded Power" now to be vested in the people—required a "Pu- rification from our Vices, and an Augmentation of our Virtues or they will be no Blessings." Yet given the extreme addiction of the people as well as the "Great" to corruption and venality, Adams could not and did not anticipate wholesale conversions.60 In this respect Mas- sachusetts or America was no exception. Early and late, John Adams understood that self-governance needs as good a people as one can muster and as many public-spirited individuals as one can press into the public's service. But to insist on that desideratum as an everyday requirement would guarantee, not the rule of the disinterested and the saintly, but the enthronement of hypocrites and knaves. Adams's steadily unsentimental view of things did not lead him to deny that there are disinterested men, but only to insist that "they are not enough in any age or any country to fill all the necessary offices." Only levelheadedness could keep the counsel of perfection in political life from turning into the triumph of madness and despotism.61 Thanks too to this sobriety, the mature Adams was spared the kind of dark despair shown by James Warren at the time of Shays's Re- bellion. "When We find ourselves disposed to think there is a total Change of manners and Principles," Adams gently demurred, "We should recollect, what the manners and Principles were before the War." There had been no golden age in Massachusetts. Looking back unsentimentally to 1760 or 1755 or even back to 1745, "You will be very sensible that our Countrymen have never merited the Character of very exalted Virtue." If Adams had hardly expected them to have grown much better, neither was he inclined to believe them to have grown much worse.62

Whatever shifts in nuance and emphasis we may detect in Adams's political thought, they remain as footnotes to his black-letter text.

60. Adams to Zabdiel Adams, 21 June 1776, in L. H. Butterfield et al., eds., *Adams Family Correspondence* II:21; Adams to Abigail Adams, 3 July 1776, ibid., 27–28.
61. Adams to John Jebb, 21 August, 10 September 1785, in C. F. Adams, ed., *Works of John Adams* IX:535, 539.
62. Adams to James Warren, 9 January 1787, in Ford, ed., *Warren–Adams Letters* II:280.

Contrary to the impression fostered by Wood's account, John Adams's writings display remarkable coherence and balance in analyzing and judging political behavior. This is no small achievement, considering the great uncertainties and frustrations that attended the American revolutionary cause as a whole and Adams's undertakings in particular. He perceived clearly and welcomed the new decree "that a more equal Liberty, than has prevail'd in other Parts of the Earth, must be established in America. That Exuberance of Pride, which has produced an insolent Domination, in a few, a very few oppulent, monopolizing Families, will be brought down nearer to the Confines of Reason and Moderation, than they have been used." That decree was irrevocable, however much the grandees and nabobs of this world might fret and foam.63 The young revolutionary, being no mere ideologue, did not permit his pleasure at that prospect to blind him to more somber vistas. Adams already knew and was increasingly troubled by the skill and ease with which the rich and unscrupulous might turn democratic sentiments, credulity, and gratitude to their own corrupt purposes. From that standpoint, a constitutional provision such as Pennsylvania's condemnation of "offices of profit" was but a land mine planted by unthinking enthusiasts. "Hang well and pay well, conveys to my understanding infinitely more sense and more virtue than this whole article of the Pennsylvania Constitution." Far from letting his unquestionable enthusiasm for the republican cause unbalance his judgment, John Adams thought from first to last that the cause demanded that "government must become something more intelligible, rational, and steady." And as though to mark that fact down to the very end, he responded to an invitation to celebrate the fiftieth anniversary of the Declaration of Independence with this fitting last reflection: "A memorable epoch in the annals of the human race; destined in future history to form the brightest or the blackest page, according to the use or the abuse of those political institutions by which they shall in time to come be shaped by the *human mind*."64 Despite the old man's shaky syntax, Adams showed by his emphasis that he was still the very model of a thinking revolutionary.

63. Adams to Patrick Henry, 3 June 1776, in Taylor et al., eds., *Papers of John Adams* IV:235.

64. Adams to John Jebb, 21 August, 10 September 1785, in C. F. Adams, ed., *Works of John Adams* IX:532–536, 542–543; Adams to John Whitney, 7 June 1826, ibid. X:417.

Recovering the Past: Its Limits and Ours

The example of John Adams, rare individual though he was, suggests the difficulties attending the modern researcher's efforts to reconstruct earlier thought. At every turn we either must discriminate or risk losing sight of our object. If, then, we are to understand the past, we must first listen with care to its distant murmurings. On this, all seem to agree. But listening from afar, like viewing from afar, requires more than specialized apparatus. Without criteria of significance, we condemn ourselves to being overwhelmed by a clutter of noise, static, and random lights that effectively conceals the thing being sought. In this respect the historian's problem resembles the astronomer's.

The shortcomings of the modes prevailing today among historians of thought may be traced in large measure to this, their studied reluctance to discriminate. The criticisms developed in the preceding pages suggest a more rewarding approach to the past. It is necessary, first, to separate the rare and thoughtful from the ordinary and banal, lest the former simply be subsumed under the latter. It is necessary, further, to distinguish the several ends and purposes being sought by those voicing common grievances, lest a richly revealing variety be reduced to a monotone. Polemics and polemicists too call for discrimination, lest all political rhetoric be indistinguishable from incantation. Finally, we modern researchers need to separate ourselves from our commonplaces lest the truisms and shortcomings of our age keep us from taking in the perspective of another.

The first act of discrimination is urged upon the student of past thought when confronting those thousands of individuals of whose doings and speeches some record remains. The investigator might begin by noting which of those historical actors were held in special regard or notoriety by contemporaries. Taking note of one's own judgment and criteria, one might further distinguish those who shape thought from those who merely market it. As suggested before, this disjunction is by no means complete. Some profound thinkers have not held themselves above the task of popularizing or even proselytizing for their conclusions. Nor ought one to underestimate the ability of an intellectual middleman to reshape the thought of a greater or more original mind even while, so to speak, transmitting it. Earlier ages may have had their own John Lennons. But these indisputable complications do not themselves render suspect or invalid the basic distinction between those who are mindful of larger issues and longer-range consequences and those who are not.

The case for paying greater heed to the former than to the latter rests, not on elitist snobbery or on fallacious intellectualism, but on down-to-earth considerations. Ultimately it is only clear and coherent thought that can be understood; the rest must to a greater or lesser extent remain obscure.[65] Further, insofar as private thought matters, insofar as it may and sometimes does alter how a larger public believes and thinks and acts, one ought to prefer the clearer and more considered expression of that thought. The distant observer needs all the help available for orientation in unfamiliar terrain—and by and large it *is* unfamiliar terrain. Or to put it more cautiously, it is a safer presumption to treat the past, including our national past, as different or as possibly even strange. In doing so we reduce the likelihood of our unwittingly smoothing away or overlooking whatever might be distinctive in that earlier period. By preserving some sense of possible alienness, we leave ourselves open to being surprised and even to learning something. Then, should we indeed find ourselves in alien territory, all the more certainly will we stand in need of any available farsighted guide.

None of this presumes anything about who such a guide might be or about where such an individual should be sought. It would be a foolish student who confined the search to eighteenth-century graduates of Harvard or William and Mary, or even to good spellers. But it would not be foolish to place greater emphasis on things said and written than on deeds performed. For although words may be spoken with forked tongue, acts are often even more ambiguous. Again, this is not to deny that a civic ritual, as analyzed by a knowing and sensitive observer, may yield a wealth of insight. But the depth of analysis displayed in the opening chapters of *The Scarlet Letter* is hardly to be expected from scholars who probably know less of their subject than did Hawthorne and who operate under a more restricted license.

It is not, however, sufficient to identify the principal and most vocal participants in a controversy. A second act of discrimination is needed, for ends, too, have to be distinguished. The fact that diverse individuals or groups concur in a political proposal or even a program is no sure

65. Nathan Tarcov, "Quentin Skinner's Method and Machiavelli's *Prince*," *Ethics* 92 (1982):693.

testimony to the identity of their objectives. Without some effort at distinguishing agreement on principles from agreement on particular political arrangements, one runs the risk of assimilating and blurring much that might be revealing. Eighteenth-century Americans seem to have perceived this fact of political life most clearly. It was not enough for them to learn that a tax had been laid or lifted. What, they insisted on knowing, was the intention behind the bare act? That would make all the difference. Thus their preoccupation with motivations, far from being a simplistic obsession, can be seen, rather, as an effort on their part to discriminate among principles in the absence of clear and explicit statements.[66]

The different grievances of that generation (for example, those of Virginia revolutionaries or New York Anti-Federalists) ought likewise to be distinguished. One suspects that those people knew at least as well as modern scholars that they were not about to be reduced to the level of that distant brutalized people of whom they had so often heard—the Turks—or of that oppressed folk whom they so often saw at their very hearths. Yet they persisted in speaking of their own potential enslavement. That decision on their part to discriminate between the burden actually borne and "the general course and tendency of things" is now commonly dismissed as an expression of eighteenth-century paranoia, frenzy, or some other form of psychosocial disorder. In this, historians err. For the standard by which a grievance is identified and measured is, not the burden itself, but the interpretation one puts on what was tolerable about one's previous condition. If Jefferson and others were correct in seeing the colonists in British America as having enjoyed virtual self-government with very limited concessions to the imperial structure, then *that* condition becomes the measure of one's discontent. The test of reasonableness asks not whether a tax of so many pence on paper, tea, or glass will bring this proud people to its knees. It asks, instead, whether the characterization of the past arrangements and the identification of what was most to be cherished in those arrangements are defensible. If they are, it is no sign of madness to feel pain at every instance in that "long train of Abuses, Prevarications, and Artifices." Then may one rightly ask, "Are the People to be blamed, if they have the sence

66. Appleby, "Republicanism," 29.

of rational Creatures, and can think of things no otherwise than as they find and feel them?"⁶⁷

It is refreshing and chastening to turn from the new historians' account of these witless prisoners of a paranoiac age to Edmund Burke's portrait of a mercurial people's "fierce spirit of liberty." Like these historians, although for very different reasons, Burke chose not to discuss the abstract doctrine of liberty. Instead, he devoted a half-dozen pages in his speech on conciliation with the colonies to convey a sense and understanding of the temper and character of American resistance. The people there depicted, "snuff[ing] the approach of tyranny in every tainted breeze," leap to life from those dazzling pages.⁶⁸ The contrast with the productions of our postpsychological age ought to be humbling.

Even in those instances where individuals great and small indulge in polemical speech, the need for discernment and distinction continues. There is a difference between those who shouted the slogans and voiced the truisms of the age and those who knew that merely following "cultural imperatives" was the road to ruination. That difference is easy to overlook when confronted, for example, by John Adams's great catalogues of authorities, ancient and modern, in support of his "revolution-principles." Yet it is a serious misreading that would conflate a young lawyer's forensic overkill with an unquestioning acceptance of conventional maxims and truths. It was one thing to seek support from whatever quarter, catching up all who might to some extent share a common spirit, even while imposing one's own understanding on those authoritative names. But it was yet another thing to do so with an awareness of the limits and risks entailed. The

67. John Locke, *Two Treatises of Government*, bk. II, §225, 230. On this, thinking revolutionaries were insistent: "How ridiculous then is it to affirm, that we are quarreling for the trifling sum of three pence a pound on tea; when it is evidently the principle against which we contend"; Alexander Hamilton, "A Full Vindication of the Measures of the Congress . . . ," 15 December 1774, in Harold C. Syrett et al., eds., *The Papers of Alexander Hamilton* I:46, 48. Similarly, James Madison: "The people of the U.S. owe their independence & their liberty, to the wisdom of descrying in the minute tax of 3 pence on tea, the magnitude of the evil comprized in the precedent"; Elizabeth Fleet, ed., "Madison's 'Detached Memoranda,'" *William and Mary Quarterly*, 3d ser., 3 (1946):557. See also the account of Franklin's views of 1775 as reported by Edmund Burke, "An Appeal from the New to the Old Whigs," 1791, in *The Works of the Right Honourable Edmund Burke* III:30.

68. Edmund Burke, "Speech on Moving His Resolutions for Conciliation with the Colonies," 22 March 1775, in ibid. I:464–469.

best among the revolutionary founders understood what the hacks and third-rate people never grasped: that there is no substitute for a clear, calm understanding of one's situation.

Far, then, from being mere reflections of their "political culture," the best took special pains to distance themselves from much of what everyone else opined. James Madison would interrupt his polemics to remind overconfident friends and foes of the proposed constitution of the limits of intellect and language in politics. He did this, not with a view to deconstructing rational discourse, but for the antiquated purpose of finding the measure of clarity and precision that the complex subject and the imperfect mind and medium would admit.[69] John Adams would distinguish the respectable and necessary uses of rhetoric from nonsensical prating and manipulative chicanery. His penetrating analysis of ideology—named as such—remains a testimony to the power of good sense to form an independent judgment.[70] It was precisely in their conscious effort not to be mere mouthers of givens that the men separated themselves from the boys.

How ironical and baffling it is that, in the cause of sophisticated rhetorical analysis as the key to meaning, the new historians should treat eighteenth-century masters of rhetoric as slaves to commonplaces. In their avidity to discover unintended meanings in the texts (and even scraps) that have come down to us, too many of these historians miss the rich subtleties to be detected in the founders' studied use of language to both persuade and teach. When a cultivated art is mistaken for children's finger painting, the consequences are predictable.

These were no garden-variety eighteenth-century ideologues flattering themselves that they had an option to create a utopia. Knowing that they could neither stop history nor command it, these founders turned their thoughts to identifying sources of danger without fancying that they might overcome those dangers once and for all. Accordingly, they took thinking clearly to be their paramount duty. It was not enough to know a truth, such as that all political authority derives

69. James Madison, *Federalist,* No. 37, in Jacob E. Cooke, ed., *The Federalist,* 233–237.

70. John Adams to Benjamin Rush, 22 June, 19 September, 11 November 1806, in Biddle, ed., *Old Family Letters,* ser. A, 99–100, 109–113, 114–117; Adams to Thomas Jefferson, 13 July 1813, in C. F. Adams, ed., *Works of John Adams* X:52–54; Adams to Jefferson, 2 March 1816, ibid., 211–212; Adams to James Madison, 22 April 1817, ibid., 256–257.

from the people, or an invaluable precept, such as that branches of government ought to be separate and distinct. Nor would it do to guide one's policies by some simplistic definitions of regimes. Unless one thought through, with care and deliberation, how those truths and precepts would work in an actual world, one stood a good chance of ending up victim of one's own principles.

These thinking revolutionaries saw their task and opportunity in fashioning a new beginning, but without presuming a magical transmutation of the species. If they were impressed that their generation had the greatest opportunity since the First Pair, they also could never ask too often, What is the genius of this people for whom and to whom we mean to propose a constitution and government? What would this all too human people accept—and follow? In displaying this awareness of boundaries and limits, the thinking revolutionaries were by no means simply parroting the conventions of the age, for within those broad limits lay a variety of paths and a variety of outcomes. It was precisely this awareness that accounts for the sense of heavy responsibility that so marks the founders' thinking and writing. They feared for the fragility of their political handiwork, not because they were caught in the grip of a paranoiac, conspiratorial age, but because their daring project was and always would be in jeopardy.

The goal, after all, was not to attain some minimal standard of cooperation and preservation. A den of wary thieves, properly organized, might manage as much for themselves. Because these thinking revolutionaries wanted so much more than that, it was all the more important that they start right, choose right, and with greatest deliberation forfend or minimize whatever might threaten or damage their new order. This meant, among other things, that the simple truths of the age—the ideologues' daily bread—had somehow or other to be qualified, even deviated from, if the cause of a self-governing people was to be preserved. The shouters of slogans, the mouthers of maxims, may have believed sincerely, may have had real grievances, but their thoughts were simple and their vision limited. They are in no way to be confused with our thinking revolutionaries, intent on complicating, refining, and elaborating those simple truths the better to make them true in practice. For this great task, no useful device would be spurned. In the case of the separation of powers, for example, they relied not only on the slogan itself (proclaimed in a half-dozen state constitutions) but on its embodiment in institutions and, not least, on the good use of power by other, later, thoughtful men and women. Here was a way by which this extraordinary experiment might correct itself and survive.

If we are, then, finally, to recover the constitution of the thinking revolutionary, we must indeed look and listen with care. Doing so may demand nothing less than shaking free of our familiar intellectual tackle, the fourth and most trying of these requisite acts of separation and discernment. We might begin by reconsidering the new historians' claim to be the first to understand the murky automatic writing of the past—and this on the basis of a new revelation coming from (of all places) the abstract theoretical works of academic social science.[71] Following the lead of those thoughtful founders who attacked ideologues for not rising above the assumptions of their age, we present-day students might make a special effort to rise above our age's maxims and think anew. Following the lead of those thoughtful founders who insisted on the difference between levels of political discourse, we might discriminate between those who dealt only in ideals and those who, without abandoning ideals, considered a world peopled with real men and women. Those thoughtful founders were not above creating a political culture, but they were intent on its being a better one. If those men of the Enlightenment, declining to rely solely on the persuasiveness of reason, chose as well to form a political culture that would instill reverence for the laws, it was out of their recognition that the citizenry were mere mortals. But since these were to be self-governing mortals, they dared not wish for a nation of automatic believers. Far from it.

Those founders believed and acted on the premise that the highest activity of the thinking revolutionary is constitution making and constitution preserving. Neither was possible where mindlessness reigned. Without thinkers, and a population receptive to thoughtful argument, the brave experiment was doomed. Hence they taught through precept and example that a people might distinguish better from worse reasons and choose the better out of its understanding. They acted as though dedicated intelligence might make a difference. Those precepts and assumptions may well be controverted. But the thinking revolutionary would probably say that their denial or denigration carries its own lesson to the broader public.[72]

71. John Patrick Diggins, *The Lost Soul of American Politics: Virtue, Self-Interest, and the Foundations of Liberalism,* 364.

72. Tocqueville, *Democracy in America,* 464–465 (II, i, 20); see also Diggins, *Lost Soul,* 357.

It takes an act of considerable will and historical imagination for a historian to shake loose of prevailing intellectual modes. Looking beyond mere numbers, we can see that ours is no great age of founding and constitution making. It is almost natural that people today should take principles for granted and find it hard to envision an earlier world in which many minds were filled with a sense of fundamentals contending as real alternatives and inviting reasoned choice. And as though this were not enough of a barrier to historical understanding and reconstruction, there is the further artificial difference between our age and that of the founders: theirs was a period when thought was believed (rightly or wrongly) to be enlightenment; ours, when thought is believed (rightly or wrongly) to be ideology. Yet even if we are persuaded that we are correct, we are not free as students of another period and another way of thinking to ignore the consequences of that difference in belief. We are compelled as students of that other period to try to imagine what differences that difference in belief makes in how thought is conducted, transmitted, and applied.

Someone might wonder, finally, whether all this talk of ideology and ideas, reasons and thoughtfulness, is not itself an exaggeration. Did all that theorizing really matter beyond the handful who delighted in such things? Such misgivings are not the monopoly of sophisticated historians, for some founders confronted those very doubts at the time. To the charge that he and his like were "disaffected" incendiaries, young John Adams chose only to deny the implied passivity of the people. His premise was that "the people are capable of understanding, seeing and feeling the difference between true and false, right and wrong, virtue and vice"; it was to "the sense of this difference" that he and those like him had recurred. It was a mistake to view the people as so much flammable matter ready at any moment to be touched off and exploded: "I appeal to all experience, and to universal history, if it has ever been in the power of popular leaders, uninvested with other authority than what is conferred by the popular suffrage, to persuade a large people, for any length of time together, to think themselves wronged, injured, and oppressed, unless they really were, and saw and felt it to be so."[73]

73. John Adams, "Novanglus," no. 1, 23 January 1775, in Taylor et al., eds., *Papers of John Adams* II:229. What began as an "apprehension" would then "arouse the attention, not only of the inquiring mind, but of the common people, and urge them to close thinking on the constitutional authority of parliament over the colonies"; Adams to Jedidiah Morse, 2 December 1815, in C. F. Adams, ed., *Works of John Adams* X:185.

For John Adams, reflection and the exchange of reasons were central to the age of founding and constitution making. Far from being an irrelevance, the capacity for thoughtful response was taken to be broadly distributed in society, albeit in different degrees and kinds. The counterpart of the thinking revolutionary in America was not some sodden peasantry. But, by the same token, neither was that population a vast, continuous seminar in political theory. Newspapers were scarce, and books no less so. "Every class of men cannot be supposed to have been aided by extensive literary views." And yet a variety of social and political arrangements made it possible for Virginians, for example, "to catch the full spirit of the theories which at the fountainhead were known only to men of studious retirement."[74] In leaving their retirement and speaking as they did, the thinking revolutionaries sought to honor themselves and their public. On this basis rested their confident invitation to all—contemporaries and successors alike—to examine their principles and acts. That invitation still stands.

74. Edmund Randolph, *History of Virginia,* 193–194.

PART ONE

SECURING

THE REPUBLIC

I

Franklin, Spectator

W̶E̶ LIVE our lives one day at a time, doing (we say) the best we can. We may have plans and expectations, we may take care to control our time, to direct our efforts. But for most of us life has its surprises, its bumps and lumps. Its disorder may please us or threaten us, but in either case life is not tidy or simple, certainly not in the way the *story* of a life may be. In speaking, then, of the life of Benjamin Franklin, let us remember that we are not speaking of the Franklin who lived that life. That Franklin is forever lost to us, was perhaps already lost to the man of sixty-five who decided to spend a few weeks' leisure in the country writing down a recollection of his life.

What we can look at and consider are the Benjamin Franklin portrayed in the *Autobiography* and the Benjamin Franklin who wrote the *Autobiography*. Each is a subtle, complex fellow—sometimes charming, sometimes astonishing, sometimes less than agreeable. Each is a man well worth knowing. I propose to begin by looking at what Franklin *says* about him, about his acts, his thoughts, his character. Then I consider what his acts and thoughts and character *tell* us about him. Finally, I look at Franklin, autobiographer, seeking evidence about the man from the way he composed his life story.

A Likely Tale

What does Franklin have to tell us about himself? What are his actions? his pleasures? his concerns? his relations with others? his religion? No one who has even hearsay knowledge of Franklin can be surprised by the principal theme of the *Autobiography:* Benjamin Franklin is a leader of men, an entrepreneur, a great projector. He is prefigured in the life and character of his English uncle, Thomas, that "ingenious" scrivener who was "a chief Mover of all publick Spirited Undertakings" for the county, town, and village where he lived, and who died four years to a day before Benjamin was born. The *Autobiography* is, so to speak, the story of a "Transmigration" (47–48).[1] Even as a lad, Franklin says, he "was generally a Leader among the Boys, and sometimes led them into Scrapes." He gives an example of what he calls "an early projecting public Spirit": "By much Trampling," Ben and his comrades had turned a favored fishing spot into "a mere Quagmire." Ben is the one who reacts to the problem by proposing a solution—build a wharf. Ben is the one who points out the suitable means—a large heap of stones intended for building a house nearby. Ben is the one who organizes and helps execute the project—assembling his playfellows "and working with them diligently like so many Emmets" or ants (54).

With one qualification, it is a scene to be repeated again and again in the *Autobiography.* Franklin founds the Junto and draws up its rules (116); writes, edits, and prints the *Pennsylvania Gazette* (120–121); proposes and prints paper currency (124); becomes a successful stationer (125–126); proposes and founds a subscription library (130, 142); proposes founding a secret sect, the Society of the Free and Easy (162–163); publishes *Poor Richard's Almanack* (163–164); proposes a better way of regulating the City Watch (173–174); proposes and organizes a fire company (174); proposes and establishes the American Philosophical Society (182); proposes and helps organize and supply a militia (182–184); invents and promotes an improved stove (191–192); proposes and helps organize and establish an academy for a more complete education of Pennsylvanian youth (192–195); promotes and helps finance a hospital by inventing the device of a conditional grant based on matching funds (199–201); promotes the paving and lighting of Philadelphia's streets (202–203); introduces sound management in the operations of the colonial post office (208); proposes and draws up "a Plan for the Union of all the Colonies, under one Government so far as might be

---

1. The page references in parentheses are to Leonard W. Labaree et al., eds., *The Autobiography of Benjamin Franklin.*

necessary for Defence, and other important general Purposes" (209–210); organizes and secures the logistical support for Braddock's ill-fated attempt to capture Fort Duquesne (217–223); and organizes and supervises the defense of Pennsylvania's northwestern frontier (230–236). The *Autobiography* is first and foremost the account of Franklin's vocation as a public-spirited projector.

But Franklin is not one who is "all business." The opening sentence of the *Autobiography* speaks, not of public duty, but of private pleasure, the pleasure he has in obtaining any little anecdotes of his ancestors (43). And not only of them, for Franklin savors any good story. One of the loveliest scenes in the *Autobiography* is that of the nineteen-year-old compositor and the elderly widow with the gout, spending their evenings together in her London room, sharing a supper of "only half an Anchovy each, on a very little Strip of Bread and Butter, and half a Pint of Ale" between them, the young lodger being regaled with his landlady's thousand reminiscences of people of distinction as far back as the times of Charles II (102). But it is not only a good story that Franklin savors; it is life itself. He would, he says, have no objection to reliving the same life from the beginning—faults and sinister accidents and all (43–44). This I take to be Franklin's considered view, rather than the confessed disappointment the twenty-one-year-old felt on recovering from a nearly fatal pleurisy, having already resigned himself to death. We may be invited to laugh at this instance of youthful impatience at having "all that disagreeable work to do over again" (107). All in all, the picture is of a man who finds pleasures in life but is enslaved to none, a man who has simple tastes (55, 145, 236). What Franklin says of his swimming holds as well for his writing and his doing: he delights in "aiming at the graceful and easy, as well as the Useful" (104, 163–164).

There is no doubt that this aim is a source of pleasure to Franklin, just as it is a source of potential delight to later generations contemplating Franklin's account. But it is much more; it is one of Franklin's intensely held ambitions. To combine the appearance of grace and ease with genuine utility is a preoccupation of the boy and the man. Speaking of himself as a sixteen-year-old, he says, "I was extreamly ambitious" to come to be "a tolerable English Writer"; and he shows us how he went at it (62). He also tells us that he wished to be—and be perceived as—a certain kind of human, and how he proceeded to work at making that come to pass. If we are to believe what we are told, Franklin knows almost from the outset that he has "a tolerable Character to begin the World with," that is, that he has a character worth cherishing and preserving. He may be faulted for certain lapses from a reasonably strict moral code, but Franklin invites us to be understanding and to not attribute these to malice or willfulness. Considering his "Youth, Inexperience, and the Knavery of others," it was almost necessary that these lapses occur, especially as he was living "remote from the Eye and Advice" of his father (115). But in speaking of his concern for his good name, Franklin (I suspect) is not thinking especially of his whoring. That he treats quite matter-of-factly as an activity into which he had been hurried by "that hard-to-be-govern'd Passion of Youth." Franklin's evaluation is limited to considerations of expense, inconvenience, and risk to health (128). No, the objects of Franklin's serious concern are rather those actions that he charmingly calls, after the style of printers, "errata." All things considered, they are not many.

The first action to be so called is Ben's breach of the contract of indenture to his overbearing older brother when he knew that James would not be in a position to assert his legal rights against the young apprentice. Franklin carefully notes later on how he made ample amends for his earlier injustice (70, 170). The second instance, what Franklin calls "one of the first great Errata of my Life," is his use of funds that had been placed in his trust (86). This act causes Franklin continuing anxiety and embarrassment; the error is "in some degree corrected" only after five years (87, 110, 114, 121–122). Another of Franklin's "great Errata" is his forgetting the promises he had exchanged with Miss Deborah Reed—or perhaps better put, his forgetting Miss Read almost altogether after he reaches London. Moved by a lack of better opportunities, as well as by pity and remorse, Franklin corrects "that great Erratum" as well as he can through a common-law marriage almost six years later (96, 129). Franklin's first stay in London is the occasion of two other errata, neither of which he could correct. One concerns "a little metaphysical Piece" he composed, his *Dissertation on Liberty and Necessity, Pleasure and Pain.* Franklin considers his *printing* of this pamphlet another of his life's errata (96). And, finally, there is an awkward incident when Franklin "attempted Familiarities" with the mistress of his deadbeat friend Ralph, "another Erratum" that costs him a friend and saves him much trouble and money (99).

All in all, this is not the narrative of a man given to regrets. His present concern is not with yesterday's misstep but with today's need and tomorrow's opportunity. When he looks at his yesterdays it is to remind himself—and us—of how far he has come. His "low Begin-ning" is a source of continuing gratification to the rising man of ambition (46, 50, 75, 197).

Franklin portrays his relations with others as complex and ambigu-ous. He gives several instances of his generosity. In one case he pays handsomely for his passage on a rowboat, prompted "perhaps thro' Fear of being thought to have but little" (75). In another place he traces his readiness to help young folk starting out in business to the gratitude and pleasure *he* felt on earning what we would call his first dollar (115–116). Still later in the *Autobiography* Franklin states a principle of generosity that leads him to decline a patent for his improved stove. It is worth noting, however, that neither generosity nor liberality nor charity figures in Franklin's list of the thirteen virtues (192, 149–150). The *Autobiography* is to a considerable ex-tent a narrative of friendships and mutual assistance, of loyalty and betrayal, and accordingly of the costs and benefits of our involvement with others. On the whole, Franklin makes very good use of his connections; the self-made man does not make it on his own. Of this there are numerous examples. No less striking, though, are the in-stances where Franklin's close friendships end in bitter dispute, as with John Collins and James Ralph. It is not clear how much Franklin holds himself to blame for the troubles these old friends bring on him (89–90, 114), but in each case Franklin loses both a friend and a burden with a clear sense of relief (84–86, 95, 98–99).

More revealing than any of this, however, is Franklin's general mode of dealing with others. He gives several instances of his conten-tiousness and indiscretion as a young man. He speaks of his "dis-putacious Turn" of mind as of an infectious disease that he had caught by reading in his father's library of religious polemics (58, 60). His precocious cleverness gives him a reputation in Boston "as a young Genius that had a Turn for Libelling and Satyr" (69), even "as an Infidel or Atheist" (71). His pamphlet on liberty and necessity leads his London employer to consider Ben "a young Man of some Ingenuity" though with abominable principles (96). The *Autobiogra-phy* is an account of how Franklin gradually overcomes his "dis-putacious Turn." The change begins when Ben is charmed by Xenophon's account of Socrates in the *Memorabilia*. Ben drops his mode of "abrupt Contradiction, and positive Argumentation, and put[s] on the humble Enquirer and Doubter" (64). This famous strat-egy of humility proves endlessly useful.

At first Franklin is enthused over the ease and even elegance with which he is able to work over his opponents, artfully ensnaring them in difficulties, contradictions, and embarrassments and gaining his victories on the cheap (64–65, 88). He also judges this method safest for himself—against the discovery by others of his true views or his errors (64, 78, 159). But in time he comes to see something more in the strategy of humility than a means of vainglorious triumph: "I continu'd this Method some few Years, but gradually left it, retaining only the Habit of expressing my self in Terms of modest Diffidence, never using when I advance any thing that may possibly be disputed, the Words, *Certainly, undoubtedly,* or any others that give the Air of Positiveness to an Opinion." By overcoming his eristic nature, Franklin is able to serve the public *and* himself. He increases his "Power of doing Good" through ingratiating speech rather than eloquence (65, 117, 159–160). He learns from his experience that humility or "the *Appearance* of it" or a low profile will make one's affair go on more smoothly. He accordingly adopts a lifelong rule of action: "I . . . put my self as much as I could out of sight" (159, 143, 193). This sacrifice of one's vanity, Franklin assures us, is both trivial and temporary: "If it remains a while uncertain to whom the Merit belongs, some one more vain than yourself will be encouraged to claim it, and then even Envy will be dispos'd to do you Justice, by plucking those assum'd Feathers, and restoring them to their right Owner" (143). It is truly consoling to know, wrapped in our humility, that our vanity and pride will be gratified after all (44, 160, 237–238).

This summary of what Franklin says about himself can properly conclude with a review of his remarks on his religion. Early in the *Autobiography,* after speaking of the gratitude owed God for human vanity, Franklin goes on in his own name to thank God for "his kind Providence, which led me to the Means I us'd and gave them Success" (44–45). It is not clear where the stress falls in this sentence, on "his kind Providence" or on "the Means *I* us'd." Nor is it altogether clear what Franklin understands by Providence: when speaking of his managing to survive in London "without any *wilful* gross Immorality or Injustice that might have been expected from my Want of Religion," Franklin credits a certain opinion he held, "with the kind hand of Providence, or some guardian Angel, or accidental favourable Circumstances and Situations, or all together" (115; cf. 193 n. 4).

It is clear, however, that Franklin is no ordinary religionist. Once he is a teenager and no longer living in his father's house, Ben evades public worship as much as he can. He still thinks such attendance a duty, "tho' I could not, as it seemed to me, afford the Time to practise it" (63). The Presbyterian or Congregationalist doctrines in which he has been educated seem to him unintelligible or doubtful. Accordingly, he spends his Sundays more profitably in study (145–146). By age fifteen he begins to doubt revelation. Some books attacking Deism have the opposite effect on Franklin, converting him into "a thorough Deist." He begins to have second thoughts when he reflects on the behavior of Deists—Collins, Ralph, Governor Keith, himself: "I began to suspect that this Doctrine tho' it might be true, was not very useful" (113–114). He now turns to consider religion from a purely human point of view. Convinced that *"Truth, Sincerity and Integrity in Dealings between Man and Man"* are indispensable for human happiness, Franklin judges each religion in accord with its tendency to support or hinder this social purpose (114). In one sense, all the religions in America are good enough. They all contain what Franklin deems to be the essential principles: God's existence, Creation, Providence, serving God by doing good to man, immortality of the soul, and reward and punishment "either here or hereafter" (146).

Franklin's private position is to respect religions differently in proportion as he finds them "more or less mix'd with other Articles which without any Tendency to inspire, promote or confirm Morality, serv'd principally to divide us and make us unfriendly to one another." Franklin's public position, based on the opinion that even the worst religion has some good effects, is "to avoid all Discourse that might tend to lessen the good Opinion another might have of his own Religion." This position, taken as a good citizen, leads Franklin never to refuse contributing his bit to help build new places of worship (146). But it in no way lessens his disgust with preachings that seem to aim "rather to make us Presbyterians than good Citizens" (147), and it in no way lessens his zealous partisanship in favor of good works (167). Indeed, Franklin insists on our seeing that his God expects him to fulfill his obligation here on earth "not for Christ's sake," but for his fellow's (153, 178–179).

Show and Tell

The *Autobiography* is filled with revealing accounts of a singular human being. Apart, then, from what Franklin says about himself, there is much to be learned from the acts and thoughts and characteristics themselves. The most obvious act to take note of is the writing of an autobiography. Many individuals find themselves endlessly interesting; only few compose the story of their life. Franklin gives several reasons for writing his story. The first is what he imagines about the addressee of the *Autobiography* (Part One is in the form of a letter, beginning "Dear Son"), namely, that his son will find agreeable what Benjamin Franklin has always found pleasurable—"obtaining any little Anecdotes" of one's ancestors. But this is not all; Franklin finds "some other Inducements." Recalling how far he has risen and the happiness he has so far enjoyed, he considers that his posterity may wish to imitate the means he has made use of "as they may find some of them suitable to their own Situations" (43). Franklin is not a ponderous ancestor sermonizing from atop a pedestal. Furthermore, as already indicated, he would relive his life if he could, in a corrected second edition if possible, but in an unrevised reprinting if need be. But as he does not expect such an offer to be made, he settles for the third-best thing—recollecting his life. Of course, if the intention were merely private, Franklin could accomplish that with his eyes closed, sitting in a lawn chair at Twyford; we all have indulged in summer afternoon recollections. But Franklin wishes "to make that Recollection as durable as possible" and so commits it to writing. Yet the *Autobiography* is not a memorandum to himself, and barely (I submit) one to his relations. Nonetheless, the large public that would find Franklin's story engrossing is not even alluded to here. Franklin closes his account of inducements with a confession that, in writing this story, "perhaps I shall a good deal gratify my own Vanity" (43–44). The mixed motives of man are a leading theme of the book.

Another leading theme is Franklin's early and continuing dedication to self-improvement. Edifying table talk was always the main course for dinner at his father's house (55). When Josiah Franklin took young Ben on walking tours to see Boston craftsmen at their work, he implanted in his son a delight in good craftsmanship and a desire to do it himself (57). Ben's "Bookish Inclination" leads him directly to his avenue of ascent; and this, not only because of what he reads—Bunyan, Plutarch, Defoe, Cotton Mather, and ever more and better books (57–59, 61–64, 72, 97, 106, 109, 112, 126)—but because of his being known to be a reader (79, 85, 117–118, 130–131, 141–143). It is through his chance encounter with an odd volume of

Addison and Steele's *Spectator* that Franklin is inspired to try to become as good a writer (61–62). He teaches himself arithmetic, geometry, logic, grammar, and foreign languages (63–64, 168–169). He learns the utility of conversation (106) and forms "a Club for mutual Improvement," the Junto, that induces its members to read with attention and speak more effectively to the purpose (116–118). And then, of course, there is Franklin's "bold and arduous Project of arriving at moral Perfection," a project at first limited to himself, but then intended to be the dedicated concern of an entire "Sect," which Franklin would have called "the Society of the *Free and Easy*" (148, 158, 161–163).

In pursuing this lifelong program of self-improvement, Franklin very early discovers the need for a proper method. As a sixteen-year-old, he devises a method for learning method (62). By the time he conceives of the project of arriving at moral perfection, he has in effect mastered the main features of the Cartesian method. One sees it in the way he studies foreign languages (168–169), and in the way he draws up a set of lectures on electricity, "in which the Experiments were rang'd in such Order and accompanied with Explanations in such Method, as that the foregoing should assist in Comprehending the following" (241). One sees it in his forming a plan, at age twenty, regulating his future conduct in life (106). Franklin understands how little reliance can be put on "the mere speculative Conviction" that we have an interest in being completely virtuous. Something more is needed, something surer; that something is what Franklin himself calls a "Method," which begins with a clear and distinct definition of the twelve or thirteen virtues Franklin believes to be necessary or desirable (148–149). With this method, anyone, cut off like Franklin from his family, may undertake this great self-reformation. By regularly examining oneself and one's little book of moral accounts, an individual may gradually and systematically "acquire the *Habitude*" of all the virtues (150–152). Franklin never actually acquires moral perfection for himself, but for that he blames himself, not his method. Even so, he believes himself "a better and a happier Man" for the attempt. He recommends his example to his descendants, and he believes that his method "might be serviceable to People in all Religions." Long after ceasing to follow the prescribed daily and weekly routines, Franklin continues always to carry his little book with the columns and the lines and the little black spots (155–157). For whose benefit is that famous little book carried? To whom is it shown?

I think it would almost be impossible to exaggerate the importance method plays in Franklin's life and thought, or the conviction with which he praises it. Indeed, one sees the highest tribute to method in what might well stand as Franklin's credo: "I have always thought that one Man of tolerable Abilities may work great Changes, and accomplish great Affairs among Mankind, if he first forms a good Plan, and, cutting off all Amusements or other Employments that would divert his Attention, makes the Execution of that same Plan his sole Study and Business" (163).

The *Autobiography* tells us a vast amount about the way Franklin executed his plan. But as is frequently the case with Franklin, the instruction comes by way of example, not exhortation. Consider these devices: sending anonymous contributions to his brother's newspaper, written in a disguised hand (67–68); keeping his whereabouts secret from his family after he escapes from Boston (79); planning secretly to compete with his Philadelphia employer while living in his house (80–81, 88); lampooning the weakest potential competitor (120); showing up the incompetence of the public printer by distributing to the legislature an elegant and correct copy of what had just been printed "in a coarse blundering manner" (121); taking care "not only to be in *Reality* Industrious and frugal, but to avoid all *Appearances* of the Contrary"—taking care "to show that I was not above my Business, I sometimes brought home the Paper purchas'd at the Stores, thro' the Streets on a Wheelbarrow" (125–126); bribing post office riders to carry and distribute his newspapers privately after the postmaster (who published the competing newspaper) was unkind enough to forbid it (127); putting himself as much as he can out of sight in proposing a public subscription library (143); proposing a secret sect to be recruited among "ingenuous well-disposed Youths, to whom with prudent Caution the Scheme should be gradually communicated" (162–163); gaining the favor and friendship of a potentially powerful opponent by the "Method" of contriving to have him do Franklin a kindness (171–172); proposing a reform of the City Watch as though it were an idea arising independently in each of the several offshoots of the Junto (173); "preparing the Minds of People" for new proposals, be they for regulating the City Watch, or forming a voluntary association for the military defence of Quaker Philadelphia, or founding an academy, or establishing a hospital (173, 182–183, 193, 200); supporting the militia association by "calling in the Aid of Religion" in the form of a proclamation for a fast (184); contriving the device of a conditional matching-funds grant that "work'd both ways," first, by securing the votes of opposing legislators who "now conceiv'd they might have the Credit of being charitable without the Expence," and second, by reinforcing the arguments of fund-raisers who now could urge that "every Man's Donation would be doubled"—altogether a maneuver that Franklin found especially pleasing (200–201).

This catalogue by no means exhausts the arsenal of cunning devices at Franklin's command, but it is a true and sufficient gloss on the meaning of the seventh virtue: "Sincerity. Use no hurtful Deceit" (150). Franklin is a master of tactics and strategy, ingratiating candor and disarming secretiveness. He delights in subterfuge and spoof, manipulation from a distance, the workings of an invisible or barely perceptible mechanism. He wishes to be a mighty mover of men, but all things considered, he would prefer they did not know it at the time. A principal lesson of the *Autobiography* is that the strategy of humility is indeed the best policy.

Franklin's thoughts and views expressed in the *Autobiography* add much to our understanding of the man. Of these, perhaps none is as revealing as Franklin's judgments of utility. He repeatedly regrets his early immersion in books of polemic theology. Compared with Plutarch's *Lives,* they are quite useless—except for polemical clergymen (58). Although Franklin does *once* become a "zealous Partisan" against orthodox Presbyterian partisan zeal (167), he generally is so revulsed by polemics as to shy away from disputation and discourage it whenever he can (118, 192). It might be fair to say that, for Franklin, polemics is totally useless and senseless, and those who indulge in it are themselves useless (60, 147, 213). An excellent illustration is provided by his reaction to an attack on his experiments and observations on electricity. A French worthy, "Preceptor in Natural Philosophy to the Royal Family," reacts to Franklin's work by first refusing to believe that such a work could come from America (thereby outbuffoning Buffon) and then challenging Franklin and defending his own theory. Franklin almost responds, but holds back. Perhaps it was Franklin's week for improving his industry: "Lose no Time. Be always employ'd in something useful. Cut off all unnecessary Actions" (149). In any event, the decision is an irresistible blend of common sense and strategy. Franklin decides to let his papers shift for themselves, believing his precious time is better spent "in making new Experiments, than in Disputing about those already made." A learned friend takes up Franklin's cause, Franklin's book is translated into three languages, and Franklin's opponent lives to see himself "the last of his Sect" except for one disciple (243–244).

There are many other instances, less splendidly triumphant, of Franklin's steady recourse to utility as the guide to conduct. Ben's early involvement with poetry is controlled by this consideration: "I approv'd the amusing one's self with Poetry now and then, so far as to improve one's Language, but no farther" (90). He knows the use in being useful to others, and he shows this brilliantly in his relations with his fellow compositors (both the drinkers and the nondrinkers) as well as with the master in the London printing house (100–101). He begins to suspect his freethinking doctrines because he doubts their utility, not their truth (114). He avoids public worship because he is otherwise, and more usefully, employed, but he still holds "an Opinion of its Propriety, and of its Utility when rightly conducted" (145–147). He is "fully persuaded of the Utility and Excellency of [his] Method" for arriving at moral perfection; one is tempted to say that its excellency consists precisely in its utility (157). Even wealth— that demon with which Franklin often is alleged to be obsessed— even wealth is considered in terms of its utility. Poor Richard tries to inculcate "Industry and Frugality, as the Means of procuring Wealth and thereby securing Virtue." The end in view is not a stuffed sack, but one that can *"stand upright"* (164).

Franklin views his own "sufficient tho' moderate Fortune" as the equipment (in Aristotle's sense) that will secure the "Leisure during the rest of my Life, for Philosophical Studies and Amusements" (196). Justice demands that we recognize this prominent feature of his thoughts. Franklin is a man of immense curiosity. Much of it is prompted, to be sure, by his awareness that "this is the Age of Experiments" and that experiments can reduce disconnected ideas and experiences to a set of rules, which can be of great use (256–257). The practical bent of his inquiring spirit also shows in his timing the work of axemen building a fort (233), examining the art by which Indians conceal their fires (234), or inquiring into the practices of the Moravians (236–237). But there is something more. Consider Franklin's first reaction on seeing some electrical experiments: "Being on a Subject quite new to me, they equally surpriz'd and pleas'd me" (240). In this capacity to be surprised and to be delighted by it, Franklin discloses one of his most endearing qualities.

The character that emerges from these pages is, as I have already suggested, resistant to simple summary. As often as not, the neat, simple statement has a concealed cutting edge. Franklin confesses his vanity, since no one would believe his denial, but then goes on to show why it would not be simply absurd "if a Man were to thank God for his Vanity among the other Comforts of Life" (44). He allows that "you" the reader will perhaps detect many instances of pride in his story, notwithstanding repeated efforts to disguise it or beat it down—but then, "even if I could conceive that I had compleatly overcome it, I should probably [be] proud of my Humility" (160). He exhibits modesty in a discussion of modesty—but only after improving on the poetry of Alexander Pope (66). His displays of modesty tend to be intermingled with displays of vanity (68, 159–160). His ambition is flattered by his advance in the world, not least because he starts from so low a beginning (197). He insists on our seeing his nonprivileged origins: "the youngest Son of the youngest Son for 5 Generations back" (46), the offspring of an "obscure Family" (50), the "unlikely Beginnings" of the hungry, tired, dirty boy who stepped onto the Market Street wharf one Sunday morning in Philadelphia long ago (75). He has come a long way, and he is proud of it.

Others view young Ben as unworldly and naive, as indeed he is to a considerable extent (82–84), but Ben can "immediately" see the difference between "a crafty old Sophister, and . . . a mere Novice" (78). He quickly learns "the Folly of being on ill Terms with those one is to live with continually" (100). He knows how to play out a line of argument the better to hook a fish like Keimer (88–89). Franklin's generosity is principled but almost always controlled (146, 177, 191–192, 201–202). His motives in arranging his marriage are a mixture of resentment at getting what he suspects might be the worse part of a bargain in other marriage negotiations, reduced expectations, a wish to avoid the inconvenience and expense of whores, pity for Deborah Read, and remorse over his earlier conduct toward her (127–129). The marriage is a settlement of mutual convenience and is depicted without the warmth Franklin otherwise shows so often in the *Autobiography*. But perhaps one ought not to make too much of this. Eighteenth-century writers tend to be reticent on this subject; in comparison with Jefferson's description of *his* marriage, Franklin's seems garrulous.

Yet the sense that Franklin is holding back on us persists and is an expression, I believe, of his politic character. Politic or prudent people know when not to speak fully (146). Franklin is on the whole pleased that his "ingenious" friend, Dr. John Browne of Burlington, New Jersey, did not publish or succeed in publishing his wicked travesty of the Bible in doggerel verse, for that "might have hurt weak minds" (74, cf. 268). With regard to his own freethinking pamphlet, Franklin comes to regret the printing. Again the issue is limited strictly to social consequences (96, 114). In evaluating his friend George Whitefield, Franklin remarks that it would have been better if that famous evangelist had never written anything. Whitefield would then have been exempt from attack, his reputation might still be growing, and "his Proselites would be left at liberty to feign for him as great a Variety of Excellencies, as their enthusiastic Admiration might wish him to have possessed" (180). The man who wrote that sentence clearly felt no need to have others feign for *him*.

Politic Artlessness

The reason that Franklin does not follow his own advice goes to the heart of the *Autobiography* and of the autobiographer. Franklin is mindful of the maxim *litera scripta manet,* "the written letter remains" (180). Having committed yourself in print, you are "bound and confin'd" and no longer free to act on better second thoughts. Rare indeed is the sect that declines to fix and publish its articles of belief because it has enough sense and modesty to realize that it holds no present monopoly on an unchanging truth, that it is as much in the fog as those around it (190–191). Believing this, then, why is it that Franklin is so emphatically a man of letters? In part, I submit, because of his awareness of his singularity. *He* can get away with it.

In one of the two letters addressed to him that he intended to insert after Part One of the *Autobiography,* his correspondent speaks of "your great age, the great caution of your character, and your peculiar style of thinking." These, Benjamin Vaughan thinks, make it unlikely "that any one besides yourself can be sufficiently master of the facts of your life, or the intentions of your mind" (139). This is a true, even profound, reading of Franklin the man. However much Franklin may insist that he intends only "to relate Facts, and not to make Apologies for them" (148), he is, in truth, doing much more—and much less. The *Autobiography* is an open book, but the same cannot quite be said for either the author or the subject.

The *Autobiography* is, of course, a story—a wonderfully told story. It follows the device of Franklin's old favorite, "Honest John" Bunyan, "who mix'd Narration and Dialogue, a Method of Writing very engaging to the Reader, who in the most interesting Parts finds himself as it were brought into the Company, and present at the Discourse" (72). Franklin is a master at this (e.g., 90–91, 122–123, 189–190, 212–214, 250–251). As *we* are brought into the company, we tend to be charmed and carried away by the action. We may become so engrossed in the vivid portrayals—of Uncle Thomas, Uncle Benjamin, Father Josiah, Governor Keith, employer Samuel Keimer—that we barely notice how blandly others are portrayed—Mother Abiah, Brother James, Wife Deborah—and we may not even notice the absence of the beloved Sister Jane and Daughter Sarah. But then again, it is not this artist's intention that we constantly be aware of his shaping hand. If we confuse this story of a life for the life itself, that is all for the good.

Franklin also is a master at ingratiating himself with his reader or auditor, believing a modest manner the best way "to *inform*, or to be *informed*, to *please* or to *persuade*" (65). As in the case of *Poor Richard's Almanack*, Benjamin Franklin's *Autobiography* is meant to be "both entertaining and useful" (163–164). Like those sensible Moravian tutors he observes, Franklin adapts his discourse to the capacities of his audience and delivers it "in a pleasing familiar Manner, coaxing them as it were to be good" (237). He follows his boyhood teacher in using "mild encouraging Methods" (53). As a result, we cannot miss the main lessons of the book.

First, Franklin takes care "that you may in your Mind compare such unlikely Beginnings with the Figure [he has] since made" in Philadelphia (75). Everyone is to get that message. Similarly, everyone is to learn the need for reasonableness and the limits of reason. Who can forget the picture of young Ben, "balanc'd some time" between his vegetarian principles and his inclination produced by the admirable smell of fish coming hot out of the frying pan? His resolution of the dilemma is presented as a triumph of "convenient"—that is to say, self-serving—reasoning and is only one of a number of memorable warnings (87–88). The "Water-American" cannot through argument convince his fellow pressman in London that strong beer will make them no stronger than the comparable amount of grain or flour dissolved in water, but his example is persuasive (99–101). Indeed, "mere speculative Conviction" is not enough even for Franklin; to keep from slipping off the path to virtue, he has to contrive a new method (148). In the end, though, we cannot be certain whether Franklin's settling for something less than extreme moral perfection is good sense or merely a case of "convenient" reasonableness: The man who concluded, after protracted grinding and polishing, that he liked a speckled ax best had learned a truth—and he was very tired (155–156). Finally, there is the great lesson to which Franklin once meant to devote a book, *The Art of Virtue,* and which he only sketches in the *Autobiography* (148–158). It is the great project of moral perfection—great and beyond the reach of reasoning and conviction, but attainable in large measure nonetheless. Ordinary folk, using the proper method, can acquire the necessary habits. No longer is perfection to be seen as the preserve of rare individuals of high character and high motivation. These, I say, are large, highly visible lessons of the *Autobiography.* We cannot help noticing them, whether or not we learn them and act on them.

Behind these, however, is another kind of instruction. Here the message is less distinct; to make out the letters, we need to put on a pair of bifocals. It is interesting to observe Franklin while he observes someone else and useful for gaining additional evidence about the man. Governor Keith, on the strength of whose promised support eighteen-year-old Ben sails to England only to be left high and dry, is summed up with exemplary fairness: "But what shall we think of a Governor's playing such pitiful Tricks, and imposing so grossly on a poor ignorant Boy! It was a Habit he had acquired. He wish'd to please every body; and having little to give, he gave Expectations. He was otherwise an ingenious sensible Man, a pretty good Writer, and a good Governor for the People, tho' not for his Constituents the Proprietaries, whose Instructions he sometimes disregarded" (95). Franklin commands admiration for his neat, nonmalicious dissection of this knave. He does not forget the wrongs that are done him, but he refuses to be petty or mean.

Now a different kind of observation: In the garret of the London house where Ben lodges there lives an elderly recluse, to all intents and purposes living as a nun in a country where there is no nunnery. "She had given all her Estate to charitable Uses, reserving only Twelve Pounds a Year to live on, and out of this Sum she still gave a great deal in Charity, living her self on Water-gruel only, and using no Fire but to boil it." It speaks volumes about Franklin that, after giving additional evidence of this lady's piety, he notes: "She look'd pale, but was never sick, and I give it as another Instance on how small an Income Life and Health may be supported" (102–103). Here, it seems to me, Franklin is not stupidly missing the point, but rather making *his* point. This gentle lady's life is no model for us to follow and has nothing to teach us other than this: that we need very little in order to enjoy the greatest goods. Knowing this, we ought to get on with the business of life, which is to be conducted not in prayerful garrets but in the workshops and fields and streets of this world.

Another instance of Franklin's determination to be an onlooker, especially where religion is concerned: He notes the enthusiasm with which "the Multitudes of all Sects and Denominations" received the Reverend Mr. Whitefield's "common Abuse of them, by assuring them they were naturally *half Beasts and half Devils.*" "From being thoughtless or indifferent about Religion, it seem'd as if all the World were growing Religious." This, says Franklin, was "matter of Speculation" to him, but he does not directly share his thoughts (175). In another case involving Whitefield, he does share his thoughts. One evening, while the preacher is speaking from the top of the court-house steps at Market and Second streets, Franklin has "the Curiosity to learn how far he could be heard" and proceeds to back away until the sound falls below his threshold of hearing. From this radius he calculates the total number of auditors such an area might contain and concludes that newspaper accounts of Whitefield's great audiences elsewhere and ancient historians' accounts of "Generals haranguing whole Armies" are credible (179). Franklin is interested in almost every aspect of Whitefield's speech and speaking other than his subject (180). I take this to be his considered judgment of the subject's relative importance and utility.

For a man so much immersed in the stream of life and so delighting in it, Franklin is also strangely distant, a spectator. He views himself (87–88, 100, 177) and he views others as opposites of himself (Keimer, 112–113; David Harry, 126). He views the croaker or anti-booster as an enemy to civic progress (116); he views the mathematician as an enemy to civil conversation (117). He views the good sense of Dunkers and Moravians (190–191, 236–237) and the bad sense of Presbyterians and Quakers (147–148, 167, 186–189). He views incompetence in high places (Braddock, 223–224; Royal Society, 242; Loudoun, 253) and in low (78–79, 121, 126, 257). Through his eyes we watch how a man's will softens and relents (177, 184). Through his eyes we come to recognize and respect the importance of "seemingly low" or trivial things (207). Indeed, with all this evidence we come to know much about Benjamin Franklin and much about the way he sees the world. But at the same time we have less confidence that we *know* him. The more he tells us, the more of him there seems to be.

Happily, artfully, Franklin does not leave us confused or uncertain about the reasons for his writing his life story. Through the remarkable device of including two letters from friends urging him to complete and publish his autobiography, Franklin compels us too to be present at this discourse. As we watch Abel James and Benjamin Vaughan make their cases so insistently and eloquently—reminding "kind, humane and benevolent Ben Franklin" that his autobiography "would be useful and entertaining not only to a few, but to millions" (134), that all that has happened to him "is also connected with the detail of the manners and situation of *a rising* people" (135), that his is a model life that shows "the poverty of glory, and the importance of regulating our minds" (138) and that proves "how little necessary all origin is to happiness, virtue, or greatness" (137)—as we watch all this going on, we may sense someone else watching *us* over his spectacles. He is smiling his little smile.

Franklin's strategy in writing this book does not require that we love him, warts and all. Nor does it require that we admire his actions and opinions in each and every particular. Not even his relatives could do that. Franklin's strategy does, however, require that we read his book, that we permit some of its episodes to impress themselves upon our memories, that we expose ourselves to its coherent point of view. To help bring that about, he assumes a role very much to his liking—that of the cool, urbane spectator. It is a role that both charms and disarms. When we first approach the *Autobiography* we are onlookers, but in the course of the book most of us come to look with different eyes. By being open with us and inviting us to laugh at his follies, Franklin puts us at our ease. We trust in our independence; we are confident that we will not be seduced into abandoning our own standards of judgment. We too, after all, are cool, urbane spectators. We can enjoy a good story as well as the next fellow. But in enjoying that good story so well told, we also adopt for the moment the perspective of the storyteller. Then there is another good story, and another, and another. Before long we are not only looking at Franklin, but looking with him.

At bottom, Franklin is as ardent a fisher for souls as Preacher

Whitefield. But he is no splendid orator; he cannot, he would not, rest his hopes on the present enthusiasm of a sudden conversion. His message must reach where his voice cannot. He must persuade from a distance. His audience must be disabused of older notions, shown the way to earthly satisfactions, and confirmed in their resolution. To accomplish all this, Franklin turns his back on long sermons, polemics, and thundering denunciations. Instead of appealing to authority, he tries to charm us into looking at the world in his way. If, in the end, his charms work and we are persuaded, it is owing to his own powerful example. By showing us how he looks at others, Franklin teaches us how to look at ourselves.

2

Jefferson's Pulse of
Republican Reformation

THOMAS JEFFERSON's striking assessment of his life's work is inscribed for all to see and contemplate. His achievements and motivations were equally objects of his anxious care, so much so that he sought to preserve the materials with which later generations might make their own assessments. Accordingly, Jefferson became the Americans' preeminent archivist-founder. But lest the sight of the forest be lost for all the trees, he also marked with studied simplicity those actions by which he wished to be remembered. The inscription he prescribed—"& not a word more"—may still be read on the plain obelisk over his grave at Monticello. He was satisfied to let his fame rest on this: that he had been the "Author of the Declaration of American Independance[,] of the Statute of Virginia for religious freedom & Father of the University of Virginia." These would suffice to establish his singularity. As for the rest—his high offices, his astonishingly varied other accomplishments—these, he apparently thought, did not reach to the core meaning of his life's work.

It is not altogether obvious why Jefferson singled out these three, and only these, as his final claim to fame. Although Jefferson was indeed "Author" and "Father," in none of these cases was he acting alone. Each of these noteworthy acts was accomplished through the medium of a committee, and at that not always in a manner that gratified its moving spirit. Each depended on the consent of a legislative body and on the political skills and labors of others who secured that consent. Yet of course each was unmistakably a production of Jefferson's mind and pen, and each formed a part of his singular vision of what America and its people might become. That vision of his, I here argue, made of those parts a whole.

It was not enough for the Declaration to proclaim—and, in proclaiming, to trace—the separate career of this people. Large principles, especially grand-sounding principles, had to be brought down to earth, translated into the institutions, procedures, and habits of mind that go to make a political regime actual. All the more was this the case if the object in view was a self-governing people. Confusing right and capacity might be fatal. If self-governance were not to become a hollow or a bitter joke, a people had to be prepared, qualified to rule itself. It is, then, in the context set by the principles and aspirations of the Declaration of Independence that we may seek the larger meaning of those other achievements that Jefferson singled out as testimonials that he had lived.

The founding of the University of Virginia was in fact Jefferson's second (and second-best) attempt at putting higher education in America on a proper footing. His earlier effort, for the thorough reformation of the College of William and Mary, disappointed his expectations but nonetheless deserves pride of place here, for that prior project was conceived by Jefferson as part of a vastly ambitious scheme, one encompassing the statute for religious freedom as well. Both were parts of Jefferson's grand design to make the promise of the Declaration a reality.

That design was much on Jefferson's mind even while composing the Declaration. In the full flush of his revolutionary ardor in the summer of 1776, he could hardly wait to be excused from the Continental Congress to return to Virginia and tend to the urgent business at hand. A great deal needed doing. Virginia's initial surge of legislative activity—among other things, abolishing entail and exempting dissenters from compulsory contributions for the support of the established Anglican church—was indeed only a beginning. Those enactments showed something of "the strength of the general pulse of reformation" but by no means all that could and should be done. Jefferson was fired "in the persuasion that our whole code must be reviewed, adapted to our republican form of government, and, now that we had no negatives of Councils, Governors & Kings to restrain us from doing right, that it should be corrected, in all it's parts, with a single eye to reason, & the good of those for whom it was framed."[1]

1. "Autobiography," in Paul Leicester Ford, ed., *The Works of Thomas Jefferson* I:66–67, hereafter cited as *Works*.

Here was a project to engage his ardor, learning, persistence, and principles.

At his prompting the Virginia General Assembly in late 1776 appointed a committee of luminaries to undertake a sober review and revisal of the entire legal legacy that had up to then shaped life and institutions in colony and commonwealth. This Committee of Revisors, composed finally of Jefferson, Edmund Pendleton, and George Wythe, would labor for two and one-half years before reporting a total of 126 bills for legislative consideration and possible enactment.[2] The result, if approved, would be the reformation—better, the virtual transformation—of an emerging republican society. On this project Jefferson lavished his astonishing concentrated energy.

To speak of this revisal as Jefferson's revisal is not to denigrate the contributions of his weighty fellow committeemen or to ignore the extent to which he had to accommodate his notions to theirs. Yet the fact remains that close to half of all the bills proposed by the committee can plausibly be held to be the products of Jefferson's drafting, that all or nearly all of the most striking bills bear his distinctive stamp, and that his dedication to this arduous project was second to none. Indeed, his singularity might seem to be confirmed by another fact: the revisal's rough journey through the Virginia General Assembly testifies to the political and psychic barriers separating Jefferson from those fellow planters in whose midst he lived and on whose votes his measures depended.[3]

Interesting as these perspectives may be, they do not take in the core of Jefferson's project. It is possible to consider the revisal as offering a rare and comprehensive view of how a founder envisioned an actual republican society. Without floating off into the fantasies of

2. The text of the 126 bills reported by the Committee of Revisors, along with much useful editorial matter, is in Julian P. Boyd et al., eds., *The Papers of Thomas Jefferson* II:305–665, hereafter cited as *Papers*. Bills will be cited by number parenthetically in the text. Most of Virginia's seventeenth- and eighteenth-century laws are collected in the edition of William W. Hening, *The Statutes at Large; Being a Collection of All the Laws of Virginia* . . . , hereafter cited as Hening.

For present purposes I accept the conclusions to which Boyd was led in trying to determine the extent of Jefferson's responsibility for the revisal; *Papers* II: 319–321. Where the bills discussed in this chapter are not attributed by Boyd to Jefferson, an asterisk follows the bill number.

3. See William Wirt, *The Letters of the British Spy*, 231–232 (also cited in *Papers* II:534–535); and Jackson Turner Main, "Government by the People: The American Revolution and the Democratization of the Legislatures," *William and Mary Quarterly*, 3d ser., 23 (1966):396, 402–403, 407.

the philosophes or sinking into a morass of sociological minutiae, Jefferson through his revisal showed the character of an emerging republican society as it was and as it might yet be. The grandness of the goal must not, however, obscure the obvious. Although an entire society was indeed to be reformed and transformed, that great work was to take place within certain legal constraints. The three revisors, representing the best legal learning in Virginia, would approach the common law with caution; they would build on existing English and colonial legislation. Precisely because the chosen instrument of change was a work of *revisal,* within a legal tradition, it presupposed that the meaning and effect of many of its prescriptions would have to be worked out in a long course of interpretation. As a whole, then (it is argued here), the proposed bills testify—sometimes eloquently, sometimes mutely—to a world of high aspiration and intractable circumstance, to a sense of open possibilities and cherished constraints. Wishing to soar, but obliged as sober legislators always to touch Virginian soil, the revisors came forward with a singular project for their colleagues to enact and their successors to ponder. In acting or failing to act as they did, each group would reveal something of itself and thereby enable us to limn a world distinguished by extraordinary equality and inequality, by complex demarcations of public and private realms, and by elaborate efforts to form and sustain a people capable of governing itself.

Unequals in a Republic of Equals

Most manifestly, that Virginian world is a society of heterogeneous parts. Its deeply ingrained habits and institutions are touched by the revisal, but only with caution. Those givens form a somber background to the revisal's efforts to accommodate equal rights and social inequality among whites; indeed, they make those efforts seem especially fragile and tenuous. We are, on the whole, more apt to be impressed by the long-standing inequalities the revisal preserves and confirms than by its often muted reforms. Yet a fuller account would have to acknowledge that the revisal does more than merely accept and somewhat mitigate existing conventional inequality. For in his elaborate education bills, Jefferson showed that he thought the active promotion of natural inequality was fully compatible with, even indispensable for, a regime of republican equals.

It is a republic with a sharp eye for making distinctions and discriminations. There are citizens and aliens, rich and poor, masters
and servants, slaveowners and slaves, and what can be called anomalies. Thus, while only whites may be citizens in Jefferson's Virginia
(No. 55), free nonwhites are not to be denominated aliens, but rather
outlaws or potential outlaws (No. 51).⁴ And while "all infants wheresoever born" may derive citizenship from either parent (No. 55),
women otherwise remain outside the politically relevant part of the
population (Nos. 2*, 118*). White males and even male citizens are
further differentiated according to the task or end in view. To qualify
as an elector of members of the General Assembly, one must be a
male citizen, over twenty-one, possessed of a certain amount of property or (if a townsman) have served as an apprentice to some trade for
five years (No. 2*). Electors are a larger population than the class of
potential members of grand juries or trial juries (No. 118*); but the
suffrage, to Jefferson's later publicly expressed chagrin, is markedly
narrower than the qualifications for service in the state militia.⁵ Bill
No. 5* not only enrolls "all free male persons, hired servants and
apprentices, between the ages of 16 and 50 years," but even takes
pains to specify the non-armsbearing employment of "free mulattoes," however evanescent that category may seem in the light of the
bill concerning slaves (No. 51).

Notwithstanding this highly unequal treatment of the inhabitants
of Virginia, the entire body of laws may be seen as forming a mantle
of procedural safeguards for all. At Jefferson's prompting, the legislature's initial call for revisal had stressed the need to accommodate the
existing system to the new constitutional circumstances created by a
republican revolution. The "republican spirit" and "liberty and the

---

4. In entitling others, who live in states that are "parties to the American confederation," to the rights, privileges, and immunities of free Virginians, Bill No. 55 is
careful to specify only free white inhabitants, "paupers, vagabonds and fugitives from
justice excepted."

The liberalization of practice implicit in Bill No. 55's offer of naturalization to "all
white persons" is easily overlooked. See the traces of Jefferson's argument and pen in
his revision of Pendleton's earlier naturalization bill of October 1776 "for the encouragement of Foreign Protestants to settle in this Countrey" (*Papers* I:558–559).

5. Thomas Jefferson, *Notes on the State of Virginia*, 118, hereafter cited as *Notes
on Virginia*. By the terms of his 1776 draft of a constitution Jefferson would have had
the state provide "every person of full age" with more than enough land in the
country to qualify as an elector; *Papers* I:358, 362. In both his 1783 draft of a
constitution and his 1794 notes for a constitution Jefferson would have guaranteed
the right to vote to anyone enrolled in the militia; see ibid., VI:296, and *Works*
VIII:159.

rights of mankind" had to be reflected in and secured by appropriate laws.[6] Jefferson's revisal seeks to achieve that end by employing a mass of insistent, detailed, sometimes apparently petty particulars whose cumulative effect might be to find a place for unequals in a society dedicated to the equal enjoyment of rights. This intention is seen as readily in a proposed system by which popularly elected aldermen nominate justices of the peace "with open doors" (No. 95*)[7] as in the preservation of a freshly articulated "natural right, which all men have of relinquishing the country, in which birth, or other accident may have thrown them, and, seeking subsistance and happiness wheresoever they may be able, or may hope to find them" (No. 55).

This note of hope and promise is much diminished, however, by the likes of the bill for the support of the poor (No. 32). In the accents of the English poor law—at once threatening and threatened—it speaks of a workhouse and of an overseer "for the government, employment, and correction of the persons subject to him, restraining him from correcting any of them with more stripes than ten, at one time, or for one offence." The bill further provides for the forcible removal of emigrants from other counties, of whom aldermen are "apprehensive" lest they become public charges. Provisions such as these view the poor as a menace to public order and to public and private funds. Yet this is not the whole story, for quite apart from that threat, and not simply derivative from it, is a challenge to which the revisal tries to rise.

Bill No. 32 authorizes local alderman to "raise competent sums of money for the necessary relief of such poor, lame, impotent, blind, and other inhabitants of the county as are not able to maintain themselves." While hardly an invitation to lavishness, these provisions are at least a public response to private distress—and without the customary badges of shame.[8] The children of the destitute, and most particularly poor orphans, are to be put out as apprentices, but only after having attended "the school of the hundred" for three years and having been clothed and boarded at the public expense if need be (Nos. 32, 60*). The whole takes place in a context of some, albeit

6. Act for the Revision of the Laws, October 1776, 9 Hening 175–177, reprinted in *Papers* I:562–563.

7. This is no empty gesture, paired as it is with a major change in a basic institution of the Virginia polity; see *Papers* II:582n, and I:361, 606–607.

8. Compare 6 Hening 478 (1755), and *Papers* II:423n. See also *Notes on Virginia*, 133–134, for the praise of local relief and local caring.

limited, public accountability and regulation and with the understanding that such children-apprentices may grow up to be qualified voters in Williamsburg or Norfolk (No. 2*). Lest their duties be overwhelmed by their poverty, the revisal provides for public purchase of arms for those members of the militia who cannot supply their own (No. 5*). And lest their rights, and the interest of "indifferent justice," be similarly frustrated, courts are given the discretion to waive fees for writs, to assign free "counsel learned in the laws," and otherwise to "help and speed poor persons in their suits" (No. 112). If this is not relief on a generous scale, perhaps it is because the poor laws are seen mainly as a charitable remedy for particular misfortune. The large remedy for poverty lay elsewhere. Given a broad land of natural plenty, its opportunities for modest sufficiency and individual independence might best be placed within most people's reach by republican policy and republican laws: land grants of up to fifty acres "in full and absolute dominion" to "every person of full age," inheritance laws encouraging the equal treatment of all brothers and sisters, and the general abolition of feudal impediments.[9]

The revisal perpetuates the traditional system of white bondage for limited periods, with its heavy penalties for misconduct, refusal to work, and running away. But the changes, such as they are, give some reason to hope for greater fairness. The contractual freedom of neither masters nor servants is absolute (No. 52). A mitigation of the rigors of servitude is effected by the revisors' provisions for the capture and return of runaways. Under Bill No. 53*, the apprehender delivers the fugitive to the owner or owner's agent. This replaced a system whereby the justice of the peace of the county where the fugitive was captured sent the hapless servant on the way back with a warrant to the neighboring constable to receive and pass along the fugitive "and give him or her such a number of lashes, as the said justice shall think fit to direct, not exceeding thirty nine, . . . and so from constable to constable, until the runaway be delivered to his or her owner or overseer" (6 Hening 363). Under both the old and new provisions for runaways, the difference between servants and slaves tended to collapse.

Needless to say, Jefferson's bill concerning slaves (No. 51) bristles with complications.[10] Its opening paragraph proclaims that "no per-

9. *Papers* I:344, 352–353, 362–363; *Notes on Virginia*, 164–165. The revisal's policy regarding the inheritance of property is treated in the following section.

10. Here, John Quincy Adams asserted (18 January 1831), lies buried one of the main reasons Jefferson displayed uncharacteristic conservatism in opposing Pen-

sons shall, henceforth, be slaves within this commonwealth," even while excepting present slaves "and the descendants of the females of them." It frees all "Negroes and mulattoes which shall hereafter be brought into this commonwealth" after they have lived in Virginia for the equivalent of one year; but then, if they have not departed the state after a further year of grace, it would put them "out of the protection of the laws." Had these proposals been enacted, they would have constituted a policy of very slow attrition, rendered speedier perhaps by the rate of lawful private manumissions. Without replenishment from abroad or from neighboring states, and with the harsh threat of outlawry hastening every free or newly freed "negro or mulatto" out of Virginia, the proportion of blacks to whites would alter.[11] Here, indeed, was the core of Jefferson's policy toward blacks.[12]

---

dleton's proposal that the revisors begin by abolishing the entire existing system of laws and then replace them with an institute of their own design. To have gone along with this plan would have meant, among other things, that the revisors would be restoring slavery after having purged it from the statute books. Speaking in their own names they would be assuming "to themselves all the odium of establishing it as a positive institution, directly in the face of all the principles they had proclaimed." But while coolly noting (27 January 1831) that Jefferson "had not the spirit of martyrdom," Adams nonetheless never doubted that the same Jefferson "could not, or would not, prostitute the faculties of his mind to the vindication of that slavery which from his soul he abhorred"; Charles Francis Adams, ed., *Memoirs of John Quincy Adams, Containing Portions of His Diary from 1795 to 1848* VIII:283–285, 299–300. Adams's reading of motives, confided to the pages of his diary, is rendered more sinister by John T. Noonan, Jr., who faults Jefferson and Wythe less for "not attempting the impossible"—abolishing slavery altogether—than for shabbily camouflaging their personal responsibility for its continuance; *Persons and Masks of the Law: Cardozo, Holmes, Jefferson, and Wythe as Makers of the Masks*, 49–54. As the following pages make clear, this is not my reading of the matter.

Even the status of the reported bill is at issue. Was it "a mere digest of the existing laws," a decoy introduced with a view to a later and more timely liberalizing amendment? (See "Autobiography," *Works* I:76; *Notes on Virginia*, 137–138.) Or, rather, was it already as Boyd would have it, "a definite proposal for a system of gradual emancipation"? (See the judicious remarks in *Papers* II:472–473n.)

11. Jefferson calculated the 1782 ratio of free inhabitants to slaves "nearly as 11 to 10," while adding immediately that natural increase "under the mild treatment our slaves experience" was furthering "this blot in our country"; *Notes on Virginia*, 87.

12. In his "Draught of a Fundamental Constitution for the Commonwealth of Virginia" of 1783, Jefferson would have forbidden the General Assembly "to permit the introduction of any more slaves to reside in this state, or the continuance of slavery beyond the generation which shall be living on the 31st. day of December 1800; all persons born after that day being hereby declared free"; *Papers* VI:298. The silent presumption—and, for Jefferson, foregone conclusion—was that this massive change would be followed by the wholesale emigration and colonization of blacks elsewhere. For Jefferson's underlying justification, see *Notes on Virginia*, 138–143.

It is no simple matter to assess the reach or even the full intentions of this bill. While the wish may be father to the deed, public wishes more often than not find expression in "short methods," in measures that even their proponents may come to rue. In this respect, Jefferson's views on slavery bear a strong resemblance to Edmund Burke's wrestlings with the slave trade: "Taking for my basis, that I had an incurable evil to deal with, I cast about how I should make it as small an evil as possible, and draw out of it some collateral good. . . . I am persuaded that it is better to allow the evil, in order to correct it, than by endeavouring to forbid, what we cannot be able wholly to prevent, to leave it under an illegal, and therefore an unreformed, existence." Still, it has been argued that Jefferson's Bill No. 51 displays a more than Burkean caution and gradualism; indeed, that unlike Burke's proposals, it deliberately shuts its eyes to slaves as human beings and to the very prospect of their enjoyment of human liberties.[13]

We are, I think, as little entitled to trace the ambiguities of the bill to its author's supposed truculence toward blacks as to its author's supposed timidity toward whites. Some of the harshest features of the bill were rejected by the legislature, but on grounds we can only surmise. That bare fact may be attributed as well to a fear that such strictness would indeed portend a major change in the numbers and character of Virginia's labor force as to a compassionate revulsion against the bill's proposed outlawry. Furthermore, however one understands the legislature's reaction to Jefferson's bill, the Virginians' perpetuation of slavery displays yet again the general truth that it is always easier to act on right principle when viewing from afar.[14]

As a statement of the proposed policy of republican Virginia, then, Bill No. 51 holds out little hope and still less generosity for present slaves and their descendants, slave or free. Virginia can be no fit home for free men or women of color; they must find their own place elsewhere if they are to live as they should and as becomes "a free and independant people."[15] Within Virginia the black has only the hard option of servitude or outlawry. On the other hand, the bill directing the method of trying slaves charged with treason or felony (No. 104*) preserves or introduces certain safeguards. The most notable of

13. Edmund Burke to Henry Dundas, 9 April 1792, in Harvey C. Mansfield, Jr., ed., *Selected Letters of Edmund Burke,* 297–300; Noonan, *Persons and Masks of the Law,* 52.
14. See below, Chap. 5, n. 6.
15. *Notes on Virginia,* 138.

these is the provision that a defendant who has commenced an action to assert his or her freedom "shall be prosecuted and tried for any such crime, in the same manner as a freeman ought to be prosecuted and tried." Where the servitude itself is in question, the procedural presumption is in favor of freedom.

Beyond this, Jefferson's revisal either would not or could not go. In his own eyes, the failure to provide a direct, if long-term, remedy to the blight of chattel slavery left a profound contradiction in the system and spirit of the laws and a source of future catastrophe. For all its proponents' brave hopes, the revisal could not transcend conditions and feelings on a matter that, if unresolved, would doom the whole republican enterprise.

The Public and Private Realms

A regime dedicated to the emancipation of the private pursuits of happiness from needless, meddlesome authority could not simply avert its eyes from the social consequences of those pursuits. Large matters might be no one's particular concern and yet, for all that, demand public attention and thought. So though the enjoyment of private freedom is a great good in Jefferson's *nomoi*, it is by no means a simple good. In the jarring or rubbing of private desire against public need, his laws detect a continuing problem, a continuing challenge. Their response, as is true of any legal system's accommodations, is evidence of a complex underlying judgment of what constitutes a just social and political order. In the case of Jefferson, that most public of our private men and most private of our public men, the judgment and the accommodations are especially complex. It is unlikely that anyone felt more keenly than he the conflicting impulses to enjoy one's own, to tend to one's proper business in peace and quiet, and yet also to take one's turn in "the commonplace drudgery of governing a single state"[16] (or, for that matter, in the arduous labors of revising its laws).

These contending impulses are clear enough in the revisal's discussions of public duties, but with the additional complication introduced by republican orthodoxy. Thus, not only ought a qualified voter to vote, an elected representative to attend, but each can prop-

---

16. Jefferson to David Rittenhouse, 19 July 1778, *Papers* II:202–203.

erly be penalized for failing to vote, for failing to attend (No. 2*). The integrity of the representative body requires that its members be (in George Mason's vexed characterization) more than "the Choice of a Handful, a Neighbourhood, or a Junto," for the prime beneficiary of general indifference is the type seen often enough in "our late Assemblies"—"a factious, bawling Fellow, who will make a noise four or five miles around him, and prevail. upon his party to attend" the election and thereby triumph over the more weighty, modest, and deserving.[17]

Ideally, then, elections ought to be so contrived as to bring forth the best the community can offer, not the worst. But even so, those choices, fine as they might be, ought not to be held hostage by the public. Thus, no one who shall have served a total of seven years in the state legislature shall be afterward compellable to serve therein (No. 2*). A somewhat different concern animates the prohibition on anyone's serving as a delegate to the Continental Congress for more than three years in any term of six years (No. 10). Here the problem appears to be a possible "danger which might arise to American freedom" and a likely loss of "the confidence of their friends," should the distant continental legislature fail to be infused regularly with new faces.[18]

The most diverse-seeming bills ring the changes on this common theme: just as there are duties owed the public, so are there rights assertable against it; but in a decent society neither claim holds undisputed sway. The salaries and fees of public officials ought to be matters of public record and posted prominently in offices and courts so as to be "visible to persons resorting thither" (No. 33*). Far from being a private matter or a public license to private enterprise, appointment to public office now is inseparable from accountability to that public.[19] In his militia bill (No. 5), Jefferson added to the list of those exempt from duty "the Presidents, Professors, and students of the College of William and Mary, and Academy of Hampden-Sidney," as well as "quakers and menonists." Even a political society at war could still afford to harbor its learned and its tender con-

17. Cited in ibid., 346 n. 5.

18. "Proposed Resolution for Rotation of Membership in the Continental Congress," 1 July 1776, ibid. I:411. See also ibid. II:17n, and Jefferson's bill for regulating the appointment of delegates to Congress, as enacted, 9 Hening 299 (1777).

19. Needless to say, the act of 1745 on which much of Bill No. 33 is modeled had made no provision for the public disclosure of salaries (5 Hening 326).

sciences.[20] That society could, with equal right, make sure that no one "shall desert wives or children, without so providing for them as that they shall not become chargeable to a county" (No. 32). In general, able-bodied persons who lack "wherewithal to maintain themselves" are forbidden to "waste their time in idle and dissolute courses, or . . . loiter or wander abroad." Proclaimed vagabonds by the law, they are impressed with a sense of their obligations to others by a confinement of up to thirty days in the poorhouse.

Not all private inclinations or passions are displayed as enemies to be overcome; some are exhibited as supports to sound policy and the public good. Thus the bill for licensing counsel, attorneys-at-law, and proctors (No. 97*) seeks to generate causes based on ordinary human drives in order to promote desired effects. It gratifies the passion of a favored class of lawyers for wealth and leisure by restricting access to the general courts. It excludes those who presently enjoy a comparative advantage, local county attorneys ("an inundation of insects") whose convenient and familiar access to clients enables them to "consume the harvest" while leaving general court lawyers weary with "incessant drudgery." In making it easy for the better sort of attorneys to earn a comfortable living and still "have leisure to acquire science," Jefferson hoped to raise the competence of the bar and make it "an excellent nursery for future judges."[21]

These features of Jefferson's socioeconomic legislation were over-shadowed in his and contemporaries' eyes by the bills concerning the transmission of wealth, the inheritance of estates. Here Jefferson saw himself as striking a mighty blow against the haughty pretensions of the privileged rich and in favor of those conditions that might best "make an opening for the aristocracy of virtue and talent, which nature has wisely provided for the direction of the interests of society, & scattered with equal hand through all it's conditions." This self-consciously republican campaign saw the enemy as the unnatural, irrational, unjustifiable restrictions embedded in the feudal common law. To rid Virginia, and America, of these would enlarge "natural right" by giving scope and expression to natural feeling.[22]

20. Compare Bill No. 5 with 9 Hening 267, 313–314 (1777), 11 Hening 477, 494 (1784); and see *Papers* II:355 n. 3.

21. Jefferson to George Wythe, 1 March 1779, *Papers* II:235. On Jefferson's possible authorship of this, the most egregious restraint of trade in the revisal, see ibid., 589 n. 2.

22. "Autobiography," *Works* I:58–59. Of considerable value in assessing this revolutionary intent are the comments of St. George Tucker, ed., *Blackstone's Com-*

Some such intention lay in the foreground of Jefferson's decision to leave Congress and go back to Virginia. One of the first products of his legislative draftsmanship on that occasion was the bill enabling "tenants in fee-tail to convey their lands in fee-simple."[23] Its intention and effect are perpetuated in the simpler language incorporated in the bill for regulating conveyances (No. 22*). With one stroke the bill does away with all restrictions placed by fathers or fathers' fathers on the sale or further bequest of land—to the advancement of good policy, family tranquillity, and the better use of the time of a legislature that no longer would have to trouble with petitions for special exemptions.[24] A system whereby an earlier generation's fancies or dreams of founding patrician dynasties lay heavy upon the desires and even necessities of their offspring could be defended by no sound principle of political economy or of political science, to say nothing of republicanism.

Equally obnoxious and hence equally fit for rapid extirpation was the common law directing the course of descents in the case of those dying intestate. Its discrimination in favor of the eldest son and his issue in preference to any other heirs is overturned, as is its rule that a bastard can inherit nothing. The general discrimination in favor of male heirs is replaced by a rule of equal division among all descendants of the same degree of consanguinity. The common-law rule that inheritance shall never lineally ascend in default of lineal descendants but shall rather escheat to the lord is rejected in accord with John Locke's reasoning on the matter: "If his Son dye without Issue, the Father has a Right in Nature to possess his Goods, and Inherit his Estate (whatever the Municipal Laws of some Countries, may ab-

---

mentaries: *With Notes of Reference, to the Constitution and Laws, of the Federal Government of the United States; and of the Commonwealth of Virginia;* see especially II:119 n. 14, and II:app., n. B, 18–24, 27–28, where the talk is repeatedly of utter incompatibility, dramatic opposition, and irreconcilability, when comparing rules that are "the offspring of feudal barbarism and prejudice" with "the policy and intention of the framers of our law." (My citation is to the volume and page numbers standard for editions of Blackstone.) A close study of wills, court records, and other transactions suggests that recourse to these feudal devices was not as widespread in Virginia as has been imagined; C. Ray Keim, "Primogeniture and Entail in Colonial Virginia," *William and Mary Quarterly,* 3d ser., 25 (1968):545–586. Their cumulative effect, however, might have been or become significant.

23. *Papers* I:560–562; 9 Hening 226–227 (1776). Since by a law of 1727 Virginia had annexed slaves to the land, rendering them too subject to limitations in tail (4 Hening 225–226), later abolitions of entail covered both land and slaves.

24. See the language of the preamble to Jefferson's earlier bill in *Papers* I:560.

surdly direct otherwise)."[25] Indeed, it is against this whole array of what he too saw as feudal absurdities that Jefferson aimed his bill directing the course of descents (No. 20). He thought it one of the most remarkable of the revisors' proposals, and with good reason, for here was yet another instance of the revisal of ordinary legislation being used to elaborate on what ought to be the fundamental principles of the regime.[26] By deflating and rejecting the grandiose claims of feudal usurpations "& such fooleries," the revisal guards against the public realm engrossing all it sees.[27]

Yet there are of course instances, all too frequent, when the government acting in the name of the public must take private property, liberty, even limb and life. When "wicked and dissolute men [resign] themselves to the dominion of inordinate passions," no one's life, liberty, and property can be safe, and the very reason for men's entering into society is put in jeopardy. A government that stood mute or helpless in the face of such domineering "would be defective in it's principal purposes" (No. 64). Of the many occasions in the revisal for reconciling the tensions between public needs and private wants, between enlightened calculations and passionate urgings, few have the immediacy and drama of this.

The purpose of Bill No. 64 is to proportion "crimes and punishments in cases heretofore capital" by arranging each "in a proper scale" with a view to enlisting men's natural inclinations in the aid of duty. Jefferson turned to this task with special enthusiasm, prompted (in the language of the preamble) by "the experience of all ages and countries . . . that cruel and sanguinary laws defeat their own purpose by engaging the benevolence of mankind to withhold prosecutions, to smother testimony, or to listen to it with bias." Rather than needlessly affront this natural fellow feeling, Jefferson sought wherever possible to replace punishments that "exterminate" with punishments that reform and restore "sound members to society." Instead of warring with their passions, citizens could then convict and punish with a clear calm conscience, and those "contemplating to perpetrate

25. John Locke, *Two Treatises of Government*, bk. I, §90.
26. This point is somewhat blurred in Boyd's otherwise excellent statement in *Papers* I:330–331. The immediately relevant provisions in Jefferson's 1776 drafts of a constitution are in ibid., 344, 352–353, 362–363. The most striking of Jefferson's assessments of the work of revisal is in "Autobiography," *Works* I:77–78.
27. See Jefferson's first draft of a constitution, *Papers* I:345; and Tucker, ed., *Blackstone's Commentaries* II:244 n. 4.

a crime would see their punishment ensuing as necessarily as effects follow their causes." Jefferson's objections to capital punishment did not, however, carry him to advocate its total abolition. It still "should be the last melancholy resource against those whose existence is become inconsistent with the safety of their fellow citizens."[28]

As a whole, however, Bill No. 64 presents itself as the studied, even artful, attempt of reason and experience to find alternatives to mindless cruelty. Julian P. Boyd's inclination is to view the bill as less a reform than a restatement of generally accepted practices concerning capital offenses; that, indeed, in its reliance on the *lex talionis,* it contrasts "shockingly" with the liberal thought of the age. The evidence he adduces of Jefferson's dissatisfaction with the bill, both at the time of its drafting and later, lends support to this judgment. But as Boyd also points out, the absence of any statement in favor of the *lex talionis* in any of the surviving documents of the revisors' proceedings is noteworthy and raises questions about Jefferson's account of its inclusion. Our efforts to take the measure of this bill are not helped much by the little we know of contemporary reactions to it. There does not appear to be any clear evidence of what the House of Delegates found obnoxious in this bill or of what amendments to render it less so they proposed during their protracted deliberations. Madison attributed its defeat, in large measure, to the legislature's "rage against Horse stealers." His bitter complaint that "our old bloody code is by this event fully restored" makes it hard to join Boyd in asserting that the "harsh features of the Bill undoubtedly contributed to its defeat." This much at least seems likely: an enlightened republican hope of measured punishment and reform foundered because the legislature took offense at what it detected behind the bill's learned citations. Lurking there was not so much the spirit of Exodus 21 as that of Beccaria.

That very spirit informs Jefferson's companion bill (No. 68) prescribing the treatment of prisoners and suffices to explain why this bill too was spurned by the legislature. Modern doctrine warns against succumbing to either cruelty or compassion when correcting the wicked. Malefactors condemned to hard labor are to be "marked out to public note," "constantly shaven," distinguished in dress from

28. *Papers* II: 506 n. 4; see also Jefferson to Pendleton, 26 August 1776, ibid. I: 505. My discussion in this and the following paragraph draws on material in ibid. II: 504–506n.

"the good citizens of this commonwealth," and this not only with a view to rendering fugitives more visible. The bill also seeks to secure equal justice by forbidding prisoners any clothing, money, property, or service beyond that supplied by their keepers, lest "the opulence of the offender, or of his friends, or the indiscreet [b]ounties of individuals . . . disarm the public justice, or alleviate those sufferings." Procedures for reviewing the behavior of jailers and the treatment of prisoners are established and assigned to some local person of "discretion, humanity and attention." The bill repeatedly seeks to guard against gross partiality or cruelty, each in its way subversive of the rationale for public punishment.

With these varied efforts at evenhandedness Jefferson and his fellow revisors hoped to strike a tolerable balance between the passionate, interested forces they meant to free and the requirements of the polity, economy, and society within which those private forces would need to be contained.

Opinion and Knowledge in Republican Society

Nowhere is the confrontation of public need and private wish more troubling and threatening than in matters relating to belief, opinion, and thought. Few issues of public policy held equal significance for Jefferson, and to none did he devote more sustained reflection and care. All the more striking is it, then, that in these very matters his revisal should contain such disparate and apparently warring elements. Some of the conflicts can perhaps be understood as inadvertent, the results of somewhat mechanical salvage and incorporation of earlier legislation or practice of long standing (and assumed to be unproblematic) in juxtaposition with novel departures. Some, but not all. What, for example, is to be made of that provision in Bill No. 64 that punishes with ducking and whipping ("not exceeding 15. stripes") "all attempts to delude the people, or to abuse their understanding by exercise of the pretended arts of witchcraft, conjuration, inchantment, or sorcery or by pretended prophecies"? One might say with Blackstone that this is "a crime of which one knows not well what account to give." Even more might one say this of its inclusion in *Jefferson's* bill. Artfully decked out with its elaborate and ancient supporting citations in Anglo-Saxon, Latin, Old French, and English, this is no merely routine copying of Virginia precedent. As matters stand, Blackstone's soft-spoken reproof of the whole business is more intelligible than the fact that the author of this provision is one who steadfastly and publicly exploded the notion that Christianity is a part of the common law.[29]

Other provisions are not so mystifying. While days of "public fasting and humiliation, or thanksgiving" were far less common in Anglican Virginia than in Congregationalist New England, the notion was familiar enough.[30] Bill No. 85* allows for such proclamations by executive order in cases where the legislature is not in session and requires further that "every minister of the gospel" preach a suitable sermon in his church on such an occasion "on pain of forfeiting fifty pounds for every failure, not having a reasonable excuse."

Much more familiar to Virginians were the provisions of Bill No. 84 punishing those who conduct business as usual on Sundays. These restrictions stem from an old line of Sabbatarian legislation, though the talk no longer is of "the holy keeping of the Lords day."[31] The bill promotes both religion and religious diversity by securing "any minister of the gospel" from arrest while engaged in public preaching or worship, and by restraining and punishing those who disturb others in their worship. As enacted in 1786, this protection is extended to "any minister of religion" (12 Hening 336–337). For a licensed minister to enjoy this immunity, the bill requires as a prior condition that he swear (the act, that he swear or affirm) fidelity to the commonwealth.

Religious interests are both protected and readjusted in other ways

---

29. Compare Tucker, ed., *Blackstone's Commentaries* IV:60–62, 436, with Thomas Jefferson, *Reports of Cases Determined in the General Court of Virginia. From 1730, to 1740; and from 1768 to 1772*, app. 137–142 (the latter is reprinted in *Works* I:453–464). A possible explanation that dissolves this incongruity and renders Jefferson's treatment of religion more consistent than the text allows would see this provision in Bill No. 64 as another instance of his self-proclaimed rational hostility to priestcraft. By this account the revisal is willing to promote diverse religions provided they are stripped of any civil powers and are respectful of civil necessity and the reason of the people.

30. Jefferson's account of how the House of Burgesses, alarmed by news of the passage of the Boston Port Act, came to proclaim a day of fasting, humiliation, and prayer appears in "Autobiography," *Works* I:11–12. (The resolution itself, 24 May 1774, is in *Papers* I:105–106.) Jefferson's narrative is more than sufficient evidence of the chasm separating Robert Carter Nicholas, who introduced the resolution, and Thomas Jefferson, who could recall how he and his political allies "rummaged over" precedents, "cooked up" a resolution, and picked Nicholas to be its mover on account of his "grave & religious character."

31. See 3 Hening 72–73 (1691), 138–139 (1696), 360–361 (1705).

as well. In the matter of the property of the once-established church, Bill No. 83 preserves the glebe lands, buildings, and other property of the "English church," conforming in this way more closely to the legislature's point of view than to Jefferson's.[32] The bill also compels the church vestries to distribute as poor-relief the excess funds levied by them in the past. Although the administration of poor-relief is rendered a purely civil matter by Bill No. 32's transfer of jurisdiction from the vestry of the parish to the aldermen of the county, the vestries themselves are not touched.[33]

Not only poor-relief is given a civil face. The registration of vital statistics (No. 63*) is no longer a responsibility of parish minister or parish clerks, nor apparently are fees to be charged for this service, as required under the prevailing law of 1713 (4 Hening 42–45). The law of marriage, too, receives a strongly secular cast. Although retaining the Levitical law regarding forbidden degrees of union, Bill No. 86* quietly does away with any need for religious solemnities. In rendering ecclesiastical authority superfluous in these matters, the revisors also would be putting an end to long-standing agitation over the Anglican clergy's monopoly over marriages, the resentment over the required threefold posting of banns, the need for special exemptions for Quakers and others, and the grudging licensing of dissenting ministers and even of "sober and discreet laymen" in the "remote parts of this commonwealth . . . on the western waters." Secularization and domestic tranquillity proceed apace.[34]

Yet Jefferson's goal, one need hardly add, was something much grander than a society of placid, comfortable burghers, squires, or

---

32. Jefferson would have discriminated between public and private donations. Where church property was traceable to public levies—"contributions on the people independent of their good will"—he would have reserved the clerical incumbents' "rights to such Glebe lands during their lives," but no longer. Private donations might be enjoyed perpetually; see *Papers* I:530–533, and 9 Hening 165 (1776).

33. See *Papers* II:423n; and Charles Ramsdell Lingley, *The Transition in Virginia from Colony to Commonwealth*, 200–211.

34. Compare the old law—3 Hening 150 (1696), 441–442 (1705); 4 Hening 245–246 (1730); 6 Hening 81–82 (1748)—to the later reluctant accommodations—10 Hening 361–363 (1780); 11 Hening 281–282 (1783), 503–504 (1784). It is not surprising that Bill No. 86 never got beyond a second reading.

Agitation over the marriage law was incessant at this time. See William Taylor Thom, *The Struggle for Religious Freedom in Virginia: The Baptists*, 62–63, 66–75; William Henry Foote, *Sketches of Virginia, Historical and Biographical (First Series)*, 329–340; and Hamilton J. Eckenrode, *Separation of Church and State in Virginia: A Study in the Development of the Revolution*, 66–73.

yeomen. To render men unlikely candidates for murderous and suicidal crusades was one thing; to dispose and fit them for the demands
of self-governance another. Here Jefferson brought more than his
formidable legislative skills to bear on the work at hand. Theme,
commitment, and art joined to produce a burst of concentrated reasoning and rhetoric that could not be contained by the dull opening
formula, "Be it enacted by the General Assembly." Nothing less than
a proem would do to set legislator and ordinary citizen in mind—
now and forever—of the reasons for, and hence the ends of, this
particular legislation. Since this part of the revisal (Nos. 79–82) had
to do with the freeing of the human mind, eloquent statement of those
reasons would equally be a support for a politics of reason. No tol-
erably alert reader of these preludes could miss that intention.[35] It
is not farfetched, then, to view two of these preambles as testaments
of Jefferson's republicanism. Therein he pronounced the principles
and reasons of his practical program, leading the reader from effects
back to causes and then from whys to hows. By considering these
preambles together with their bills' detailed provisions, we may better
grasp the political science through which Jefferson hoped to make
republicans.

Bill No. 79 does more than nod smilingly in the direction of republican government. Without Jefferson's needing to mention that
favored form by name, we know that it is surely among those that are
"better calculated than others to protect individuals in the free exercise of their natural rights, and are at the same time themselves better
guarded against degeneracy." Despite this favorable prospect, Jefferson's sequel turns out to be less an expression of congratulation than
of concern, caution, even alarm, for experience testifies to the gradual
corruption of public trustees and to their perversion of even the best
forms into tyranny. To forfend what has happened everywhere and
always is the objective of the "bill for the more general diffusion of
knowledge."

The best preventive, it is believed, "would be, to illuminate, as far

---

35. Of the 126 bills in the revisal, only seven have preambles: No. 7* (giving
emergency powers to the governor and council), No. 64 (proportioning crimes and
punishments), No. 79 (for the more general diffusion of knowledge), No. 80 (amending the charter of the College of William and Mary), No. 82 (establishing religious
freedom), No. 112 (providing help for paupers in their suits), and No. 120* (changing
to the Gregorian calendar). Most (or arguably, all) of these bear Jefferson's unmistakable mark. On the function of legislative preludes, see Plato *Laws* 722D–723D.

as practicable, the minds of the people at large." Being forewarned, as it were, by the exhibits of history, they would be forearmed. By coming to "know ambition under all its shapes," they would be "prompt to exert their natural powers to defeat its purposes." The most famous gloss on the revisal puts it best: "Of all the views of this law none is more important, none more legitimate, than that of rendering the people the safe, as they are the ultimate, guardians of their own liberty."[36] Yet by itself this precautionary instruction cannot suffice, at least if one has in mind something more than frustration of potential tyrants. More is wanted, and more is possible; not only the free exercise of natural rights—not only the pursuit of happiness, one is tempted to say—but the real happiness of the people is to be sought. And that search (Jefferson's preamble asserts) compels one to look beyond the people at large to "those persons, whom nature hath endowed with genius and virtue." Without this better sort to form wise laws and to administer them honestly, the people cannot be as happy as they might be. The bill for the more general diffusion of knowledge is thus inevitably also a bill for the "liberal education" of the indispensable few who will thereby become better "able to guard the sacred deposit of the rights and liberties of their fellow citizens." To find those few, then, is a public necessity and a public charge.

Precisely because the public need for them is so great, and precisely because so few are worthy of receiving such an education, sound public policy dictates that the joining of promising genius and proper education not be left to chance. To the extent that barriers of wealth, birth, or other accidental circumstances might prevent that happy conjunction, they ought to be overcome. Jefferson took for granted as basic social facts both "the indigence of the greater number" and the random distribution of rare genius. To identify, nourish, and educate those children "whom nature hath fitly formed and disposed to become useful instruments for the public" requires a social policy at once generous and tough. The preamble defends that generosity on grounds of political economy. Without some form of public assistance, the able children of the poor will not receive the education of which they are worthy—to the public's own great loss: "It is better that such should be sought for and educated at the common expence

36. *Notes on Virginia,* 148. Had this bill been enacted, Jefferson mused some thirty-five years later, "our work [of laying "the axe to the root of Pseudo-aristocracy"] would have been compleat"; letter to John Adams, 28 October 1813, in Lester J. Cappon, ed., *The Adams–Jefferson Letters* II:389–390.

of all, than that the happiness of all should be confided to the weak or wicked." The toughness of the policy is clear enough from the bill. The annual selection of scholarship students for the next higher stage, "after the most diligent and impartial examination and enquiry," constitutes what Jefferson characterizes elsewhere as raking the best genuises from "the rubbish."[37] In creating a system whereby a poor man's gifted son would deservedly receive what any rich man's son could afford, Jefferson held to a totally unsentimental view of entitlement.

One of the striking features of Bill No. 79 is its great detail in prescribing the manner of defining school districts, determining the location of the schools, prescribing the modes of condemning property for public use, and the like. Almost two-thirds of the bill proper is devoted to administrative details of this kind, descending even to the minutiae of the grammar school steward's job description and the exact time and manner for selecting scholarship students. The details bespeak an intention to impress upon local electors, aldermen, and overseers the gravity of their educational responsibilities; if the legislature takes such pains with every detail, imparting to each an almost ritual significance, every detail of educational administration must indeed be somehow terribly important for the success of the whole. Electors of the hundreds are charged with determining where the local schoolhouse shall be located or relocated. Aldermen are charged with determining and regulating the boundaries of local districts; further, they are to conduct the public interrogation of nominations for grammar school scholarships. Overseers have the "business and duty" of appointing and (if necessary) removing teachers, examining the scholars, and fixing a centrally situated place for a grammar (or secondary) school. Visitors of the grammar schools are charged with hiring and firing the master and steward of the school, setting tuition,

---

37. *Notes on Virginia*, 146. Julian P. Boyd asserts that elitism of this kind "never became and possibly could not become an explicit object of any democratic society"; *Papers* II:534n. Jefferson clearly thought otherwise. He chose to proclaim rather than conceal his judgment that popular government could not possibly do without the very thing that threatened it—the talents and ambitions of its rarest types. In this respect Jefferson did not differ from other founders as politically diverse as John Adams, Alexander Hamilton, James Madison, and George Washington. Jefferson, however, chose to defend this policy in terms that stressed what today's jargon would call its "cost effectiveness." The reluctance of the legislature to establish, and then of the county governments to implement, a public education system suggests that Jefferson did not mistake the obstacle to success.

and examining the school, its staff, and its students. Both the over-seers of the schools of the hundreds and the visitors of the grammar schools are charged with seeing to it that any general instructional plan recommended by the visitors of William and Mary College shall be observed. Teachers are accountable for their performance, just as they are for their fidelity to the commonwealth; overseers are accountable for their recommendations and appointments; scholars are accountable for making the best of whatever genius they have. In short, the entire scheme for establishing and maintaining an educa-tional system constitutes in itself an education in responsible self-governance. In lavishing these details upon the bill, Jefferson also gave his fullest explanation by example of what he meant by self-government. The scheme's elaborations thus make it of a piece with a curriculum that would teach the three R's to all the free boys and girls of the commonwealth by drawing on useful lessons from Greek, Roman, English, and American history. For their own safety and that of others, for their own happiness and that of their children, a free people must be qualified "as judges of the actions and designs of men."[38] Jefferson's bill encompasses that intention at every level.

"In order that grammar schools may be rendered convenient to the youth in every part of the commonwealth," Bill No. 79 arrays all the counties of the state into twenty fairly compact districts. In each of these is to be established a school where students would be taught "the Latin and Greek languages, English grammar, geography, and the higher part of numerical arithmetic." With half of these districts entitled to a choice every other year, those ten among the select grammar school seniors adjudged annually to be "of the best learning and most hopeful genius and disposition" would be sent to William and Mary College, there to be educated, boarded, and clothed for three years at the public expense. But the college they would attend, along with fifty or so sons of the well-to-do, would differ significantly from the William and Mary of Jefferson's undergraduate days (1758–1760), or George Wythe's (1746). To effect that change and to justify it is the object of Bill No. 80. Doing so takes no few words; indeed the preamble of this bill for "amending the constitution of the college of William and Mary and substituting more certain revenues for its support" is about the length of all the other six preambles combined. It begins by telling a long story in a tone and style that have been

---

38. *Notes on Virginia*, 148.

found unworthy of its author.[39] It is a narrative of hopes and frustrations, of generosity and misguided intentions, all told with tedious particularity by a man who detested pleonasms and legalistic involutions, who was obliged to follow the revisors' general rule of draftsmanship "not to insert an unnecessary word, nor omit a useful one," and who was more adept than most at saying much in few words.[40]

One need not puzzle long over this departure from pithiness, especially since Jefferson in effect accounted for it all when drawing the necessary and useful lessons from this history of the college. The narrative of "the experience of near an hundred years hath proved" that, as presently constituted, William and Mary can only continue to disappoint; further, that its defects are fundamental and hence beyond the ordinary powers of its trustees to remedy; still further, that its reliance on public exertions and public benefactions going back to its very origins and foundation entitles one to view that endowment as "no wise in nature of a private grant."[41] Accordingly, the present General Assembly and governor of Virginia, acting as the public's "legal fiduciary for such purposes," not only may but of right ought to reconstitute the college's charter "until such form be devised as will render the institution publicly advantageous, in proportion as it is publicly expensive." To dispose of any lingering misgivings or scruples that might impede full consent to this project to alter a private corporation's charter, the preamble ends in an appeal to the revolutionary moment and its revolutionary promise: "The late change in the form of our government, as well as the contest of arms in which we are at present engaged, calling for extraordinary abilities both in council and field, it becomes the peculiar duty of the Legislature, at this time, to aid and improve that seminary, in which those who are to be the future guardians of the rights and liberties of their

39. "The historical introduction is soured by an unworthy and unnecessary resentment of the past for not being what Jefferson would have liked it to be, and this biliousness seems to have affected the author as he worked on the body of the text so that his habitual lucidity for once escaped him and the whole draft reads like a parody of those acts of which he himself had complained" [then quoting from "Autobiography," *Works* I:70]; J. E. Morpurgo, *Their Majesties' Royall Colledge: William and Mary in the Seventeenth and Eighteenth Centuries*, 185.

40. *Papers* II:325, 599 (Bill No. 102 opening), and 320–321.

41. The breadth and sweep of Jefferson's reasoning here ought to be compared to the cautious arguments of opposing counsel in *Bracken* v. *The Visitors of William & Mary College*, 3 Call's Reports (Va.) 573 (1790), especially 590 (John Taylor), and 592–594 (John Marshall).

country may be endowed with science and virtue, to watch and preserve the sacred deposit." It is only after all this necessary justification that Jefferson permitted the enacting clause to hover into sight.

What follows in the body of the bill may seem only to reinforce the initial impression that the whole effort is overwrought, out of proportion, and therefore out of character with its author. But Jefferson took pains within the overall confines of the bill to depict the "after" as vividly as the "before" of William and Mary. In fact the "after," the potentially far-reaching effects of the revolutionary changes being legislated for a private Anglican foundation, can be said to be emphasized by the very intermixture of details large and small. Consider, for example, the provisions specifying procedures for removing professors "for breach or neglect of duty, immorality, severity, contumacy, or other good cause"; for replacing the college's revenue from state duties on skins, furs, and liquors with a more reliable and steady "impost of 9d on every hogshead of tobacco to be exported from this commonwealth by land or water"; for authorizing, indeed directing, the visitors to engage "that greatest of astronomers, David Ryttenhouse," to make and erect a mechanical model of the solar system "that this commonwealth may not be without so great an ornament, nor its youth such an help towards attaining astronomical science." In such and such ways, prescribed by law, shall the visitors, chancellors, and faculty perform their offices. As in the case of the lower schools, the legal detail exemplifies a conception of republican governance applied to a central institution. The visitors or governors of the college are now to be appointees of the state legislature. Their sworn assurance of fidelity to the commonwealth, their tenure of office at the legislature's pleasure, their liberation from the original charter's restrictions based on "the royal prerogative, or the laws of the kingdom of England; or the canons or constitution of the English Church"—all these point to a public, politically accountable superintendence over the college's principal policies.

Most prominent, partly owing to the typographical arrangement of the bill's appendix, is Jefferson's reconstitution of the college's curriculum. Here especially lay the heart of Jefferson's project to take a training school for Anglicans, "to enlarge it's sphere of science, and to make it in fact an University." The old arrangement of six professorships into four schools (Sacred Theology, Philosophy, Latin and Greek, Indian) is no more. Holy scripture falls out of the curriculum, as do "the common places of divinity, and the controversies with

[8 3]

heretics," and the teaching of metaphysics. Ecclesiastical law and ecclesiastical history are folded into those larger disciplines of which they are now seen to be only a part. The teaching of Latin and Greek is transferred to the grammar schools where it belongs, thereby ridding the college of "children," freeing the college's resources, which had been "exhausted in accommodating those who came only to acquire the rudiments of science," and giving those "young and tender subjects" enrolled in the grammar schools a program of secular studies more suited to their powers and needs.[42] The Indian school, founded on the private bequest of the pious chemist Robert Boyle and dedicated to teaching Indian boys the three R's and the Christian catechism, is abolished and its professor replaced by "a missionary, of approved veracity," who is charged with collecting anthropological and especially linguistic materials for the college library.

The description of the eight professorships as given in the bill's appendix is hardly a New Organon, but it does display clearly enough what Jefferson found wanting in the existing arrangement. The old professorship of rhetoric, law, and ethics is replaced by one of ethics (moral philosophy, law of nature, law of nations) and fine arts (sculpture, painting, gardening, music, architecture, poetry, oratory, criticism). Present necessity might compel a union of subjects that future legislative leisure and generosity would subdivide, but this particular joining is far from arbitrary or accidental.[43] An altogether new professorship of law and police is established, encompassing "Municipal" law (the teaching of common law, equity, and mercantile, maritime, and ecclesiastical law) and "Oeconomical" law (the teaching of politics and commerce). Also altogether new are three professorships of anatomy and medicine, of natural philosophy and natural history, and of modern languages (French, Italian, German). Whereas Hebrew was earlier taught by the professor charged with expounding the holy scriptures in the School of Sacred Theology, now it is in the domain of a professor of ancient languages, "oriental and northern." This philological polymath is responsible for teaching Hebrew, Chaldee, Syriac, Moeso-Gothic, Anglo-Saxon, and Old Icelandic.

---

42. "Autobiography," *Works* I:75–76; *Notes on Virginia*, 147–148, 150–151.
43. Classifications were not a matter that Jefferson took lightly. See the perceptive discussion by Douglas L. Wilson in "Sowerby Revisited: The Unfinished Catalogue of Thomas Jefferson's Library," *William and Mary Quarterly*, 3d ser., 41 (1984):619–625.

The implications of this reorganization for the kinds of questions to be asked and the kinds of answers to be sought are no mystery. If the William and Mary of the 1693 charter faithfully exhibited the contours of a prelatical establishment and the hopes and vision of its royal or pious benefactors, so too would the new William and Mary exhibit the new contours of the republic of learning and the hopes and vision of its learned republican benefactor. The "liberal minded" impulse that first led Virginians to petition their rulers for a college would now at last be fulfilled in a seminary of science, rights, and liberties.

The third of Jefferson's bills to free the human mind proposes the establishment of a public library (No. 81). Its particulars are rather sparse and, at that, somewhat at odds with his two glosses on the bill. As presented in the "Autobiography," the library would be the third stage of an educational system that rose from elementary schools to colleges to "an ultimate grade for teaching the sciences generally, & in their highest degree." In *Notes on Virginia* the bill is described as proposing "to begin a public library and gallery, by laying out a certain sum annually in books, paintings, and statues." The text of the bill, however, says nothing that would suggest an art gallery or a teaching institute of advanced studies. It speaks instead of books and maps, intelligently selected and properly preserved; of a noncirculating collection "made useful by indulging the researches of the learned and curious, within the said library, without fee or reward." The library is public in the sense that two thousand pounds per annum is to be paid out of the state treasury for its acquisitions and operations. It is public in the sense that access to its riches is to be without charge or favor. But this is not a library *for* the public. Admission is to be limited to the qualified; furthering *their* already advanced researches is the great object in view. In proposing to devote substantial public funds to the advancement of rare private minds, Jefferson displayed his confessed "zeal of a true Whig in science." The sight of such splendor, like the sight of beautiful buildings, might enlarge and enrich an entire country. A people boasting such adornments would be worthy of self-respect and of the respect of others.[44]

Finally there is Bill No. 82, whose enactment by the General Assembly Jefferson accounted as one of the three pillars on which he was content to rest his everlasting fame. Its enacting clause relieves

44. *Works* I:75; *Notes on Virginia*, 149; *Papers* II:203.

everyone from compulsory attendance in or compulsory support for any form of religious worship and from any manner of penalties on account of religious opinions or belief. At the same time it guarantees to all the freedom "to profess, and by argument to maintain, their opinions in matters of religion," having equated religious opinions with "opinions in physics or geometry" as matters independent of civil rights.[45] With such simplicity and directness would Jefferson establish religious freedom in Virginia. But that plain prose, far from standing alone and austere (and for all that, memorable) is encased in a text of throbbing eloquence and conviction. The bill's opening and conclusion may stand as definitive statements of Jefferson's republican creed, inviting one to consider No. 82 as the capstone of those bills in the revisal directed to freeing the human mind.[46]

Singularly, the preamble dispenses with the customary "Whereas" and seems to begin in the very midst of an argument: "Well aware that the opinions and belief of men depend not on their own will, but follow involuntarily the evidence proposed to their minds."[47] All the fourteen or so parallel clauses that follow either depend on that awareness or common knowledge, or lend credence to that assertion, or trace the evil

45. The revisal's silence about freedom of political opinion and of the press must at least be noted. To the extent that it touches on these concerns, it is in the form of requiring assurances of fidelity to the commonwealth from electors, civil officials, militia officers, clerics, lawyers, teachers, and professors. In his 1776 drafts of a constitution Jefferson would have guaranteed that printing presses be free, limiting exceptions to private action for private injury; *Papers* I:344–345, 353, 363. But consider this ardent revolutionary's uncertain thoughts about "seditious preaching or conversation against the authority of the civil government"; ibid., 344, 347 n. 10, 353.

46. By this account, No. 79 (more general diffusion of knowledge), No. 80 (William and Mary), No. 81 (public library), and No. 82 (religious freedom) belong together as serving a single intention—enabling free men to be their own best guardians of their rights. Alternatively, No. 82 would be the first of a series of bills devoted to supporting religion and including No. 83 (saving Anglican church property), No. 84 (punishing disturbers of religious worship and Sabbath breakers), No. 85* (appointing days of public fasting and thanksgiving), and No. 86* (annulling marriages prohibited by the Levitical law). It is possible to assert that the arrangement of the 126 bills is not simply random without being obliged to account for all its details and without being driven to overly ingenious explanations. As sensible and conscientious draftsmen, the revisors took the trouble to group bills bearing on related topics before presenting the legislature with the results of their labors of two and one-half years. This is not to say that the logic of their groupings is always obvious. In support of the reading offered in my text, consider James Madison to Thomas Jefferson, 22 January 1786, quoted in ibid. II:549n.

47. Differences between the bill as proposed and the act as adopted (12 Hening 84–86) are detailed in the numbered notes in *Papers* II:552–553.

consequences of ignoring that truth. In sum they show that it is futile or impious or tyrannical, or some combination of all these, to coerce others in matters of opinion, belief, religion, persuasion, or worship. Echoing Milton, the preamble suggests that reason is but choosing and holds "that truth is great and will prevail if left to herself . . . unless by human interposition disarmed of her natural weapons, free argument and debate." Echoing Locke and Shaftesbury, the preamble proclaims "that the opinions of men are not the object of civil government, nor under its jurisdiction." And echoing Adam Smith, it holds that monopolistic privileges corrupt minister and religion alike. For in depriving parishioners of "the comfortable liberty" of contributing to whomever they please, the old law of compulsory religious assessments simultaneously withdraws "from the ministry those tempora[l] rewards, which proceeding from an approbation of their personal conduct, are an additional incitement to earnest and unremitting labours for the instruction of mankind."[48]

Equally singular is the presence in Bill No. 82 of a coda. As though loath to part and leave the enactment to stand on its own, Jefferson showed plainly enough that this bill, if any, would be his candidate for an irrevocable law. Put once and forever beyond the tamperings and temporizings of future generations, this law would confirm and secure most precious "natural rights." But such a wish is absurd: "We well know that this Assembly, elected by the people for the ordinary purposes of legislation only, have no power to restrain the acts of succeeding Assemblies, constituted with powers equal to our own." The proper bottoming of republican society requires the authorization of a power greater than that of "this Assembly" but other than that of "Almighty God," "the holy author of our religion."[49]

48. Jefferson's notes on Locke and Shaftesbury are in *Papers* I:544–550; Adam Smith, *An Inquiry into the Nature and Causes of the Wealth of Nations*, 743–745. For the textual emendation, see *Papers* II:552 n. 5.

49. On the sole authority of Jefferson's later gloss, these two phrases from the preamble of Bill No. 82 are to be read as appositional, leading one to wonder what that religion is; see *Papers* II:552 n. 3.

The limits of a legislative sanction probably account for the absence from the Report of the Committee of Revisors of the two most prominent pieces of Virginian lawmaking. Neither the Declaration of Rights (9 Hening 109–112) nor the Constitution of 1776 (9 Hening 112–119) is proposed for reenactment. They figure only as the report's last word, so to speak, as the most visible and notable exceptions listed in the bill repealing earlier acts of Parliament and of the General Assembly (No. 126*). In making these particular exceptions, the revisors in effect only reasserted Jefferson's belief that those necessary but extralegal actions of the interregnum legislature ex-

Yet however more secure and solemn such a guarantee may be as compared to an ordinary enactment, even a constitutional provision grounded on explicit popular consent still would be subject to later revision by another convention. Would "the natural rights of mankind" then be proof against a constitutional majority's desire to repeal or narrow the enjoyment of those rights? The coda suggests that there are fundamentals, such as the rights asserted in this bill, that are beyond the legitimate reach of laws or even constitutions. The argument for establishing natural rights by law and constitution is not that the latter are sufficient but that they are indispensable for helping to educate the people in the principles of their regime. Thus, even while guarding Virginians against any imminent infringement of their rights, the bill for establishing religious freedom helps educate a society that will cherish such guarantees now and in the future.

The Philosophical Legislator's Long View

Jefferson's *nomoi* display in all their richness and complexity the intersections of his intelligence, principle, and circumstance. The society they portray and prescribe is at once harsh and tender, calculating and lofty. It whips bodies and cossets consciences; it honors genius from behind a wharf of tobacco hogsheads. It cherishes institutional safeguards not of its making, while finding the past instructive mostly for its failures and disasters.

Above all Jefferson's *nomoi* anticipate a society that faces forward. That society is invited to raise its hopes, even while mired in a system of chattel slavery that promises to swamp or befoul every brave plan. Those hopes are centered on itself, its land, and the finest of its children. Here all is promise, another kind of promise, a promise anchored in a sense of past achievements and present dedication. The

---

posed Virginians to "the hazard of having no fundamental rights at all." A proper basis could not be found in ordinary acts of legislation: "To render a form of government unalterable by ordinary acts of assembly, the people must delegate persons with special powers"; *Notes on Virginia,* 121–125. Thus, leaving those foundations of Virginian liberty in place without reenacting them was tantamount to declaring that only an authority superior to that of any legislature, the authority or personal consent of the people, could set matters on a solid and proper footing. This is a persistent Jeffersonian theme; see *Papers* I:347, 354, 357, 364, VI:294–295.

indeterminacies of the present and of the distant future seem hardly to matter. In the midst of a war of uncertain duration and outcome, the revisal's preoccupation is with the kind of society Virginia means to be.

That society, if it is to be at all worth forming and preserving, must be self-governed by truly free men. The simple directness of that stipulation cannot conceal the complexity of the means needed to realize it. For Virginia to become a commonwealth in fact and not merely in name, all segments of the body politic need to be instructed. Schooling is only a part of that instruction and (I am inclined to believe) not even the greater part. The three years of common schooling that all would get, the few years in secondary school that some would enjoy, even the college instruction of the privileged handful— all that could only alert and forewarn, cajole and predispose a people to wish to be their own best guardians of their rights. To make that wish a fact, lessons learned would have to be applied. Institutions had to be contrived that would draw individuals together, compel them to speak and listen to one another, accustom them to judging men and measures, confirm them in the habits of being accountable for their acts. With apparently hopeless circularity, the problem seemed to demand simultaneously that society be made worthy of free men and that individuals be made fit for free society. Here was a challenge that would drive a Rousseau to seek an unspoiled people on an island by themselves; only such a people would be fit for the best a philosophical legislator could contrive. Jefferson, in contrast, needed no mythic Corsica to elicit his greatest efforts. The ground he stood on, the people in whose midst he had always lived—these would be, had to be, the makings of the promising society.

More than his hopeful temperament sustained Jefferson in this bold project. For to a greater degree than the revisal allows (or my account discloses), Jefferson assumed a people already long accustomed to the forms and habits of English law, "a people fostered & fixed in principles of freedom."[50] Similarly, he could take for granted that the extensions of public accountability and local self-government called for in the revisal would be perceived as precisely that—extensions of what had in one form or another existed in Virginia for over a century and a half, not bewildering or alien novelties. What *was* new and in

50. See *Jefferson's* "Declaration of Independence," *Papers* I:318, 426.

need of careful explanation and ardent justification was a heightened spirit of dedication. To legislate that spirit in matters large and small was the great challenge to which Jefferson tried to rise.

Here was a goal worthy of his revolutionary impulse. Making the people aware of what it took to be and to remain their own masters was a considerable undertaking. Each type of person had to be addressed in a manner suitable to its capacities, even while those capacities were themselves being stretched and developed. Furthermore, all this was to be done in a setting where a thousand daily circumstances drew citizens' thoughts and energies earthward and inward, where the enticements of immediate material reward threatened to drain public life of the indispensable involvement of the many and the indispensable contribution of the best. For Jefferson such wholesale indifference would be the very hemorrhaging of public life. A nation of private calculators with short memories would forget the long-term consequences of not tending to the public business. More than anything else they needed to be instructed and confirmed in their present resolve not to be the wards of others.

In seeking to effect that outcome, the revisal nowhere carelessly takes for granted an easy harmony of public need and private interest, not even when suggesting their congruence. To establish a network of connecting secondary postal service for "the more general diffusion of public intelligence among the citizens of this commonwealth and the maintenance of correspondence between friends and merchants" requires, after all, an act of legislation—and is no simple matter at that (No. 19). To be sure, the revisal does not eschew using private interest to further a public purpose (as when licensing counsel, No. 97*), but it would hardly mistake such support for the bedrock of a self-governing society. More is needed.

Here enter the great proems that introduce those bills most critical to Jefferson's project and most characteristic of his legislating art. Inspiring and inspired, they could rouse a people to a sense of what that people might be. They could remind a people of the evils self-governance helps them avoid—and of the possibilities for good and ill it puts within their reach. Commercial opportunities and free consciences, public accountability and participation in public duties, the freeing of private life and the public utility of private excellence—here were benefits to be cherished by all, both atop Monticello and in the valleys below. It took a rare, long perspective to make that evident and point out the way.

3

The Supreme Court as Republican Schoolmaster

FOR THINKING revolutionaries it was axiomatic that securing the republic depended on first forming a certain kind of citizenry. This was not a task to which responsible governors might affect indifference or remain aloof. Accordingly, every organ of the new republican government could be expected to do its part, each in the mode most becoming to it.

In the case of the judiciary this obligation entailed, among other things, a test of the narrow limits within which the judge and his public customarily met and took one another's measure. Judges, after all, were empowered primarily to deal with the particular case or controversy at hand. Their license to adjudicate hardly predisposed prudent judges or their wary publics to expect a relaxation of those restraints. The picture of a sitting judge as propagandist, haranguer, or part-time philosopher would warm few hearts, then or now.

And yet a thoughtful judge, reflecting on the close connection between judicial power and public opinion, might have reason to wonder whether the judge's task narrowly conceived is adequately conceived. All the more would this doubt arise in the context of democratic politics. It is enough to recognize that no regime can safely or for long avoid hard, politically unpopular decisions—and, with that, to ponder the means by which such necessary measures may be rendered palatable to a modern democratic people. These are difficulties more readily stirred than resolved.[1]

---

1. The vast secondary literature that has been spawned by this issue gives no sign of abating. This is to be expected, since the proper relation between judicial power

It comes as no surprise to learn that Alexis de Tocqueville was acutely alert to this problem. In conceiving of a democratic people as benevolently inclined but little given to self-denial, he was expressing some of his profoundest preoccupations and misgivings. Here, it seemed to him, lawyers generally and judges in particular have much to contribute. Their quasi-aristocratic habits of mind fit them to serve as needed and politically acceptable counterweights to popular impatience and injustice.

The consequence of so regarding the judge is to thrust him (and the whole machinery of justice) into the role of an educator, molder, or guardian of those manners, morals, and beliefs that sustain republican government. And yet, of course, the political effectiveness of a judge in gently shaping and even checking democratic opinion is itself dependent on that very opinion. Thus, for Tocqueville, while their ordinary jurisdiction offers justices of the Supreme Court vast opportunities for the exercise of power,

> it is power springing from opinion. They are all-powerful so long as the people consent to obey the law; they can do nothing when they scorn it. Now, of all powers, that of opinion is the hardest to use, for it is impossible to say exactly where its limits come. Often it is as dangerous to lag behind as to outstrip it.
>
> The federal judges therefore must not only be good citizens and men of education and integrity, qualities necessary for all magistrates, but must also be statesmen; they must know how to understand the spirit of the age, to confront those obstacles that can be overcome, and to steer out of the current when the tide threatens to carry them away, and with them the sovereignty of the Union and obedience to its laws.[2]

A democratic regime, then, requires a judiciary that is both upright and subtle, equally attentive to its opportunities and dangers, and averse to seeming either diffident or overbearing. So Tocqueville maintained, and so too did some of the shapers and leaders of the early national judiciary. Less obvious is whether the earliest generation of national judges consciously acted as statesmen-teachers or, indeed, whether they were supposed to assume any such role. In

---

and public opinion remains a problem, live and urgent, if mocking of final formulations.

2. Alexis de Tocqueville, *Democracy in America,* 137, 247–248, 252–254 (I, pt. i, chap. 8; ii, 8).

seeking to recover and assess that historical evidence, one looks, not for a ready-made model for the modern judge, but for a deeper understanding of the founders' political science.

Itinerant Sermonizing: Use and Abuse

The legislative history of Senate Bill 1 of the first session of the First Congress must, in many interesting particulars of motive and intention, remain hidden from us. The genesis of what was to be called the Judiciary Act of 1789 has been examined and reexamined, sometimes with great care,[3] but always with a number of questions unanswered and perhaps unanswerable. The secrecy in which the Senate then conducted its business and the heedless indifference with which Americans long treated their public records obscure the purposes Congress intended to serve in enacting the Judiciary Act. What broad political functions were the justices of the highest court of the land expected to perform? We can give at best a probable answer. To what extent were the political and psychological premises underlying the national judicial establishment of a piece with those on which the other parts of the new government were founded? On such a fundamental question we are obliged to speak with no less caution. We are dealing with matters that not only admit of speculation but fairly require it.

It is not only such large questions that are difficult to answer with confidence. Many narrower problems are equally beset with ambiguities and uncertainties. Consider the simple question, What led Congress to send members of the Supreme Court riding circuit over the length and breadth of the land? There may be parallels between the organization of the circuit courts and the English assize system or the colonial or state courts.[4] But earlier practice contained no precise analogy to the way members of the nation's highest court were brought directly into the milieu of local laws and usages, local law-

3. See, above all, Charles Warren, "New Light on the History of the Federal Judiciary Act of 1789," *Harvard Law Review* 37 (1923):49–132.

4. *Register of Debates in Congress*, 19th Cong., 1st sess., 2, pt. 1:1101 (Kerr), hereafter cited as *Congressional Debates*; Felix Frankfurter and James M. Landis, *The Business of the Supreme Court*, 12–13; Peter Archer, *The Queen's Courts*, 250–251; Roscoe Pound, *Organization of Courts*, 107; and "A Democratic Federalist" (17 October 1787), in Herbert J. Storing, ed., *The Complete Anti-Federalist* III:61. But see *Congressional Debates*, 19th Cong., 1st sess., 2, pt. 1:873–874 (Webster).

yers and jurors. Members of the Supreme Court, sitting as circuit court judges, instructed grand juries and presided over trials while disposing of the considerable original jurisdiction vested in the circuit courts. It bespeaks some legislative purpose, not to say single-mindedness, to compel the disgruntled members of the highest national tribunal to perform tiring and hazardous circuit duties. It is plausible, even likely, that nothing more lies behind this feature of the judicial system than a close-fisted Connecticut concern to get value for money. The early expectations for the Supreme Court's business, both original and appellate, suggested that ennui rather than exhaustion would be the justices' probable occupational hazard. Jealous guardians of the public purse may very well have seen circuit riding as a cure to boredom and a way of serving both justice and economy, to neither's disadvantage.[5]

However onerous members of the Supreme Court felt their circuit duties to be, it cannot be said that they failed to take advantage of the opportunities thus presented. The justices of the Federalist period sensed and were reminded of the novelty of giving substance to the Constitutional Convention's founding act. It is not farfetched to suspect that the justices saw themselves as having a unique responsibility, beyond those shared by other courts in the system. They were all Federalists. They were not narrow professional lawyers but revolutionary patriots and statesmen whose involvement in the founding and ratification controversies made it natural for them to think politically and to feel some proprietary relationship to the new order. The justices were quick to see and seize the chance to proselytize for the new government and to inculcate habits and teachings most necessary in their view for the maintenance of self-government. (In so doing they left later interpreters with the problem of distinguishing a defense of the regime and of the Constitution from a defense of an administration and of a party.) The main vehicle for this instruction was the charge to the grand jury, with which the presiding judge formally opened the proceedings of a circuit court session.

The prevailing practice was for a judge to summarize for a newly empaneled grand jury the statutes and, in the state courts, the com-

5. The story of complaints, recommendations, and responses is summarized, along with much relevant historical background, in Frankfurter and Landis, *Business of the Supreme Court*, 4–30. (See also Leonard D. White, *The Federalists*, 483–484; Charles Warren, *The Supreme Court in United States History* I:85–90.) *Congressional Debates*, 19th Cong., 1st sess., 2, pt. 1:977 (Powell).

mon law relevant to the performance of their duty. It was the grand jury's duty to return such indictments and presentments alleging violations of the laws as in its judgment were warranted by the evidence already known to it or presented to it. In the state courts it was common for the grand jury to present grievances about poor administration of the laws and the need for new laws, reaching down to matters of narrow local concern and great specificity.[6] None of this was new or extraordinary. But out of the years of stress that preceded and led to the break with Britain, another kind of dialogue between judge and jurors matured. In a growing number of instances the judge came to regard himself as an exhorter and teacher, obliged at all times (but above all at moments of crisis) "boldly [to] declare the law to the people, and instruct them in their civil rights." By 1785 John Dickinson could write to members of the Pennsylvania Supreme Court, about to go on circuit, "that besides the Terror of legal Penalties, all the Influence to be derived from your Characters, and the Dignity of your Stations, might be applied in disseminating the best Principles & setting forward the most effectual Regulations for the prevention of offences. You Gentlemen, well know how vain are Laws without Manners."[7]

That the judges would respond to such instructions with differing degrees of avidity may safely be presumed. But for two reasons we can be quite certain that when they did undertake political education they did so with self-awareness. The political charge was a deviation from the ordinary and recognized as such by the judges who used it. James Iredell, at the time a North Carolina judge, could cut short, after five pages, a sermon on natural rights and patriotism—itself a sort of prelude to a brief grand jury charge—by recalling that "the time, and even the occasion, [would] not properly permit" his elaborating on these themes. Another North Carolina judge could surround a long and impassioned plea that "the love of our country rise superior to the turpid and base passion for gain" with unmistakable signs that he knew his political charge was not of a piece with his just-

---

6. Alexander Addison, *Reports of Cases in the County Courts of the Fifth Circuit . . . of Pennsylvania. And Charges to Grand Juries of those County Courts* [pt. 2], 75–76 (June 1793).

7. Grand jury charge of South Carolina judge William Henry Drayton (November 1774), in Peter Force, comp., *American Archives*, 4th ser., I:959–960; John Dickinson, President of the State of Pennsylvania, to the Chief Justice and other Judges of the Pennsylvania Supreme Court, 8 October 1785, in Samuel Hazard, ed., *Pennsylvania Archives* [1st ser.], X:523–524.

concluded statement of the law: "Gentlemen, give me leave now, before you retire to business, to address a few words to you in another character." "Gentlemen, you will, I hope, excuse my traveling out of the line of Business for which you have been summoned here at this time."[8] This self-consciousness when delivering political charges persisted. Indeed, this open self-consciousness was in later days often a sign of sensible use of the political charge. American oratory at large may have made this kind of speech familiar, but not to the extent that the members of the new national judiciary could forget the customary bounds of judicial propriety, even while exceeding them.

Chief Justice John Jay defended himself by saying in the charge delivered on his first circuit, "These remarks may not appear very pertinent to the present occasion, and yet it will be readily admitted that occasions of promoting good-will, and good-temper, and the progress of useful truths among our fellow-citizens should not be omitted." Similarly, a district judge could declare to a grand jury that "to forbear to speak of this government on this occasion, (altho it may not be necessary to the business for which you are now assembled) might argue an insensibility towards it, which no citizen should ever feel." Having said this much, he was free to extol the new Constitution through contrast with the old and through hopeful anticipation of public prosperity.[9]

It was not only the novelty of the political charge that led the judges to signal their auditors (and themselves) of a departure from customary decorum. At least as powerful an inducement to judicial self-awareness and self-control were the uneven and fluctuating reactions to the practice by grand juries. If there were times when judge and jurors sang in beautiful harmony—now in outrage against the British, then in stirring defense of the revolutionary cause—there were other times when cacophony prevailed. The political charge could and did exacerbate political differences—most evidently before the Revolu-

8. Griffith J. McRee, ed., *Life and Correspondence of James Iredell* I:387–388 (1 May 1778); grand jury charge of Judge Samuel Ashe (11 June 1778), in Walter Clark, ed., *The State Records of North Carolina* XIII:443, 441, 444.

9. Henry P. Johnston, ed., *The Correspondence and Public Papers of John Jay* III:390 (April–May 1790); grand jury charge of District Judge John Sitgreaves, *Gazette of the United States* (Philadelphia), 4 May 1791.

On occasion, Pennsylvania judge Alexander Addison gave clear signs of knowing that his use of the charge went beyond his official capacity; Addison, *Reports of Cases* [pt. 2], 165–166 (September 1795), 187 (September 1796). But his is a case where self-awareness was not always accompanied by moderation.

tion when Loyalist judges chastised grand juries for failing to make presentments and indictments against libelers and tea burners and other local revolutionaries, less dramatically after the Revolution when state judges' urgings of moderation in the treatment of Loyalists were received with little enthusiasm by grand jurors.[10] During the first decade of the national judiciary, the political charge was subjected yet again to the full cycle of popular applause and disdain. Toward the end of the period, one state judge could exhort a grand jury to steer clear of political presentments, "not [to] think of introducing politics into a court of justice which *cannot* or *ought not* to have anything to do with it," and to keep to the business of grand juries as defined by the state legislature. By the end of the period, the publication of another state judge's collected grand jury charges required this kind of prefatory defense:

A stronger evidence of a disposition in some men, to monopolize the direction of public opinion, can hardly be given, than the harsh censures which have been propagated on what are called *Political Charges;* nor of the depravity of public opinion, than the approbation with which those censures have been received. While so many set themselves up as political instructors, and, in this capacity, with all the confidence, industry, and zeal of inspired missionaries, preach error and sedition; it would seem hard, if men whose education, habits, and experience, may have qualified them to think justly on public affairs, should be condemned to silence; or, while interposing their sentiments against the torrent of delusion, deny them the solemnity of a public station. I flatter myself, that such censures come not from the wisest and best part of the community.[11]

But by then the days of the political charge (and of Judge Addison's tenure) were numbered.

The reports of the manner in which these charges were delivered and received suggest a cross between a political sermon and a speech

10. For Chief Justice Thomas Hutchinson, see Josiah Quincy, Jr., comp., *Reports of Cases . . . of the Province of Massachusetts Bay, between 1761 and 1772,* 262–270, 309. For Chief Justice Frederick Smyth, see Richard S. Field, *The Provincial Courts of New Jersey, with Sketches of the Bench and Bar* (New Jersey Historical Society, *Collections,* III [1849]), 175, 180–181. For postwar resentment, see Richard D. Younger, *The People's Panel: The Grand Jury in the United States, 1634–1941,* 41.

11. Grand jury charge of Virginia judge Richard Parker, *Palladium* (Frankfort, Ky.), 23 October 1798; Addison, *Reports of Cases* [pt. 2], iii–iv.

from the throne.[12] It would be a mistake, as the substance of the statements shows, to dismiss these charges as the merest Federalist propaganda, although one of their intended effects was to bolster Federalist theories and practices. Lumping all these charges and reducing them to simple apologetic would make it hard to discriminate between Chief Justice Jay's use and Justice Samuel Chase's abuse of the judicial charge. Some of these political sermons ought to be considered rather as carefully composed, self-conscious appeals to that portion of the population which was then politically influential— appeals to be good republicans coupled with some rules for being good republicans. Depending on the judge and the occasion, the political charges presented the full range from judicial elevation to intemperate special pleading. These appeals were often printed in the newspapers at the request of the grand jurors and then reprinted farther afield. The justices knew that their audience extended beyond the confines of the courtroom. An occasion for a ceremonial pronouncement was seized, the pronouncement itself given a character both judicial and political—like, yet unlike, what a president might say— and a certain conception of the public good promoted through a calculated exhortation. Before one can judge the adequacy and fairness of the conception of the public good implicit in the exhortation, one has to see precisely what the judicial teaching was.

Chief Justice Jay, in his charge to grand juries repeated throughout the Eastern Circuit on the occasion of his first convening these courts in the spring of 1790, opened appropriately enough with the question to which the history of the United States was to provide the answer. In accents reminiscent of the initial paragraph of *Federalist,* No. 1, the chief justice began:

> Whether any people can long govern themselves in an equal, uniform, and orderly manner, is a question which the advocates for free government justly consider as being exceedingly important to the cause of liberty. This question, like others whose solution depends on facts, can only be determined by experience. It is a question on which many think some room for doubt still remains.

. 12. Descriptions of those occasions may be found in Frank Monaghan, *John Jay,* 314; McRee, ed., *Life of Iredell* II:435; George Van Santvoord, *Sketches of the Lives and Judicial Services of the Chief-Justices of the Supreme Court of the United States,* 262–263; William Garrott Brown, *The Life of Oliver Ellsworth,* 245; Frankfurter and Landis, *Business of the Supreme Court,* 20; Warren, *Supreme Court in United States History* I:59 n. 1.

It has fallen—providentially fallen—to the Americans to have "more perfect opportunities of choosing, and more effectual means of establishing their own government, than any other nation has hitherto enjoyed." The force and fraud that seem to have shaped constitutions and governments in most other times and places appear to have been frustrated, at least for the while. The sometimes painful experiences of establishing and correcting state governments "have operated as useful experiments, and conspired to promote our advancement in this interesting science." Similarly, the future lessons of time and experience will be applied to improve this new national government as long as the people rely—and have reason to rely—on their own good sense.[13]

Other Supreme Court justices, such as Iredell and Oliver Ellsworth, elaborated upon this theme. "The noble experiment" that the Americans had undertaken would test the limits of human nature as well as the cause of "a government of reason." "A higher degree of freedom [than that provided by the Constitution], consistent with any government at all, is not exerciseable by human nature." At the same time, "no people . . . can rationally desire more than that they should themselves choose the government under which they are to live." Jay cautioned his audience to temper their theory with some sober practice, just as Jefferson was to appeal to his fellow citizens not to abandon the experiment represented by "this Government, the world's best hope," on the basis of some "theoretic and visionary fear." "If, then," Jay continued, "so much depends on our rightly improving the before-mentioned opportunities, if the most discerning and enlightened minds may be mistaken relative to theories unconfirmed by practice, if on such difficult questions men may differ in opinion and yet be patriots, and if the merits of our opinions can only be ascertained by experience, let us patiently abide the trial, and unite our endeavors to render it a fair and an impartial one." It was in this mixed spirit of high hope and sober sense, equally removed from the doctrinaire and from cold legalism, that some justices instructed the people in republicanism.[14]

---

13. Johnston, ed., *Correspondence of Jay* III:387–389 (April–May 1790); see also grand jury charges of district judges in New Hampshire and Maine printed in *Columbian Centinel* (Boston), 31 July 1790 (John Sullivan), and 25 August 1790 (David Sewall).

14. McRee, ed., *Life of Iredell* II:394 (May 1793), 484 (May 1796); Brown, *Life of Ellsworth*, 247 (April 1796); Johnston, ed., *Correspondence of Jay* III:389–390

The foremost of the themes repeated and elaborated upon by the justices was that of the close connection between self-restraint and true liberty. The justices showed an awareness that the civil liberty of a people freè to choose its governors cannot for long be restrained in a manner that is not generally accepted. No matter how well born or high toned they are, governors dependent on the popular franchise cannot expect simply to prescribe opinions and codes that will be authoritative. The more intelligent justices recognized this from the outset and took such steps as they could to persuade others to adopt their opinions. While the courtroom circumstances in which the charges were delivered could have brought to mind ex cathedra pronouncement, the rhetoric actually employed shows that the justices chose not to rest with appeals to their authority. They began, rather, by appealing to fairly narrow calculations of self-interest, broadening the range of considerations as the argument moved from self to nation to type of regime: "It cannot be too strongly impressed on the minds of us all how greatly our individual prosperity depends on our national prosperity, and how greatly our national prosperity depends on a well organized, vigorous government." Jay was quick to reassure his listeners that such a government is not "unfriendly to liberty—to that liberty which is really inestimable." And, having gone so far, he proceeded to define civil liberty as "an equal right to all the citizens to have, enjoy, and to do . . . whatever the equal and constitutional laws of the country admit to be consistent with the public good." It is true that Jay, like Iredell and Ellsworth, was prone to see a divine plan (or the tracks of one) in political affairs, but that was not the sole or main thrust of his argument. If an appeal was to be made to his contemporaries, it had to be to both "the duty and the interest . . . of all good citizens."[15] Once led to see the connection between their material well-being and law-abidingness, they would be less apt to be

---

(April–May 1790). Compare Thomas Jefferson, First Inaugural Address, 4 March 1801, in James D. Richardson, ed., *A Compilation of the Messages and Papers of the Presidents, 1789–1897* I:322.

15. Johnston, ed., *Correspondence of Jay*, III:394–395 (April–May 1790); see also *Pennsylvania Gazette* (Philadelphia), 14 April 1790 (Wilson), and *Columbian Centinel* (Boston), 28 July 1792 (Jay). Justice Wilson was especially insistent on developing a kind of patriotism and law-abidingness that grew out of "rationally beloved" laws: "I mean not . . . to recommend to you an implicit and an undistinguishing approbation of the laws of your country. Admire; but admire with reason on your side"; Robert Green McCloskey, ed., *The Works of James Wilson* II:823 (May 1791).

startled by false alarms. They would be better able to distinguish "true liberty" from the "unbounded liberty of the strongest man," or the "unlimited sway of a majority," or "unlicensed indulgence to all the passions of men." "Let each man consider, that his liberty and his property cannot be secured without forming a common interest with all the other members of the society to which he belongs." The cultivation of this common interest, the adjustment as far as possible of "the common welfare of the whole jointly" to the welfare of the individuals and states forming the whole, are tasks to which "moderation and good sense" are indispensable.[16]

The recent history of American public affairs might well have contained important and even salutary lessons, but as can be seen here those lessons were subject to interpretations. That the cause of individual liberty requires that a price be paid to a larger whole and that genuine liberty is fundamentally dependent on law-abidingness are propositions to which no thinking person could take exception. But thoughtful people could and did disagree about the environment most favorable to liberty. It was a frequent Anti-Federalist argument—and one with respectable theoretical credentials—that liberty was neither safe nor securable under a single government extending over so large and varied a country. More than one response was possible, and more than one was made. A comparison of Ellsworth's language (voiced while on circuit at Savannah) with Jay's in *Federalist,* No. 2, reveals not that one response was more mythopoeic than the other but that the voice of the judge speaking as judge had a rhetoric of its own. To the contention that America was too extensive and heterogeneous to have one will (unless it were coerced by Janizaries), Jay, writing as Publius, replied by denying the significance and even the existence of barriers to union. Ellsworth, in contrast, speaking as chief justice, turned the argument around. Far from being too vast to be bound together by good laws, this country would be held together precisely and above all by good laws. Not the ties of kinship, not the memories of common disasters and victories—important as these were—but the ligatures of national laws were most to be relied on. It was for a judge, a teaching judge, to make this point and to create the occasions for reiterating it. Beneath the laws lay political preconditions; beyond the laws stretched political consequences. For a moment there merged

16. McRee, ed., *Life of Iredell* II:365–366 (12 October 1792); see also ibid., 484 (23 May 1796).

the inclination and the opportunity to expound these matters to the citizenry.[17]

Implicit and often explicit in the Supreme Court justices' political charges was the advocacy of a certain kind of conduct, corresponding to a certain type of citizen: plainspoken, self-possessed, manly in a quiet rather than gallus-tugging fashion; jealous of his rights, but aware of his duties and the self-esteem of others. It is arguable that the justices were at least as concerned with sustaining an already existing type as with creating a model republican. The republic itself showed such moderation and presupposed it in its citizens.[18]

This confidence, however, was not to be taken for granted. Popular government, more than other forms, tries citizens' capacities for enduring disappointment gracefully. After being invited—indeed, obliged—to declare their views on the public business, the citizens of a republic are further obliged "cheerfully [to] submit" to constitutional majority determinations. This "deference of private sentiment to that of the public" is "the very basis of all republican governments." The greater diffusion of political rights carries with it a need for a more broadly distributed sense of political responsibility, the quality of which is seen most clearly perhaps in the way public discussion is conducted. The freer the government, the greater its dependence on popular confidence; and that confidence, to be worth anything, requires that each citizen exercise the right of public comment so "that he may neither be unwarily misled himself, nor unwarily mislead others." Such considerations—to say nothing for the moment of the special problem of those who deliberately deceive the public—point to "that salutary caution with which all public measures ought to be discussed." Nowhere is this more needed than in discussions of policy, "because nothing is more fallible than human judgment when it extends its views into a futurity." Diffidence, moderation, and a cautious weighing of inconveniences and advantages are in order: "Any other mode of considering great questions of public policy is idle and insignificant." Above all, the enlightened citizen will remember that "things and not names ought to decide our judgments."[19]

---

17. Brown, *Life of Ellsworth*, 246 (April 1796); Jacob E. Cooke, ed., *The Federalist*, Nos. 2, 9, hereafter cited as *Federalist*. Compare Henry Adams, *History of the United States during the Administrations of Thomas Jefferson and James Madison* I:1–11, for another view of Jay's providentially blessed land.

18. *Columbian Centinel* (Boston), 28 July 1792 (Jay).

19. McRee, ed., *Life of Iredell* II:467 (12 April 1796), 506–508 (22 May 1797), 484–485 (23 May 1796); *Columbian Centinel* (Boston), 28 July 1792 (Jay).

There are lessons to be drawn from the past, lessons to be passed on to present and future generations. In this continuous process of extraction and transmission, many of the justices saw their relations to the grand jury as central. Every nation, but especially "an extensive country," has to learn to cope with those who, "impelled by avarice or ambition, or by both," are prepared to gratify their longings at the expense of the public good. Add to this peril the natural effects of partisanship on even "the best men": "our wishes and partialities becoming inflamed by opposition, often cause indiscretions, and lead us to say and to do things that had better have been omitted." Between these arts of the deceitful and the weaknesses of the honest, republics have come to ruin. For these old dangers, remedies—both old and new—are needed: government by representatives, a divided and balancing legislature, a vigorous executive. As fundamental as any of these are the qualities called for by Ellsworth: "vigilance, constant diligence, and fidelity for the execution of laws"—traits needed in any good republican, but especially in a republican grand juror.[20] And from the grand juror would go forth the law, both the knowledge of it and the spirit of it. "I offer no apology, gentlemen, for the nature or the length of this address," Justice James Wilson said in concluding a charge whose printed version could not easily have taken less than an hour to deliver. "In the situation, in which I have the honour to be placed, I deem it my duty to embrace every proper opportunity of disseminating the knowledge of [the criminal code] far and speedily. Can this be done with more propriety than in an address to a grand jury?" And later: "Inform and practically convince every one within your respective spheres of action and intercourse, that, as excellent laws improve the virtue of the citizens, so the virtue of the citizens has a reciprocal and benign energy in heightening the excellence of the law."[21]

20. McRee, ed., *Life of Iredell* II:485 (23 May 1796); Francis Wharton, ed., *State Trials of the United States during the Administrations of Washington and Adams,* 57 (Jay); Brown, *Life of Ellsworth,* 247 (April 1796).

21. McCloskey, ed., *Works of Wilson* II:822–823 (May 1791). See also Wharton, ed., *State Trials,* 62; Wilson spoke of the useful lessons to be taught and learned in the courtroom so that "a practical knowledge and a just sense" of a free people's duties might be "diffused universally among the citizens." This theme of the grand jurors' duty to instruct others "when you blend yourselves again among your neighbors" is well stated by Chief Justice William Henry Drayton of South Carolina in some of his charges to Charleston grand juries; see Hezekiah Niles, ed., *Principles and Acts of the Revolution in America,* 333 (23 April 1776), 347, 352 (21 October 1777); see also Addison, *Reports of Cases* [pt. 2], 110 (September 1794).

These admonitions and appeals ought not to be mistaken for simple declarations of the need for vigorous administration and good government. Some measure of popular self-restraint is indispensable for good government, while one of the surest effects of good administration is the way it secures the voluntary attachment of the people. If there can be no good government without some citizen virtue, there can be no highly developed sense of citizenship without good government. The itinerant justice, in this early stage of national life, improved the judicial occasion by drawing out the deeper implications of national law enforcement for both liberty and union. When he did his work with finesse, the teaching judge was more than a scrupulous craftsman, if less than a philosopher-king, and quite other than the partisan. It is not hard to see that the task of political education would be complicated and even defeated once it fell to the hands of coarse judges and once harsher party conflicts emerged. For however salutary the lessons to be conveyed, a sensible teacher first pays heed to the context of the instruction. In the measure of care that the justices took in considering those limits, we find a way of discriminating the use from the abuse of the judicial charge. By examining two of the instances where judicial pronouncements ran counter to strong popular and partisan opinion, we can get a sense of the strengths and weaknesses of this variety of judicial politics.

The conduct of foreign policy became a theme of judicial teaching in two ways. To the extent that the grand jury's duty to investigate suspected breaches of the laws of the United States touched upon treaties, the law of nations, and the like, it was beyond debate that the justices should instruct the grand jury out of their superior judicial understanding of international law. This the justices did, but not only this. Prompted by the occasion, and by the passions quickened by Washington's proclamation of neutrality of 22 April 1793, the justices went on to pronounce some lessons in foreign policy. In their remarks they tried to steer a narrow course between an examination of the particulars that vexed domestic politics throughout most of the first decade of the new government and an overly vague statement of what constituted good manners in international conduct. Chief Justice Jay's grand jury charge at Richmond, delivered a month after Washington's proclamation, is a fair sample of the concerns for policy and professional duty that merged in the political charge.22

22. There are two texts in print. The original draft is in Johnston, ed., *Correspondence of Jay* III:478–485 (22 May 1793). The final version, which was delivered and

The grand theme running through Jay's charge is that the demands of duty and interest coincide, that neither individuals nor nation will find their genuine interests slighted when they act in an honorable fashion. The aptness of this theme is illustrated in various ways. Thus the old maxim that one should use one's own property so as not to harm others is generalized beyond the realm of property to comprehend liberty, power, "and other blessings of every kind." The very purpose of free government is to restrain people to act in accord with this maxim. It is precisely in a regime where all powers are derived from the popular will that the need for strong government is most acute, for it is there that the number of rights to be protected and the difficulty in restraining the citizenry are greatest. It is above all in a free government that "the duty and interest of us all, that the laws be observed, and irresistibly executed," are clearest, for it is above all in such a government that the laws express the will, and secure the benefit, of the citizens as a whole.23

In reviewing the laws of which the grand jurors ought to take cognizance, Jay was careful to instruct the jurors in the "general principles" that guided relations among the nations and, going beyond this, to argue that utility and justice coincided in recommending a policy of neutrality for the United States. The bulk of the charge is taken up with a discussion of the relevant laws, under the headings of treaties, law of nations, and the Constitution and statutes. Treaties ought not to be mistaken for statutes; the unilateral discretion available for changing and repealing the latter does not apply to the former. The special standing that treaties enjoy as part of the supreme law of the land is a token of the practical restrictions on each contracting power. There are maxims and principles of the law of nations that prescribe and define fidelity to treaties. Not who the parties are, but the fact of their mutual pledge, makes the obligation binding. Similarly, the law of nations imposes duties as well as rights on the United States. In urging "a conduct friendly and impartial towards the belligerent powers," Washington's proclamation "is exactly consistent with and declaratory of the conduct enjoined by the law of nations." Its domestic consequences, restricting citizens and aliens alike from behaving in a manner that jeopardizes that neutrality, are well supported by the law of nations. "The respect which every na-

---

then "printed by the government for the purpose of explaining abroad the position of the United States," appears in Wharton, ed., *State Trials*, 49–59.

23. Wharton, ed., *State Trials*, 49–52, 58–59 (Jay).

tion owes to itself imposes a duty on its government to cause all its laws to be respected and obeyed." Considerations of duty, interest, and disposition all support a policy of neutrality and bind the grand jurors to ferret out those seeking to frustrate that policy. As though this would not suffice, Jay proceeded to defend the wisdom of the proclamation of neutrality in terms going beyond the judge's or jurors' province strictly defined. It is not enough to "be faithful to all—kind to all—but let us also be just to ourselves." America now enjoyed peace, liberty, safety, and unparalleled prosperity. A policy of neutrality left her free to pursue her offices of humanity and benevolence—as well as her commerce—toward all belligerents. An enlightened self-interest also dictated that Americans act with an awareness of the domestic causes that might lead the country into war. There was a possibility of war arising from the narrowly self-regarding actions of those who would "not hesitate to gratify [their] passions [of avarice or ambition or both] at the expense of the blood and tears even of those who are free from blame." Or war might equally arise out of the partisan indiscretions from which even the best citizens are not exempt. "Prudence directs us to look forward to such an event, and to endeavour not only to avert, but also to be prepared for it." The principal precaution is "union in sentiments and measures relative to national objects," the avoidance of parties that are partisans of one foreign power or another. There is, in short, a kind of conduct becoming a free people in peace and war:

> But, if neither integrity nor prudence on our part should prove sufficient to shield us from war, we may then meet it with fortitude, and a firm dependence on the Divine protection; whenever it shall become impossible to preserve peace by avoiding offences, it will be our duty to refuse to purchase it by sacrifices and humiliations, unworthy of a free and magnanimous people, either to demand or submit to.[24]

However one regards the law of nations—as rules for relations between states or (with Justice Wilson) as "the duties which a nation owes to itself"—it is to be understood in the light of a few well-known facts. In Chief Justice Jay's words, "nations are, in respect to each other, in the same situation as independent individuals in a state of nature." Having no common judge on earth, these nations "have a perfect right to establish such governments and build such houses as

24. Ibid., 52–58 (Jay).

they prefer, and their neighbors have no right to pull down either because not fashioned according to their ideas of perfection." The indisputably superior merit and justice of the American form of government (and none of the justices was shy about so judging it) ought to commend it to the world, but they do not entail a general commission to remake the world after the American likeness. Nonintervention and self-determination seem, rather, to be the standing order. But if "strict impartiality" is the rule—"it is no less our interest than our duty to act accordingly"—it is a rule open to qualifications and, in any event, is not to be mistaken for indifference. There are standards of conduct, standards of civility, to which nations, no less than individuals, ought to be held. Unless prior treaty commitments require it, Americans ought not to be partisans of one belligerent or the other. If the war is about objects in which America is not interested, Americans ought not to interfere except as mediators and friends to peace.[25]

It also is to be borne in mind that in Wilson's formulation there are certain self-regarding duties that neither states nor individuals can properly shirk. Predictably, "self-preservation is a primary duty." Beyond that is the duty to "love and to deserve an honest fame." In the midst of the controversy over the proclamation of neutrality, Jay could declare in a grand jury charge: "A just war is an evil, but it is not the greatest; oppression and disgrace are greater. War is not to be sought, but it is not to be fled from. Let us do exactly what is just and right, and then remain without fear, but not without care about the consequences." Honest fame, a due regard for national dignity and character, all required a state of mind that would neither give nor brook insult and disgrace.[26]

The justices' international and domestic teachings were as one. They saw a need in each case to elevate self-interest into republican virtue, manly independence, self-respect, and patriotism. In the course of reciting the reasoning that in his judgment gave issue to the Washingtonian policy, the chief justice could not but be aware of the fact that the merits of that policy were a subject of bitter partisan dispute. Yet even here there was a lesson to be learned, a moral to be

25. Ibid., 62–63 (Wilson); Johnston, ed., *Correspondence of Jay* III:481–482 (22 May 1793). Nothing in Jay's charge runs counter to Hamilton's argument in "Pacificus," No. 4 (10 July 1793), on the limits or inappropriateness of gratitude as a principle of international conduct.

26. Wharton, ed., *State Trials*, 62 (Wilson); Johnston, ed., *Correspondence of Jay* III:482.

drawn. However heated the controversy and debatable the policy, as law of the land the proclamation bound judge and juror alike. The duty to enforce the law overbore individual scruples and misgivings. Outside the courtroom, in the political forum, "as free citizens we have a right to think and speak our sentiments on this subject, in terms becoming freemen—that is, in terms explicit, plain, and decorous." Within the courtroom, in the very act of performing an unpleasant duty, grand jurors would have occasion to learn the truth of "the excellent principle" that "the interests and the duties of men are inseparable."27

There seems to be general agreement that the use of the charge as a means of political education was the introduction of a new purpose to what originally had been a mere abstract of crimes and punishments. But not every such introduction is impudent meddling. What saves Jay's charges (and those like his) from the scorn justly directed toward hot-headed political preachments from the bench is precisely the consciousness that he "was treading on delicate ground." Jay enacted in the courtroom the very spirit and teaching he would inculcate in others. He knew, and acted and spoke as though he knew, that "on such difficult questions men may differ in opinion and yet be patriots." It is one thing to declaim (like Ellsworth) against the evil effects of disorganization and impiety, showing that, "unhinged and imperious, the mind revolts at every institution which can preserve order, or protect right, while the heart, demoralized, becomes insensible to social and civil obligations." But it is another, and more difficult, thing to avoid both the erroneous doctrine and the erroneous manner of "heated divines" and of "some enthusiastic politicians."28

The troubles of Justice Chase flowed from various causes, some of them peculiar to that able but intemperate man. The larger political controversies behind the impeachment are not my concern now. Nor do I mean to assert—what cannot be proved one way or the other— that more cautious charges could long have preserved the Federalist judiciary from the watchful hostility of the Jeffersonian administration and Congress. Nonetheless, it is possible and even useful to try to

27. Johnston, ed., *Correspondence of Jay* III:485; *Columbian Centinel* (Boston), 28 July 1792 (Jay).

28. Wharton, ed., *State Trials,* 58 (Jay); Johnston, ed., *Correspondence of Jay* III:389–390 (April–May 1790); Henry Flanders, *The Lives and Times of the Chief Justices of the Supreme Court of the United States* II:192 (Ellsworth); McRee, ed., *Life of Iredell* II:467 (12 April 1796).

detect that respect in which Chase's style in his political charges differed from Jay's.[29]

Justice Chase's scandalizing charge may be considered in its three parts: an exordium stating the problem and the speaker's credentials to speak to it; a critique of three accomplished or proposed changes in the laws; and finally, an analysis and rejection of the theoretical foundations of those changes in the laws. The political charge itself is seen as extra matter, the delivery of which was prompted by a concern for the welfare of the country. Chase saw his task as countering pleasant-sounding nonsense, even at the risk of saying things "repugnant to popular prejudice." Yet there is more than a consciousness of good intentions; he identified himself as a man of 1776, an authentic long-time republican. The problem as it emerges in the charge is that a change is occurring in the ordinary understanding of representation and liberty; and that change is such, according to Chase, that the "fast approaching" result will be that "the people are *not free,* wh[a]tever may be their form of government."

Indicative of this evil end are the institutional changes condemned and deplored by Chase in the central part of his charge:

> You know, gentlemen, that our state and national institutions were framed to secure to every member of the society, equal liberty and equal rights; but the late alteration of the federal judiciary by the abolition of the offices of the sixteen circuit judges, and the recent change in our state [Maryland] constitution, by the establishing of universal suffrage, and the further alteration that is contemplated in our state judiciary (if adopted) will, in my judgment, take away all security for property and personal liberty. The independence of the national judiciary, is already shaken to its foundation, and the virtue of the people alone can restore it. The independence of the judges of this state will be entirely destroyed, if the bill for the abolition of the two supreme courts should be ratified by the next general assembly. The change of the state constitution, by allowing universal suffrage, will, in my opinion, certainly and rapidly destroy all protection to property, and all security to personal liberty; and our republican constitution will sink into a mobocracy, the worst of all possible governments.

29. The text of Justice Chase's offending grand jury charge of 2 May 1803 is reproduced in Charles Evans, *Report of the Trial of the Hon. Samuel Chase . . . ,* app., exhibit no. VIII, 60–62. The Samuel H. Smith–Thomas Lloyd transcription of the Chase impeachment is printed in *Debates and Proceedings in the Congress of the United States, 1789–1824,* 8th Cong., 2d sess., hereafter cited as *Annals of Congress.* The charge appears at 673–676.

I can only lament, that the main pillar of our state constitution, has
already been thrown down by the establishment of universal suffrage.
By this shock alone, the whole building totters to its base, and will
crumble into ruins, before many years elapse, unless it be restored to its
original state. If the independency of your state judges, which your bill
of rights wisely declares "to be essential to the impartial administration
of justice, and the great security to the rights and liberties of the people," shall be taken away by the ratification of the bill passed for that
purpose, it will precipitate the destruction of your whole state constitution; and there will be nothing left in it, worthy the care or support of
freemen.

What is one to make of this prose? Let us grant that the Judiciary
Act of 1802 threatened the independence of the national judiciary,
though this is a proposition not easily supported by Chase's behavior
here or by that of a unanimous Supreme Court less than ten weeks
before in *Marbury* v. *Madison* (1 Cranch 137 [1803]), or by the
Court's acquiescence in *Stuart* v. *Laird* (1 Cranch 299 [1803]) in the
reestablishment of the circuit-riding system prescribed by the Judiciary Act of 1789. Even granting this, though, what can be intended by
the appeal to the virtue of the people? Could Chase have expected
that those who had entrusted and reentrusted their affairs to the
Jeffersonians would throw the rascals out the next time around for
their repeal of the Judiciary Act of 1801?[30] The attack on the extension of the Maryland suffrage to a population beyond those "who
have property in, a common interest with, and an attachment to, the
community" seems, if anything, even more futile than the attack on
the Judiciary Act of 1802. By what stretch of a political imagination
can the narrowing of a once-extended suffrage be envisioned through

30. Yet such was Justice Chase's hope. See his gloss on this text in Evans, *Report of
the Chase Trial,* app., 39, and in *Annals of Congress,* 8th Cong., 2d sess., 148. Henry
Adams comments on this passage of the charge in his *John Randolph,* 136: "There
was gross absurdity in the idea that the people who, by an immense majority, had
decided to carry on their government in one way should be forced by one of their
servants to turn about and go in the opposite direction; and the indecorum was
greater than the absurdity, for if Judge Chase or any other official held such doctrines,
even though he were right, he was bound not to insult officially the people who
employed him." There was absurdity enough, perhaps, without exaggerating the
matter. Chase did not entertain the delusion that the people could "be forced" to
adopt contrary principles, but he obviously acted as though he believed that they had
been persuaded out of one set of opinions and into another set.

reinstituted property qualifications? To what majority is such an appeal addressed?

The practices Chase censured stem from bad opinions, and it was to those opinions, or rather to the theoretical underpinnings of those opinions, that he turned in the final part of his charge:

> The declarations, respecting the natural rights of man, which originated from the claim of the British parliament to make laws to bind America in all cases whatsoever; the publications, since that period, of visionary and theoretical writers, asserting that men, in a state of society, are entitled to exercise rights which they possessed in a state of nature; and the modern doctrines by our late reformers, that all men, in a state of society, are entitled to enjoy equal liberty and equal rights, have brought this mighty mischief upon us; and I fear that it will rapidly progress, until peace and order, freedom and property, shall be destroyed. Our people are taught as a political creed, that men, living under an established government, are nevertheless entitled to exercise certain rights which they possessed in a state of nature; and also, that every member of this government is entitled to enjoy an equality of liberty and rights.

The justice's critique of these opinions would not seem strange to anyone who knew *Reflections on the Revolution in France,* yet Chase's attack, if similar to Burke's, is also more extreme than Burke's. Chase mounted an attack against a fallacious doctrine—but he did so in the name of a doctrine or from a doctrinal position. His critique displays an insufficient regard to what Burke held to be of central importance—circumstances. To the assertion of the natural rights of man, Chase brought the counterassertion that there are no natural rights; nor, in his view, is there any state of nature. "I really consider a state of nature as a creature of the imagination only, although great names give a sanction to a contrary opinion." In this categorical denial, Chase went beyond Burke; and—what is more revealing—Chase was recklessly separating himself from such "founding Federalists" as Jay and Wilson by rejecting one of the fundamentals of the Revolution. To the views of those "visionary and theoretical writers" who argued that men could enjoy their natural rights in society, Chase replied with a denial that there could be any personal liberty and rights before, or outside of, society. All rights are social, conventional. And to the egalitarian doctrines of latter-day reformers, Chase replied in a fashion that can best be summarized by Burke's dictum: "In this partnership all men have equal rights; but not to equal things."[31]

What is most striking about Chase's grand jury charge, if compared with that of Jay, is not that his teaching was bizarre but that it was propounded immoderately. Jay was upholding the law and calling for obedience; Chase was attacking the laws and calling for resistance, repeal, and restoration. Although Chase's teaching perhaps resembled Jonathan Boucher's too much to suit contemporary tastes, it must be said that his general political position was sound Federalism. Chase was not playing Sir Robert Filmer to nineteenth-century Americans, but his words give little sign that he appreciated how irrelevant his mode of teaching had been rendered by the change in opinions that he was deploring. In the eyes of Jefferson and his followers, the results of the election of 1800 were as momentous as the events of 1776 (more than a few Federalists agreed). The principles of '76 were now triumphant, the last vestiges of monocratic power would be erased, and the promise of the great documents and pamphlets of the revolutionary struggle would be fulfilled. Yet if the election of 1800 was a political revolution, it was one secured by a margin of eight electoral votes. It was an election in which Maryland had split evenly and following which the state Federalist party retained significant strength. Chase, however, showed no sign of acting on the premise that a more moderate political charge would be likely to receive a respectful hearing or have the desired effect. Instead, he mounted a frontal attack against Jeffersonian doctrine. That exhilarating teaching (however remote from Jeffersonian practice) had kindled the imaginations and aspirations of New England and Appalachia alike. In the face of widespread expectations that political life was to be restored, purified, raised to new heights, how could Chase have expected to move men with a categorical rejection of Jeffersonian doctrine and with an appeal of this sort?

> I cannot but remember the great and patriotic characters, by whom your state constitution was framed. I cannot but recollect that attempts

---

31. Edmund Burke, "Reflections on the Revolution in France," in *The Works of the Right Honourable Edmund Burke* II:282, 332–334. The earliest published account of Chase's charge found its theorizing repulsive and attacked it for its "unjust reproaches cast upon . . . the fundamental and characteristic principles of the nation itself"; *National Intelligencer and Washington Advertiser* (Washington), 20 May 1803.

were then made in favor of universal suffrage; and to render the judges dependent upon the legislature. You may believe, that the gentlemen who framed your constitution, possessed the full confidence of the people of Maryland, and that they were esteemed for their talents and patriotism, and for their public and private virtues. You must have heard that many of them held the highest civil and military stations, and that they, at every risk and danger, assisted to obtain and establish your independence. Their names are enrolled on the journals of the first Congress, and may be seen in the proceedings of the convention that framed our form of government. With great concern I observe, that the sons of some of these characters have united to pull down the beautiful fabric of wisdom and republicanism, that their fathers erected!

Chase, a leading framer of the Maryland constitution of 1776, found all the more rankling the participation of the sons (many of them young Federalists) in the undoing of their fathers' handiwork. But his appeal from the new to the old Federalists fell on deaf ears. Starting not from where his audience was, but from where (in his judgment) they ought to be, Chase made his argument out of exhortation, remonstrance, and appeal to venerable authority. His impatience with the errors of his audience deprived him of the ingratiating arts and courteous consideration that might have moved his audience to recognize some reasonableness in his position. Even more did his impatience deprive him of a recognition of the deeper calculations that would lead one of the most aristocratic of states to introduce the most democratic forms.[32] Taking arms, as he did, against a sea of troubles, Justice Chase would have drowned—had not his firm but prudent counsel adopted another style in addressing the Senate when it sat as a court of impeachments.

It is easy to see that Chase's excesses and subsequent impeachment would have effects that went beyond merely cooling intemperate judges. Both sides at his trial held to the tacit premise that the day of the political charge had passed. Even Chase's counsel felt obliged to say that using the grand jury charge as a vehicle for arguing against a public measure "may, perhaps, be ill-judged indiscreet or ill-timed. I am ready to admit that it is so: for I am one of those who have always

32. See the evidence of Maryland aristocrats "exciting the favor of the people they associate with on no other occasion," in Chilton Williamson, *American Suffrage: From Property to Democracy, 1760–1860,* 140–146. A sufficient explanation of aristocratic acquiescence in suffrage reform is given by Tocqueville, *Democracy in America,* 52 (I, i, 4).

thought, that political subjects ought never to be mentioned in courts of justice." The real issue, however, was criminality, and here the defense raised was that the political charge had become customary and that its use had been explicitly and implicitly approved. "From the time of Judge Drayton to the time of Judge Chase, it has been considered as innocent." In Chase's own words:

> It has been the practice in this country, ever since the beginning of the revolution, which separated us from Great Britain, for the judges to express from the bench, by way of charge to the grand jury, and to enforce to the utmost of their ability, such political opinions as they thought correct and useful. There have been instances in which the legislative bodies of this country, have recommended this practice of the judges; and it was adopted by the judges of the supreme court of the United States, as soon as the present judicial system was established.

If this was prescription, it was not old prescription. Nor was the appeal to practice a sufficient response to the allegation of impropriety. This was not a strong defense against an attack that could point to "a judge of the United States, passing judgment of condemnation on the laws which he was bound to conform to, and execute, and with the policy of which, in his judicial character, he had nothing to do."[33]

A comparison of Jay and Chase in their capacity as teaching judges supports the truth and aptness of Tocqueville's standard for measuring judicial behavior. In the passage quoted near the beginning of this chapter, Tocqueville stressed the need for judges who combined legal learning, civic rectitude, and political adroitness. The manner in which the judge performed his duties was of decisive importance. Jay tied his political teaching, however broadly stated, to the proper business of a grand jury—in this instance, enforcing the Neutrality Proclamation as declared national policy. He combined his character as judge with his larger function. Chase, in contrast, appeared more nakedly as a partisan political advocate, and at that as an opponent of the laws of the land. His sense of the rightness of his intentions could not make up for the lack of prudence displayed in his exhortation.

It took high political finesse to use the grand jury charge as a means

33. Evans, *Report of the Chase Trial*, 242*–244* (Harper), app., 37–38 (Chase); *Annals of Congress*, 8th Cong., 2d sess., 556–558 (Harper), 146 (Chase), 639 (Rodney).

of political education. Abuse led to disuse, and disuse led to a kind of forgetfulness. Barely four decades after one chief justice could speak of not omitting occasions for promoting good will, good temper, and the progress of useful truths among the citizenry, another chief justice could opine confidently to a grand jury that "it would be a waste of time in the court to engage itself in discussing principles, and enlarging upon topics which are not to lead us to some practical result. . . . Not a moment should be wasted in unnecessary forms."[34]

Judges and the Perpetuation of Political Institutions

Members of the pre-Marshall Supreme Court could, while on circuit, fairly be called teachers to the citizenry. In this phase of its role as republican schoolmaster, the Supreme Court seized upon the expedient of the grand jury charge, but with this it had uneven success. A series of bitter partisan conflicts—centering on the Neutrality Proclamation, the Alien and Sedition Acts, and the overthrow of Federalist hegemony—contributed to the disappearance of the political charge. The unfashionable became repulsive, finally foolhardy. Chase's impeachment only ratified that result. Nonetheless, the fact remains that the first justices of the Supreme Court—among them men such as Jay, Wilson, and Ellsworth, who had been singularly important in the drafting or defense of the Constitution and of the Judiciary Act of 1789—adopted this mode of political education as fitting, even necessary. I now look beyond the sermon charge (a passing phase), beyond the circuit riding (only one aspect of the judicial role), to the larger problem subsuming all these, and more. The temporary and particular draw our attention to the fundamental reasoning for an institution designed to play a broad and permanent part in the life of the nation. That fundamental reasoning touches circuit duties only incidentally and outright political preaching to the people only by remote construction. Political preaching presumes a kind of superiority in the judge. Was that superiority (as distinguished from the explicit preaching) taken to be an essential feature of the national judiciary?

34. Chief Justice Taney's charge to a grand jury, 30 Federal Cases 998, at 999, Case No. 18,257 (1836).

The question is not so much whether the courts, and more particularly the Supreme Court, were expected to be "a bevy of Platonic Guardians"[35] as whether the authors and defenders of the Constitution conceived of the courts, and of the Supreme Court more than any, as acting and speaking on principles of public-spiritedness and civic devotion beyond the probable range of other governmental officials, to say nothing of the ordinary citizens. To what extent did the new plan of government require a body of judges disposed and able to transcend considerations of enlightened self-interest? That question, in turn, raises the larger issue: How did the framers of the Constitution expect to sustain and perpetuate a republican regime? The manner in which the Federalists addressed themselves to this question leaves much to be desired. The Anti-Federalist complaint that there was a profound disharmony in the new system was neither forced nor fatuous. The preconditions of republican virtue, as then understood, were not fulfilled in the extended republic envisaged by the apologists for the Constitution. When Federalist debaters chose to speak on this theme, they did not meet the issue in a uniformly candid or persuasive manner. In the preceding pages I have examined the connection between extraordinary qualities of leadership and the need for widespread citizen virtue by considering how judicial statesmen, through their teaching, tried to promote and sustain republican virtue. Here I am concerned with identifying the kind of citizen virtue and the kind of statesmanship the Federalists believed necessary for the perpetuation of their political institutions.

Though all—Federalists and Anti-Federalists—agreed that the new government, whatever form it might take, had to accord with the temper and genius of the American people, there were great differences on what that temper and genius were. Franklin could argue against paying the executive, adducing foreign examples and that of General Washington "to shew that the pleasure of doing good & serving their Country and the respect such conduct entitles them to, are sufficient motives with some minds to give up a great portion of their time to the Public, without the mean inducement of pecuniary satisfaction." On the other hand, Noah Webster could propose improving the "system of the great Montesquieu" by striking out the word "virtue" wherever it appeared in the *Spirit of Laws* and substituting "property or lands in fee simple." "*Virtue*, patriotism, or

35. Learned Hand, *The Bill of Rights*, 73.

love of country, never was and never will be, till mens' natures are changed, a fixed, permanent principle and support of government."36

In the midst of a heated debate, Patrick Henry could lament the Constitution's dangerously delusive reliance on the governors' "fair, disinterested patriotism" and on good, but naturally weak, "luminous characters." "The real rock of political salvation is self-love, perpetuated from age to age in every human breast, and manifested in every action." To rely on men's higher motives (and to the extent Henry saw the Constitution as doing that) was in effect to turn the government over to the watchful wicked, notwithstanding the republican virtue of the people at large. This argument—a strange marriage of ward-politics reasoning and deserted-house imaginings— was answered by two of the least starry-eyed defenders of the Constitution. According to John Marshall, Henry could search in vain for some American analogue to the British "exclusive personal stock of interest." The American way was so to blend public and private interests that all men (or most) would have a sense of their stake in society. When the American "promotes his own [interest], he promotes that of the community. When we consult the common good, we consult our own." With such a population—alert, wary, and interested—one might establish a government of sufficient energy to rule an extensive republic, relatively safe in the confidence that its abuses would be checked. Madison went even further in challenging Henry's pitting of the cunningly corrupt against the drowsily virtuous; it was neither a fair match nor a credible one:

> I go on this great republican principle, that the people will have virtue and intelligence to select men of virtue and wisdom. Is there no virtue among us? If there be not, we are in a wretched situation. No theoretical checks, no form of government, can render us secure. To suppose that any form of government will secure liberty or happiness without any virtue in the people, is a chimerical idea. If there be sufficient virtue and intelligence in the community, it will be exercised in the selection of these men; so that we do not depend on their virtue, or put confidence in our rulers, but in the people who are to choose them.37

36. Max Farrand, ed., *The Records of the Federal Convention of 1787* I:84; [Noah Webster], "An Examination into the Leading Principles of the Federal Constitution . . . ," in Paul Leicester Ford, ed., *Pamphlets on the Constitution of the United States . . . 1787–1788,* 59.

37. Jonathan Elliot, ed., *The Debates in the Several State Conventions on the Adoption of the Federal Constitution . . .* III:164–165, 232, 536–537.

Words like these suggest that Madison was carried very far indeed by the mood and movement of the Virginia debate. It would be hard to find in this language a concession that there was a political task involved in sustaining the virtue of the people. Is then the people's republican virtue a given—enduring, available, sufficient? Not quite. Though in speaking at all to the issue Madison differed from many Federalists, his discussion remains incomplete and hence problematic. The Federalists surely were aware of the insufficiency of their response to nagging Anti-Federalist questions about republican virtue. They may well have avoided a detailed discussion of that theme out of fear that the answer they would be obliged to give could only harm the more urgent cause of ratification. Moreover, since the main attack on the Constitution was mounted in the name of popular liberty, the Federalists were supplied with a double opportunity to thrash the Anti-Federalists on that issue while eluding a confrontation on the problem of sustaining popular virtue.

What I have identified as the larger issue—how best to sustain and perpetuate the regime—is connected with the need for republican virtue, but the Federalists did not always choose to dwell on that connection. Hamilton, for example, could address himself to the need for statesmen and uncommon leaders (and did so repeatedly) without appearing to have to discuss popular virtue as a problem. Even when the attachment and confidence of the people were taken up as an explicit theme by him in the New York debates, the problem seemed to turn less on the need for a certain kind of citizen than on the need for a certain kind of ruler:

> All governments, even the most despotic, depend, in a great degree, on opinion. In free republics, it is most peculiarly the case. In these, the will of the people makes the essential principle of the government; and the laws which control the community receive their tone and spirit from the public wishes. It is the fortunate situation of our country, that the minds of the people are exceedingly enlightened and refined. Here, then, we may expect the laws to be proportionably agreeable to the standard of perfect policy, and the wisdom of public measures to consist with the most intimate conformity between the views of the representative and his constituent. . . .
>
> It was remarked yesterday, that a numerous representation was necessary to obtain the confidence of the people. This is not generally true. The confidence of the people will easily be gained by a good administration. This is the true touchstone. . . . The popular confidence depends

on circumstances very distinct from considerations of number. Probably the public attachment is more strongly secured by a train of prosperous events, which are the result of wise deliberation and vigorous execution, and to which large bodies are much less competent than small ones.[38]

The intelligence needed to produce "a chain of prosperous events" is to be found in the men whom the people have chosen. This was a subject to which Hamilton warmed and spoke at length. At a considerably lower level is the popular intelligence that sees or feels the advantages of "a chain of prosperous events" and knows enough to connect the presence or absence of such advantages with what the government does. This was not a subject requiring much elaboration.

We are left to wonder at the Federalists' discussion. When sustaining republican virtue is the theme, the treatment is muted and surprisingly incomplete. When the question is how to sustain the necessary conditions for popular government, the Federalists usually move the emphasis away from the need for statesmanship and uncommon leadership without quite ruling out the possibility that such leadership may be indispensable. Why they should have followed this tack is another of those problems admitting of more speculation than certainty. It might be said that, by arguing in a manner that neither foreclosed nor required statesmanship for the conduct of the new republic, the Federalists' thinking showed its origins and its limits. The leading founders were not philosophers but gentlemen. Their thinking, while precise and often acute, was not thorough; their goal was a sufficient understanding, not an elaborated theory. In this sense, what they thought and argued and built was very good indeed. They envisioned a government whose business would be conducted by men such as themselves; in such hands the public business would be well placed and diligently executed. "A Federalist gentleman differed only in his political views from a Republican gentleman."[39]

Credible as such an interpretation is, it is not altogether convincing. An analysis of the argument of *The Federalist* shows that its authors relied on quasi-aristocratic leaders and teachers, like the national judiciary, to sustain and guide the kind of public their regime presup-

---

38. Ibid. II:252, 254.
39. Leonard D. White, *The Jeffersonians*, 550. White argues explicitly (547–550) that the same social class dominated public life throughout the first forty years of the national government and implicitly that the political differences among them were of only secondary importance.

posed. Why the defenders of the Constitution, in the stress of hard fights for state ratification, would prefer to emphasize those features that made it appear to be a self-sustaining system is immediately intelligible. It was, they argued, a constitution peculiarly fit for this particular people. And, in truth, the framers, in their clear-eyed, unsentimental way, had cut the Constitution to the pattern of ordinary American citizens (as they were or were likely to become). But aware of the extraordinary efforts they themselves had had to make in order to have a constitution to recommend, did they believe that their constitution would obviate such efforts by future generations? More narrowly, would the system "wholly popular" survive, even thrive, on talents wholly popular? A review of Publius's calculations and anticipations in *The Federalist*—and though polemical, they were no less careful—suggests that the answer is no. The founding of the American regime was an act of men whose talents were both great and not wholly popular. Those men thought the preservation of that regime under their Constitution, if it did not require equally great men, at least stood in need of some men who were not wholly popular.

Publius was calm by nature, not given to exaggerated enthusiasms or fears, though not above playing on such feelings. In judging human nature, he was inclined to be less, rather than more, sanguine about its capacities and about its inclination with respect to good and bad; but in this judgment, as in so many other matters, he aimed at some kind of balance: "As there is a degree of depravity in mankind which requires a certain degree of circumspection and distrust: So there are other qualities in human nature, which justify a certain portion of esteem and confidence." That portion might not be very great; neither did Publius trouble himself to name or describe those "other qualities." But it was certain that republican government, more than any other form, depended on their existence. In all such political calculations, excess was to be avoided: "The supposition of universal venality in human nature is little less an error in political reasoning than the supposition of universal rectitude." The famous and distinctive solution of *Federalist,* No. 51, based on the "policy of supplying by opposite and rival interests, the defect of better motives," does not deny the existence of those motives, still less declare them superfluous. If the insufficiency of virtue and honor is repeatedly shown, if a reliance on "superior virtue" is misplaced in republics, that does not settle the question.[40] True, the Constitution presupposes that its powers will be administered with only "a common share of prudence." The virtue of the citizens may be little more than this: that they "understand their rights and are disposed to defend them." And yet Publius showed, again and again, that he was indifferent to neither the utility, beauty, nor necessity of higher and finer motives. He knew and admired "men, who under any circumstances will have the courage to do their duty at every hazard." But he also knew that "this stern virtue is the growth of few soils." Its presence, therefore, was not to be depended on, if that could be avoided. Still, Publius had no a priori way of knowing that all problems likely to arise under the new Constitution would be capable of being accommodated satisfactorily by merely self-interested groups. He surely must have considered whether a nation could do without some leaders (like those in the Constitutional Convention itself) who had "a deep conviction of the necessity of sacrificing private opinions and partial interests to the public good."[41] In fact, the promotion of the public happiness, indeed the republican cause, requires men who have "courage and magnanimity enough" to serve the people while risking popular displeasure. Why, we may ask, do these men act as they do—saving the people's interests from the consequences of their foolish inclinations—under a cloud of popular scorn and blame? Is it likely that the "lasting monuments of their gratitude" with which the people may ultimately reward their guardians are a sufficient inducement? And wherein lies the magnanimity of these guardians? Might they as easily, perhaps more easily, have set snares for the unwary, flattering their prejudices to betray their interests?[42] In these lines, I suggest, there is presupposed a sense of duty—rare, needful of institutional support, but in the last (and desperate) instant, indispensable. Hypocritical self-serving governors and a mean-spirited populace were

40. *Federalist*, No. 55, 378, No. 76, 513–514, No. 51, 349, No. 22, 142.
41. Ibid., No. 27, 175, No. 28, 179, No. 73, 497, 493, No. 37, 239.
42. Ibid., No. 71, 482–483. Compare Lincoln's "Young Men's Lyceum Address" on the perpetuation of our political institutions (27 January 1838) for another analysis of the motivations of those leaders whose "*all* was staked" on demonstrating in practice that the people were capable of self-government; Roy F. Basler et al., eds., *The Collected Works of Abraham Lincoln* I:113. Consider, in the light of Lincoln's statement of the problem posed by ambition, Publius's exception of "a few aspiring characters" (*Federalist*, No. 57, 386) and his explicit silence about his own motives (*Federalist*, No. 1, 6).

Publius's Scylla and Charybdis. He dared not separate the case for good government from the case for popular government. He knew that severally and together those cases needed something more in both the leaders and the people than an overpowering absorption in self-interest. Uniting those cases was at once a political necessity and an act of high statesmanship.

No branch of government was more likely to shelter and provide a political platform for that presupposed sense of duty as a regular matter of course than the judiciary. There especially might this rare, nonpopular, and often unpopular virtue be fostered and used to best effect. Little, it had to be confessed, was to be expected of the House of Representatives in this respect. Although not utterly devoid of elevation, its virtue would be its commonness, its similitude to the interests and sentiments of the great body of the people. Similitude does not mean perfect congruence. If it is true "that the people commonly *intend* the PUBLIC GOOD," the House may be said to borrow that intent, refining it a bit, but also possibly deflecting it by its own special humors. Its commonness, moreover, would best be secured by *avoiding* commonness as the proper basis of representation. Publius could defend the House against attack by showing that the interests and feelings of all classes of the people would best be expressed in that body by representatives drawn from certain particular classes. "Bound to fidelity and sympathy" with the people by cords of "duty, gratitude, interest, [and] ambition itself," it was to be presumed that "in general" these men, "distinguished by the preference" of their fellows, would be "somewhat distinguished also, by those qualities which entitle them to it."[43]

Somewhat more might be hoped for in the Senate: "There is reason to presume" that the state legislatures will choose "those men only who have become the most distinguished by their abilities and virtue." In such a small body, where each member can receive "a sensible degree" of praise and blame, there is the motive to devote oneself to studying and attending to the public business. It is not altogether clear whether the Senate would have a "permanent motive" to do so, and if so, what that motive would be. A properly constituted Senate should supply "the want of a due sense of national character," thus providing a remedy for the unenlightened, variable, and blundering policies of the Confederation. The special responsibility in foreign

43. *Federalist*, No. 71, 482, No. 35, 218–222, No. 57, 385–387.

affairs with which the Senate (in association with the president) is charged gives added weight to the peculiar virtues that are needed and expected in that body. But the very motives of patriotism and national dignity that might encourage a Senate to take a strong stand for the national honor would also lead it to eschew "absolute inflexibility." In resisting the will of the more popular branch, it would be "particularly sensible to every prospect of public danger, or of a dishonorable stagnation in public affairs." The Senate will moderate its intransigence so as to avoid deadlock because of "the interest which [the senators] will individually feel in whatever concerns the government."[44]

In comparison with either branch of the legislature, the president appears likely to be much better situated to give public expression to his "livelier sense of duty" and his "more exact regard to reputation." Publius foresaw "a constant probability" that the presidency would be occupied by "characters pre-eminent for ability and virtue." One of the marks of the national government's superiority to that of the states is the knowledge that "other talents and a different kind of merit" would be needed to raise a man to "first honors" in the nation as a whole. Yet in contemplating a president's temptations "to sacrifice his duty to his interest, which it would require superlative virtue to withstand," Publius, sensibly enough, did not make gratuitous assumptions: "The history of human conduct does not warrant that exalted opinion of human virtue." His discussion of the executive veto gives a fair measure of his expectations:

> In the case for which it is chiefly designed, that of an immediate attack upon the constitutional rights of the executive, or in a case in which the public good was evidently and palpably sacrificed, a man of tolerable firmness would avail himself of his constitutional means of defence, and would listen to the admonitions of duty and responsibility. In the former supposition, his fortitude would be stimulated by his immediate interest in the power of his office; in the latter by the probability of the sanction of his constituents; who though they would naturally incline to the legislative body in a doubtful case, would hardly suffer their partiality to delude them in a very plain case. I speak now with an eye to a magistrate possessing only a common share of firmness. There are men, who under any circumstances will have the courage to do their duty at every hazard.

44. Ibid., No. 64, 433, No. 63, 422–423, No. 62, 419, No. 58, 395.

What sustains a president of tolerable, common firmness in his inclination to protect the common good? Not the certainty of popular approbation; not any immediate self-interest. Standing alone, a president can count on only the probability of public approval; yet that approval, if it comes, is his alone. We ought not to be surprised to find the president considering himself both "under stronger obligations, and more interested" to fulfill his responsibilities.45 But striking as the effects of executive leadership can be, especially in critical cases, the motivations to such public-spirited acts are unreliable and insufficient. We have not yet before us the full union of private motives, institutional supports, and special training.

Of the judges, and only of the judges, did Publius declare that they would be "too far removed from the people to share much in their prepossessions." It was precisely this dissimilarity, this nonpopular character, that would especially qualify the judiciary to be "an intermediate body between the people and the legislature." The judiciary is the only branch of the government whose members require special training and competence, and one of the effects of that training is to set those individuals apart from the populace. The judicial function itself occupies some sort of middle ground between a technician's deductions from general rules and a legislator's pure reason prescribing such general rules. In construing the Constitution, the judge performs a political duty through the exercise of a technical duty. When Publius rejected the theory according to which each branch of government would make an authoritative construction of its powers binding upon the other branches, he at the same time candidly avowed that the courts would stand in a closer relation to the deliberate will of the people as expressed in the Constitution than would the representatives of the people. The courts would be peculiarly fit to discover in the Constitution what the will of the people was. Even bolder was his conjuring of a situation in which the judges would stand in need of "an uncommon portion of fortitude":

> Until the people have by some solemn and authoritative act annulled or changed the established form, it is binding upon themselves collectively, as well as individually; and no presumption, or *even knowledge of their sentiments,* can warrant their representatives in a departure from it, prior to such an act. But it is easy to see that it would require an uncommon portion of fortitude in the judges to do their duty as faithful

45. Ibid., No. 76, 510–511, No. 68, 460–461, No. 75, 505, No. 73, 497.

guardians of the constitution, where legislative invasions of it had been instigated by the major voice of the community.

One may still speak of the sense of the people ruling, but in a manner that vividly brings to mind the "courage and magnanimity" it takes to serve the people "at the peril of their displeasure."[46]

If it was Publius's wish to suggest that in the national courts would be found a locus of high statesmanship—cautious, politic, yet able and willing to cope with popular excesses—he did not leave it at only these indirections. His general, thematic discussion of the judiciary anticipates, and surely does not preclude, judges who would view themselves as teachers of republicanism using the text of the Constitution and the national laws interpreted in a judicial spirit of moderation and fairness. The preliminary impression conveyed by Publius's account is that elements somewhat incompatible are being stirred together. If the judiciary was the least dangerous branch, it might well also be considered the least to be trusted.[47] To complicate

46. Ibid., No. 49, 341, No. 78, 525, 527–528 (emphasis added), No. 71, 483.

47. A fair, even inevitable, objection would be, Was there in fact, in 1787, any wary distrust of the judiciary on grounds of its "nondemocratic" character? According to Jackson Turner Main, "the argument which developed a hundred years later, that the [Supreme] Court was undemocratic because of its lack of responsibility, and that it was biased against changes desired by the majority, while implied by a few [Anti-Federalist] writers, was never clearly stated"; *The Antifederalists: Critics of the Constitution, 1781–1788*, 156. One might also question whether there was much political sensitivity to a judiciary as independent as the one proposed by the Constitutional Convention by recalling that, at the time, a majority of the states (including New York) provided for judicial tenure during good behavior, and that all the states filled their highest courts by appointment, not election; William Clarence Webster, "A Comparative Study of the State Constitutions of the American Revolution," *Annals* 9 (1897):401–403; James Schouler, *Constitutional Studies, State and Federal*, 64–65; but see Roscoe Pound, *The Formative Era of American Law*, 91–92, on the prevailing distrust of judges. Note, too, the forebodings of Federal Farmer, Nos. 3 and 15 (10 October 1787, 18 January 1788), and of Brutus, Nos. 11 and 15 (31 January, 20 March 1788), in Storing, ed., *Complete Anti-Federalist* II:244, 315–316, 321, 422, 438, 442.

No moderately sensitive reader of *Federalist*, No. 78, can overlook the defensive character of its rhetoric. Publius wrote as though prevailing opinion were hostile to (or uncertain of the wisdom of) the judicial arrangement embodied in the Constitution. What leads a partisan to answer objections the opposition has not yet raised? (a) to provide as thorough a defense as he can for what is to him a supremely important cause; (b) to avoid having to dwell on other objections, more or equally important; (c) to defend a position clearly seen by him as vulnerable because of his expectations (in this instance, of the political role of the Supreme Court), though not yet recognized as such by the opposition. All three considerations may well be present here. I incline to the opinion that the tone and mode of argument of No. 78 are sufficiently understood by holding that Hamilton's hopes and fears took in a longer futurity than did his foes'.

matters further, there was no prima facie evidence to show that it would be the least influential branch. The subject had to be treated judiciously. Perhaps nothing illustrates this quite as well as those famous lines:

> Whoever attentively considers the different departments of power must perceive, that in a government in which they are separated from each other, the judiciary, from the nature of its functions, will always be the least dangerous to the political rights of the constitution; because it will be least in a capacity to annoy or injure them. . . . The judiciary . . . has no influence over either the sword or the purse, no direction either of the strength or of the wealth of the society, and can take no active resolution whatever. It may truly be said to have neither Force nor Will, but merely judgment; and must ultimately depend upon the aid of the executive arm even for the efficacy of its judgments.[48]

One doubts whether we smile much more at this comparison than did Publius. His very next sentence begins with the words "this simple view of the matter." Although the argument is offered in a spirit that does not disgrace the cause of truth, this view is indeed simple even considered on the premises of Publius's psychology; the view is kept simple because of the demands of Publius's rhetoric. The too sharp distinction between will and judgment defied, then as now, the good sense of any discerning mind. Madison could speak in the Constitutional Convention of the analogy between the executive and judiciary, while stressing that one of the differences was that "in the administration of the [executive] much greater latitude is left to opinion and discretion than in the administration of the [judiciary]." There is no suggestion here that the judicial function is free of every influence of opinion and discretion. Nor is Publius one to mistake names for things; he knows better:

> The faculties of the mind itself have never yet been distinguished and defined, with satisfactory precision, by all the efforts of the most acute and metaphysical Philosophers. Sense, perception, *judgment,* desire, *volition,* memory, imagination, are found to be separated by such delicate shades, and minute gradations, that their boundaries have eluded the most subtle investigations, and remain a pregnant source of ingenious disquisition and controversy.[49]

48. *Federalist,* No. 78, 522–523.
49. Farrand, ed., *Records* II:34; *Federalist,* No. 37, 235 (emphasis added). Publius is not of two minds on this matter; the author of No. 78 could say in No. 79, 533,

It is unreasonable, then, to assume that Publius thought of judicial decision making as a thin-blooded exercise in deduction in which discretion and will had no place or effect. He chose to speak in this manner, rather, in order to strengthen the impression that the judiciary could safely be accorded special, extraordinary supports and defenses. And, let it be added, he could speak in this manner because what he said was essentially, though not simply, true. That very statement characterizing the judiciary as "least dangerous" does not assert that it is weak. The Supreme Court will be innocuous: "the political rights of the constitution," "the general liberty of the people," will not be threatened by an independent and separate judiciary. But the Supreme Court will not be weak or ineffectual, save in the most extreme political controversies in which its will (for we must call it that) is pitted against the constitutional will of the representatives of the people. The provisions of the Constitution and the prudence of the judges will warn off the courts from most such confrontations. But within the large domain remaining, the judiciary will hardly be unnoticed. Leaving aside the problem of judicial review of national legislation, the judiciary will serve as an instrument of national supremacy. Publius never suggested any weakness in the Supreme Court's carrying the authority of the Constitution and the laws to the people and in its facing local injustice and plain localism backed by popular feelings. In its capacity for harming individuals, even large numbers of individuals, the judiciary is, as Montesquieu had said, terrible. But the judiciary cannot (or is not likely to) take over the government the way the other branches of government can, and in that specifically political sense it is "next to nothing." The full force of the words is to be accorded Publius's statement of why the Supreme Court was not united with the Senate to form a court of impeachments: "I forbear to remark upon the additional pretext for clamour, against the Judiciary, which so considerable an augmentation of its authority would have afforded." There were already pretexts enough.[50]

Publius's case for an independent judiciary is inseparable from, even as it goes beyond, his case for the separation of powers. By "contriving the interior structure of the government" in the proper

---

"The mensuration of the faculties of the mind has, I believe, no place in the catalogue of known arts." In No. 51, 348–349, there is a discussion of the will (and, for that matter, of the ambition and interest) of the several departments of government without any exemption of the judiciary.

50. *Federalist*, No. 78, 522–523, No. 81, 545, No. 65, 441, 443.

way, it is possible to achieve that measure of a separation of powers that is "admitted on all hands to be essential to the preservation of liberty." The basis of that separation is, more fundamentally, the desired independence of each of the branches of government. By being in a position and of a mind to resist the encroachments of the others, each branch is able to perform its distinctive function and also serve as an effective element in the system of checks and balances. A prerequisite, then, to the separation of powers is that each branch "should have a will of its own"; this in turn requires, strictly speaking, that all appointments to the three branches "be drawn from the same fountain of authority, the people, through channels, having no communication whatever with one another." The separation of powers presupposes separate derivations from the people, if only to prevent any one branch from preempting the right to speak in the name of the people. In a government wholly popular, the independence of the branches of government vis-à-vis one another rests on the separate dependence of each on the sovereign people.[51] It is, however, a separate but unequal dependence.

Although each branch of government has its connection with the people, each also has a certain measure of distance or separation from them. It is *"the total exclusion of the people in their collective capacity* from any share" in the American republics that forms the "true distinction" between them and the ancient republics. Decisive as this difference may be, there are further distinctions to be drawn, no less interesting, within the structure of the American republic. Nowhere is the separation from the people more complete and more necessary than in the judicial branch. If there is to be a judiciary equal to its tasks and adequate for the preservation of liberty, there must be some relaxation of the principle of unmediated derivations from the people. That this relaxation is politically safe is suggested by two considerations. The peculiar qualifications and qualities of the judges remind us that we are discussing the "least dangerous" branch and hence the one in least need of direct popular control. Then, too, the permanent tenure with which judges hold office entails the least risk that their will may be hostage to the appointing power. There must, moreover, be a departure from "the characteristic policy of republican government" (popular election of rulers) and from the "most effectual" means of maintaining "a proper responsibility to the people" (limited

51. Ibid., No. 51, 347–349.

terms of appointment).52 The cause of free government requires a qualification of popular government.

Adherence to the republican principle, to the spirit of a government wholly popular, in no way entails "an unqualified complaisance to every sudden breeze of passion, or to every transient impulse which the people may receive from the arts of men, who flatter their prejudices to betray their interests." Publius, like Rousseau, knew that while "the people commonly *intend* the PUBLIC GOOD," they do not always "*reason right* about the *means* of promoting it." Indeed, we may say that the deepest justification of a separate and independent judiciary is the expectation that, more often than is politically safe, "the interests of the people are at variance with their inclinations." If the "republican principle demands, that the deliberate sense of the community should govern the conduct of those to whom they entrust the management of their affairs," it also imposes a "duty" on "the guardians of those interests" to call the people to their senses or at least to give the people the chance to come to their senses. A government ought to have an unlimited range of powers, adequate to its objects and "free from every other control, but a regard to the public good and to the sense of the people."53 A free government is one in which the sense of the people or the sense of the majority is controlling. But to secure the public good in a manner compatible with the republican principle requires that the deliberate sense of the community prevail. And that sense is not taken simply or unqualifiedly from what the people or a majority say to their legislative representatives at any given moment. The "deliberate sense" is found in a blend of voices, from the people and their representatives, direct and remote, present and past.54 In the extreme, critical, and interesting case, that sense may be taken from what "men, who [have] courage and magnanimity enough to serve them at the peril of their displeasure" declare to be in the people's interest. Insofar as these forms of resistance to temporary passions refer to the protection of minorities, it may be said that securing the rights of all has a democratic source. Thus the popular credentials of the American regime are in no way impugned by asserting "that the whole power of the proposed government is to

52. Ibid., No. 63, 428, No. 51, 348, No. 57, 384.
53. Ibid., No. 71, 482–483, No. 31, 195. See Jean-Jacques Rousseau, *Du contrat social,* bk. II, chap. 3.
54. *Federalist,* No. 22, 139, No. 58, 397, No. 71, 482.

be in the hands of the representatives of the people" rather than in the hands of the people themselves. More than this was neither necessary nor safe, in Publius's eyes. Ultimately, the people's "cool and deliberate sense" prevails over the views of their rulers; but, at any given moment, their freely chosen rulers act "to suspend the blow meditated by the people against themselves."[55]

It is in such a context that Publius could look forward to the judiciary's "faithful performance of so arduous a duty" as guarding the Constitution against legislative encroachments, and to the thwarting of certain popular "ill humours" by the judges. When the separate judicial establishment performs its distinct function and when it serves as a complicating element in the system of checks and balances, the judiciary is but one of the three branches of the government and as such is unexceptionable. But at still another level—transcending its other functions, and implied in the technical knowledge needed by this branch of government alone—the judiciary acts as special guardian of the principles of the Constitution. In this role it is no longer merely one of three, and no longer weak. To the extent that it can remove itself from its popular source of power, the judiciary is able to display and act in its unique character. Ultimately, the judges ought to hold their office with permanent tenure in order to sustain their "necessary independence" of the executive and the legislature and the people. If such tenure did not in fact "soon destroy all sense of dependence," if fear and a concern for popularity were to affect the quality of justice, the complications and safeguards of the Constitution would be a hollow joke.[56] Uniquely situated and uniquely protected, the judges were not expected to behave like ordinary men.

For Publius it was sufficient to remind "considerate men of every description" of the larger political benefits to be derived from a judiciary whose temper was marked by "integrity and moderation." The tone and quality of the highest national court would prove decisive for the entire administration of justice, since "the national and state systems are to be regarded as ONE WHOLE. The courts of the latter will of course be natural auxiliaries to the execution of the laws of the union, and an appeal from them will as naturally lie to that tribunal,

---

55. Ibid., No. 71, 483, No. 28, 178 (cf. No. 21, 131–132), No. 63, 425. Publius had no difficulty in speaking of "the sense of the people" being operative where that sense is determined by a select body popularly chosen; see the discussion of the electoral college in No. 68, 458.

56. Ibid., No. 78, 526–529, No. 51, 348.

which is destined to unite and assimilate the principles of national justice and the rules of national decisions." Such a tribunal, so placed, could display political wisdom as well as legal craftsmanship. Its opportunities and risks would be correlative. Publius could safely have adopted as his own Aratus's understanding of the political position of the North Carolina courts:

> The *Judicial* of our democracy runs an equal pace with a monarchical judiciary, but steps forward to an almost undetermined distance—not only acting in all law occurrences . . . as the monarchical judiciary; but from the nature of our government, as may be easily deduced from the constitution itself, *pro salutate reipublicae,* it advances higher, and becomes the *equilibrium* or *pendulum* thereof.[57]

It was expected that the national judiciary—independent, public-spirited, and impelled by a pride in its special competence—would serve as an instrument and symbol of the power of "a more perfect Union." Such an understanding was clear and widespread.[58] But it was debatable whether more should be expected of the justices, that is, whether their political counsel should be sought and indeed required for making public policy. The Constitutional Convention repeatedly discussed a "council of revision" (first proposed by Governor Randolph in his presentation of the Virginia Plan and presumably modeled after the New York arrangement); these discussions revealed quite differing views about the province and function of judicial power. According to the Virginia Plan, a council of revision, composed of the national executive and "a convenient number" of the national judiciary, would possess a qualified veto over every act of the national legislature, including the latter's act of negativing any state law "contravening in the opinion of the National Legislature the articles of Union." The involvement of the judiciary in this automatic review of all national legislative authority was the occasion of much debate. Madison saw in this involvement an apt way of bolstering a chief executive who was all too likely to be in need of whatever support he could get and perhaps also in need of being reminded of

57. Ibid., No. 78, 528, No. 82, 556; Aratus, No. 3, *State Gazette of North-Carolina* (Edenton), 4 June 1789.
58. See Brutus, No. 11 (31 January 1788), in Storing, ed., *Complete Anti-Federalist* II:418, 420; Elliot, ed., *Debates* IV:258 (C. Pinckney); *Federalist,* No. 16, 102, No. 22, 143–144, No. 80, 535, 537–538.

his duty. According to this argument, the American chief executive, representing the monarchic principle (and the responsibilities and temptations of solitary rule), needed to be supported and restrained in a manner that took due account of the overall republican setting in which he would act. "Mr. Elseworth," who was to be the principal draftsman of the Judiciary Act and its jealous manager through committee and floor debates, "approved heartily of the motion" for a council of revision: "The aid of the Judges will give more wisdom & firmness to the Executive." Madison, early in the debates, drew attention to a power of review that was not exhausted by considerations of constitutionality: "In short, whether the object of the revisionary power was to restrain the Legislature from encroaching on the other co-ordinate Departments, or on the rights of the people at large; or from passing laws unwise in their principle, or incorrect in their form, the utility of annexing the wisdom and weight of the Judiciary to the Executive seemed incontestable." This expectation that the judges would not limit themselves to judgments of constitutionality—and ought not to so limit themselves—was made even more forcefully by Wilson:

> Laws may be unjust, may be unwise, may be dangerous, may be destructive; and yet not be so unconstitutional as to justify the Judges in refusing to give them effect. Let them have a share in the Revisionary power, and they will have an opportunity of taking notice of these characters of a law, and of counteracting, by the weight of their opinions the improper views of the Legislature.[59]

These arguments, however, were unavailing. The notion that judges ought to be charged explicitly with the delicate task of assessing the wisdom of proposed legislation was successfully attacked on grounds of competence and propriety. Gorham doubted whether as judges they were "to be presumed to possess any peculiar knowledge of the mere policy of public measures." Gerry saw in the proposal "an improper coalition": "It was making Statesmen of the Judges; and setting them up as the guardians of the Rights of the people." So far was this trust mistaken, that he feared that the executive could rather "be covered by the sanction & seduced by the sophistry of the Judges." Although the council of revision lacked nothing in the way of able and persistent advocates, it was decisively rejected. In a final

59. Farrand, ed., *Records* I:21, 138–139, II:73–74.

effort to extend the formal influence of the judiciary in the new government, Gouverneur Morris proposed a "council of state" to assist and advise the president. Heading the list of cabinet officers was to be the "Chief Justice of the Supreme Court, who shall from time to time recommend such alterations of and additions to the laws of the U.S. as may in his opinion be necessary to the due administration of Justice, and such as may promote useful learning and inculcate sound morality throughout the Union." Having once been referred to the Committee of Detail, this proposal never emerged again. Faced with clearly stated alternatives, the majority of the Convention appear to have been of the mind that "it is impossible to keep the Judges too distinct from every other avocation than that of expounding the laws."[60]

We are left with an equivocal conclusion: While some of the leading framers of the Constitution proposed making use of the judges' political wisdom—and indeed implied in so recommending that the judges would not otherwise have these broader duties or opportunities—the majority of the Constitutional Convention (and even the leading defenders of its work) emphatically rejected such a plan on the grounds that judges ought to be kept "judicial." The attack on the revisionary power, then, was mounted mainly for the sake of securing the proper separation of powers, that is, for the sake of an effective check on the other branches of government. But the ground of that attack was the notion that it is best that judges do what they are trained for.[61] Yet that technical competence points to another, higher judicial function—safeguarding the legal and political principles of the regime. Indeed, those very characteristics of the judiciary so well set forth in *Federalist,* No. 78, make it more likely that the purposes envisioned for the council of revision are better served under the present arrangement. The judiciary can better perform its higher function indirectly, through its more "technical" acts, than directly. The judges—and the judges alone, of all government officials— needed to have special training and character in order to do their job at all. Set apart from most citizens by temperament, education, acquired tastes, and responsibilities, the judges (at their best) could

---

60. Ibid. II:73, 75, I:139, II:342; *Federalist,* No. 73, 499.

61. This need not utterly rule out any judicial activity beyond deciding cases and controversies; see the careful discussion in Russell Wheeler, "The Extrajudicial Activities of the Early Supreme Court," in Philip B. Kurland, ed., *1973 The Supreme Court Review,* 123–158, esp. 127–131.

make the most of such opportunities as came their way to act as faithful sustainers and guardians of the regime. The political grand jury charge was one response to that challenge, but not the last.

Political Limits and Judicial Discretion

An examination of the Supreme Court's work during its first decade of circuit riding discloses that the judges were concerned to educate their audience politically. Further, evidence of the early intentions and expectations for the national judiciary points to a political role for the courts. This conception starts from the premise that "government must be framed for man as he is, and not for man as he would be if he were free from vice." It is not embarrassed when discussing the likelihood that "the faithful discharge" of the judicial power will not win the general acclaim and support of a people no longer virtuous; rather, this conception of judicial power flatly accepts the great probability of some significant political tension when the court acts as an equilibrium *pro salutate reipublicae*: "We are well aware this doctrine will sound ruffly in the ears of many of our demagogues of power."[62]

Recognizing the near certainty of heated confrontations, the early justices took it upon themselves to mold public sentiment to the degree that it lay in their power to do so. Teaching a people how to be good republicans meant more than making judicial power secure. It would have the far greater effect of making the republicans safe for the republic. The justices (in this respect anticipating Lincoln) acted on the understanding that "in this and like communities, public sentiment is everything." It was on this premise that they sought to mold and educate that public. Doing so presupposed an educable people as well as a population who are emphatically citizens. For yet another member of the second generation, John Quincy Adams, this was the lesson to be drawn from the revolutionary generation's deeds:

> This was the platform upon which the Constitution of the United States had been erected. Its VIRTUES, its republican character, consisted

---

62. James Kent, *Commentaries on American Law*, lect. XIV, I:273–274; Aratus, No. 3, *State Gazette of North-Carolina* (Edenton), 4 June 1789.

in its conformity to the principles proclaimed in the Declaration of Independence, and as its administration must necessarily be always pliable to the fluctuating varieties of public opinion; its stability and duration by a like overruling and irresistible necessity, was to depend upon the stability and duration in the hearts and minds of the people of that *virtue,* or in other words, of those principles proclaimed in the Declaration of Independence, and embodied in the Constitution of the United States.

The first justices of the Supreme Court acted in such a way as to counter the habit of mind that insisted that "there is no right principle of action but *self-interest*" and to inculcate civic virtue. More, perhaps, than any other branch of the government, they were in a position and of a character to do so.[63]

Subsequent changes in the organization of the courts and in the style of political discourse led the Supreme Court to give up the political charge. Yet in so doing, the justices merely replaced one mode of shaping public beliefs and opinions with another—one that could be equally, probably more, effective. Much of Chief Justice Marshall's greatness lies in his success in, so to speak, putting the Supreme Court as a whole on circuit. By explicitly taking the higher role of guardian of the principles of the regime and by speaking with one voice through opinions of the court, the Supreme Court, under Marshall's politic and artful guidance, was able to survive and even prevail in ways not easily foreseeable in 1801. Today the Supreme Court is, in some respects, more evidently and continuously on circuit and its work more often before the public eye than the warmest supporters of circuit riding could have hoped.

One of the reasons Congress persisted in requiring members of the Supreme Court to ride circuit in the nineteenth century was a fear of the political consequences of isolating the judiciary from its public. The argument that was made pointed perhaps as much to judges learning as to judges teaching. It is precisely because judges have "political functions to discharge" that they should be attentive to their political support; "they should be conversant with public opinion, and imbibe the spirit of the times." But it is not alone important

---

63. Abraham Lincoln, Reply to Douglas, Ottawa, Ill. (21 August 1858), in Basler et al., eds., *Collected Works of Lincoln* III:27; John Quincy Adams, *The Jubilee of the Constitution,* 54. See Lincoln, "The Repeal of the Missouri Compromise" (16 October 1854), in Basler et al., eds., *Collected Works of Lincoln* II:255.

that the judges have a clear and vivid sense of being tethered but not shackled to public opinion. It is perhaps even more important, in the long run, that the people at large have a clear and vivid sense that there is "a harmony of opinion and of action" between the Supreme Court and the inferior courts, and between the judiciary and the people for whom it is meant to establish justice. "In a Government founded on opinion, it is necessary that the People should be satisfied with judicial decisions."[64]

In requiring circuit duty, Congress acted as though it believed that this harmony could be fostered by the confrontation of judges with a larger public of lawyers, court officials, litigants, and bystanders. In that encounter, the political charge after the Chase impeachment was neither appropriate nor significant; but the judges could resort to another way of teaching, more politic and effective because more obviously "judicial," and hence less visible. Then, as now, the judges had the option of teaching by cases. By their decisions, and especially through a coherent explanation of the grounds of their decisions, the judges could partially introduce the language of the law into the vulgar tongue. What is more important, they could transfer to the minds of the citizens the modes of thought lying behind legal language and the notions of right fundamental to the regime. The political sophistication needed, then and now, for conveying these lessons is surpassed only by the sense of political responsibility that continues to set judges the task of being republican schoolmasters.

64. *Congressional Debates,* 19th Cong., 1st sess., 2, pt. 1:554 (Harper), 878 (Webster), 1100 (Kerr). I have adapted the language of Lord Devlin—"A judge is tethered to the positive law but not shackled to it"—as conveying quite precisely the kind of relation between judge and public opinion that the early Congresses envisioned; Sir Patrick Devlin, *The Enforcement of Morals,* 94.

PART TWO

THE BURDEN
OF COLOR

4

Reds and Whites:
Rights and Wrongs

THE ENCOUNTER of Indians and whites in this country has been a
moral-political problem of high drama and extraordinary complexity. Too often, however, that encounter has been viewed from
one of three patently inadequate points of view—that of avaricious
Indian-haters, or of sentimental white humanitarians, or of sullen and
beleaguered natives. A more appropriate perspective is that of the
white statesmen who tried to shape national policy toward the Indians in the early years of the republic. For these statesmen, the presence of the red man was both a threat and a challenge.

Among their own people the white leaders saw greed, energy, and a
genius for turning the soil and a dollar. Looking beyond the frontier,
they saw men filled with exalted notions of their own honor, many
still ruthless and high-spirited warriors, some already physically and
morally dependent on the Europeans' technology and distillates, and
none adept at the Europeans' various dismal sciences. A high degree
of individualism prevailed in the camps of the frontier whites and
reds; only rarely were the efforts of either coordinated through effective leadership. Yet the broad outcome of a confrontation between
these peoples—the triumph of the whites through the absorption or
elimination of the Indians, the reworking of the landscape, and the
replacement of a world of hunting and subsistence farming by a
commercial empire—was perfectly predictable. That this would be
the outcome no white leader doubted; nor did any doubt its desirability.

A reminder at the outset of the fundamental economic and political problem is in order. Red and white uses of the land were not only different but incompatible. Neither of these peoples could follow their accustomed ways in the vicinity of the other. Moreover, it seemed clear that national authority and security could not be maintained consistently with populous, self-governing enclaves of alien peoples. This concern went beyond issues of color and would have arisen had the reds been whites maintaining a territorial, cultural, and political separateness within the bounds of the United States (such as the French population in Louisiana, the Russian in California, the Spanish in Florida, California, and the Southwest). If the one alternative of full recognition of the Indians' equal rights as Indians was unacceptable, so too was the other alternative of outright extermination. Given the objective of conquest, statesmen still had to consider the manner of triumph and transformation. The range of political choices was limited and the choices were difficult. Yet fidelity to republican principles required mighty efforts to include the Indians in the new political society, to persuade them to accept the offer, to proceed in this task with the utmost patience. Even if one doubted the likelihood of amalgamation, even if one considered the collective protagonist and antagonist fated to act out their tragic roles to a predetermined end, there still remained the demands of the general moral standards that govern the relations of man and man. At least some national leaders believed that the character and reputation of the United States depended on meeting such tests by keeping promises, by restraining arbitrary acts of violence and fraud, and by treating the vanquished with generosity and a regard for their self-respect. The whites, as the more knowing party, as the immediate cause of Indian dislocation and distress, may well have felt obligated to concede more to Indians than to other whites. The very exercise of what were alleged to be white rights might entail a grievous wrong toward the Indians. The question had to be met: Were the whites being as scrupulously fair as they ought to be, or even as they could afford to be?

The men who made the American Revolution and founded a new nation inherited a problem not of their own making even as they assumed full responsibility for it. Much of what had been done in the course of 175 years of colonial settlement could not be undone— whatever their preferences. Indian displacement from areas of concentrated white settlement, the piecemeal acquisition of land titles to vast territories once claimed by the native Americans, the creation of a free and acquisitive society whose westward expansion into Indian country was irresistible by any normal legal means—these were limits indeed, and already unalterably fixed by 1776. Above all, there was the belief in the inevitability and rightness of the triumph of white civilization over red barbarism. Under these severe limits, it still remained for the statesmen of the new republic to determine what their national circumstances, interests, and principles required of them in dealing with perhaps one hundred thousand Indians living east of the Mississippi. The particular choices were complex and difficult; the general result of Indian policy was brutally simple. The mass expulsion of the Indians from the eastern half of the country in the 1830s under Andrew Jackson and Martin Van Buren effectively completed a process begun under the Confederation. During that half-century, Indians fell from the status of formidable enemies to nuisances. In the 1780s and 1790s, the government's preoccupation with Indian affairs, while hardly totally engrossing, was substantial, such affairs forming a large and pressing part of the business of the secretary of war. By the end of the period, the eastern Indians had been overrun. With the exception of a few costly campaigns, armed operations against the natives partook less of the character of war than of a police action. Throughout the period, the Indian question was subsumed on the nation's agenda under the headings of security, land, and trade. Comprehensive thinking about the large issue of red-white relations was episodic. It was as though, having fixed the ends, white leaders could only rarely bring themselves to question the justification for those ends, even though unable to avoid the practical problems raised by their adoption. Then, too, policy was more often set by events than the reverse; all too often, policy was reactive and confirmatory rather than an expression of what leaders believed to be timely and right.

I propose to consider the encounter of reds and whites from the vantage of those white leaders. In trying to reconstruct their ways of looking and judging, I examine their more or less public record of hopes and frustrations and disgust. That record is reviewed in several of its forms: initially in that mode of decision making furthest removed from the passions and dangers of the frontier—appellate adjudication; then in the statesmen's assessments of the opposing peoples' characters; next in the prevailing opinions (and consequent actions) deduced from those assessments of character; finally in the tangled thoughts of the most knowing statesmen of the age. But whatever form of the public record we scrutinize, whatever our final judgment of those men's pronouncements and practices, we must ask whether the problem posed by the encounter of Indians and whites admitted of any simply just solution.

Weighing Rights and Wrongs

In their hapless appeals to the better angels of the white man's nature, Indians often found themselves in the white man's court. The reports of those deliberations record judgments at once patronizing and fair-minded, neither severe nor generous. The opinions in the leading cases in the early part of the nineteenth century—Chancellor James Kent's in *Goodell* v. *Jackson* (20 Johnson's Reports [N.Y.] 693 [1823]) and Chief Justice John Marshall's in *Johnson* v. *M'Intosh* (8 Wheaton 543 [1823]), *Cherokee Nation* v. *Georgia* (5 Peters 1 [1831]), and *Worcester* v. *Georgia* (6 Peters 515 [1832])—mirror the narrow confines within which Indian policy could realistically be considered and judicial politics could safely be conducted. These opinions leave the impression that may be confirmed by a general review of legislative and executive actions, namely, that here was no mere malfunction of the political machine. The controversy involved the stuff of political life, the assertion and counterassertion of intransigent interests, each with some measure of justice to its credit, if not as much as each claimed. There was, to be sure, no parity between the warring parties; it was a white man's tribunal. But those courts were quick to point out that the disparity implied an obligation. Corresponding to the Indians' "dependence and imbecility" was a claim upon the whites for protection against Indian weakness and white intelligence and cupidity. Chancellor Kent of New York went so far as to argue that enforcing the Indian "right to protection from us as against our own people"—in this instance a matter of land transfer—was not only a duty that the powerful owed the weak but a requital prompted by gratitude for earlier kindnesses shown by "these generous barbarians."[1] The court felt no embarrassment in treating the Indians in a patronizing and paternalistic way. Presidents had indeed

1. *Goodell* v. *Jackson*, 20 Johnson's Reports (N.Y.) 693, at 715, 720, 723–725. As was common at the time, "imbecility" as used by Kent referred to impotence and incompetence and not to feeblemindedness.

long given up the habit of addressing visiting chiefs as "brothers" and adopted the title "my children." In the view of whites, in and out of court, the Indians had not yet reached the age of discretion.

However much this incompetence might affect the enjoyment of rights, it had limited relevance to the complicated controversy over title to the land of North America. The heart of the issue was that such conflicting claims involved "not singly those principles of abstract justice, which the Creator of all things has impressed on the mind of his creature man, . . . but those principles also which our own government has adopted in the particular case." Neither set of principles ought to be considered to the exclusion of the other. For example, a preoccupation with the question of the "right, on abstract principles," of white farmers and traders to supplant Indian hunters could lead to acts of doubtful justice. The Europeans' claim to America might well be "pompous," their pretensions to converting discovery into rightful conquest "extravagant," their unilateral demotion of Indians from owners to occupants "opposed to natural right." But the fact remained that "conquest gives a title which the courts of the conqueror cannot deny." The political limits to a theoretical investigation were undeniable. A principle might be vulnerable to logical and moral objections, and yet, "if a country has been acquired and held under it; if the property of the great mass of the community originates in it, it becomes the law of the land, and cannot be questioned." As judge, Marshall shunned the clear light of theory, for its clarity was as much vice as virtue. Instead he "glanced" at the origins of white claims and rights and passed on, leaving the question stated but unanswered. This was, however, more than a polite nod in the direction of the principles of right. A full acknowledgment of the realities was no cause for a single-minded celebration of the new sovereign's will. By insisting that that will be held accountable, by embarking on a public examination of some of the rights and wrongs of red-white relations—all the while recognizing the practical bounds to such inquiries—the judges acted in a manner illustrative of the strengths and limits of adjudication.[2]

These early cases are significant in settling the Indians' status at law: they were to be dependents, but not simply subjects. In reaching

2. *Johnson* v. *M'Intosh*, 8 Wheaton 543, at 572, 588–592; *Worcester* v. *Georgia*, 6 Peters 515, at 543. See also James Kent, *Commentaries on American Law* III:310–311.

this conclusion the judges had first to appraise the claims of the whites. Those claims, derived from European discovery of America, took the form of a right asserted against other European nations and recognized by them, an exclusive right to extinguish the Indians' title to the land by purchase or conquest. Simple calculations of self-interest had recommended such a principle to the contending European powers, but its assertion could hardly be binding upon the Indians. The principle underlying Europe's carving up of America for purposes of conquest and colonization was "not one which could annul the previous rights of those who had not agreed to it." In practice, however, "the rights of the original inhabitants . . . were necessarily, to a considerable extent, impaired." Reduced from rightful owners to rightful occupants of the land, the Indians found their rights at once confirmed and diminished. To neither Indian eyes nor white was it always clear where the natives' rights ended and European sufferance began.[3]

Looking back at the claims raised by the Europeans, Marshall found it "difficult to comprehend the proposition that the inhabitants of either quarter of the globe could have rightful original claims of dominion over the inhabitants of the other, or over the lands they occupied; or that the discovery of either by the other should give the discoverer rights in the country discovered which annulled the pre-existing rights of the ancient possessors." In fact, he concluded that "the extravagant and absurd idea that the feeble settlements made on the sea-coast" entitled the whites to rule the land and its inhabitants "from sea to sea, did not enter the mind of any man." There were absurdities enough in the Europeans' pretensions. The discovery of America was both a result of European enterprise and ambition and a lure to them. If the whites needed an "apology" for asserting their dominion, it was supplied by the Indians' character and religion. "The potentates of the old world found no difficulty in convincing themselves that they made ample compensation to the inhabitants of the new, by bestowing on them civilization and Christianity, in exchange for unlimited independence."[4] Causes good and true, interests

3. *Johnson* v. *M'Intosh,* 8 Wheaton at 573–574, 587; *Worcester* v. *Georgia,* 6 Peters at 543–544, 546, 559; Joseph Story, *Commentaries on the Constitution of the United States* I:5. For a nice discussion of "Marshall's doctrine that the Federal Government and the Indians both had exclusive title to the same land at the same time," see Felix S. Cohen, *The Legal Conscience: Selected Papers of Felix S. Cohen,* 293–294.

4. *Worcester* v. *Georgia,* 6 Peters at 543–545; *Johnson* v. *M'Intosh,* 8 Wheaton at 572–573. Marshall's muted criticism here, in *Johnson* v. *M'Intosh,* is put more baldly

large and small, all (it was asserted or believed) would be served by Europe's absorption of America. Marshall declined to defend this line of white reasoning, though he thought that "some excuse, if not justification," might be found in the character and habits of the Indians. In the face of an altogether extraordinary situation, the usual rules that ought to govern relations of conqueror and conquered seemed inapplicable. Here was a case where the conquered could neither be blended with the conquerors nor safely be governed as a separate people. "Every rule which can be suggested will be found to be attended with great difficulty." The stark, simple choices were European abandonment of the country and of their "pompous claims to it," or enforcement of those claims by the sword and the adoption of certain admittedly defective principles, or exposure to "the perpetual hazard of being massacred." With such alternatives, a simple-minded indictment of white morality was too easy—and less than fair.[5]

Marshall was reluctant to accept arguments presupposing a providential plan for America "to be subdued and cultivated, and to become the residence of civilized nations."[6] Neither the pompous

in Story, *Commentaries on the Constitution* I:6: The European nations "were content to take counsel of their interests, their prejudices, and their passions, and felt no necessity of vindicating their conduct before cabinets, which were already eager to recognise its justice and its policy." For an even severer attack on European subterfuges "by which royal ambition sought to disguise its real objects," see Joseph Story, "Discourse Pronounced . . . September 18, 1828, in Commemoration of the First Settlement of Salem, Mass.," in *The Miscellaneous Writings . . . of Joseph Story*, 75–76, hereafter cited as "Centennial Discourse."

5. *Johnson* v. *M'Intosh*, 8 Wheaton at 589–591. "The conduct of our forefathers in expelling the original occupants of the soil grew out of so many mixed motives that any censure which philanthropy may bestow upon it ought to be qualified"; John Marshall to Joseph Story, 29 October 1828, Massachusetts Historical Society, *Proceedings*, 2d ser., 14 (1900–1901):337.

6. Kent, *Commentaries* III:312. This was a theme dear to John Quincy Adams's heart, as is clear from the following diary entry (25 September 1814): "On the other hand, in repelling an insolent charge of the British Plenipotentiaries against the Government of the United States, of a system of perpetual encroachment upon the Indians under the pretence of purchases, I had taken the ground of the moral and religious duty of a nation to settle, cultivate, and improve their territory—a principle perfectly recognized by the laws of nations, and, in my own opinion, the only solid and unanswerable defence against the charge in the British note. Gallatin saw and admitted the weight of the argument, but was afraid of ridicule. Bayard, too, since he has been reading Vattel, agreed in the argument, and was willing to say it was a duty. But the terms God, and Providence, and Heaven, Mr. Clay thought were canting, and Russell laughed at them. I was obliged to give them up, and with them what I thought the best argument we had"; Charles Francis Adams, ed., *Memoirs of John Quincy Adams* III:41–42. See also the quotation in the text below, at n. 39.

claims nor the condemnation of those claims would do. The whites' governance of the Indians had to be informed by principles more modest and more humane. The time had come when the whites could morally afford to do no less.

Having appraised, in this manner, the rights of the whites to claim America for themselves, the judges went on to describe and prescribe the legal relationship between the United States and the Indians. It does not appear from the opinions that the whites' government had any general commission to rule directly over individual Indians. Dependent they might be, but as allies, tribes, national communities, as diminished rather than extinguished sovereignties. In this anomalous relationship the Indians retained "their original natural rights," governing themselves according to their own lights.[7] There was no denying that the enjoyment of those rights was qualified by the whites' possession of "irresistible power" that not only restricted the manner in which Indians could alienate their land but also subjected them to "our coercion, [though only] so far as the public safety required it, and no further" and even—indeed going further—punished individuals "without the consent, and against the will of their own governments" when the behavior was "shocking to humanity, and . . . not to be tolerated in the neighborhood, and under the eye of a civilized and Christian people."[8] It was a peculiar, even unique, relationship. "Judicially considered," the Indians appeared to be a foreign nation, if "foreign" were viewed as a political relationship rather than as a territorial location; but "with strict accuracy" it was hard to call a people living within the boundaries of the United States by that name. A more correct designation would be "domestic dependent nations"; a more correct analogy would be the relation of "a ward to his guardian." Once a people "too powerful and brave not to be dreaded," the Indians were now in their unhappy latter days no less a distinct people. Having fulfilled the demands prompted by a respect for their own safety, only now were the white American people free "to give full

7. *Goodell v. Jackson,* 20 Johnson's Repts. at 710, 712, 714; *Johnson v. M'Intosh,* 8 Wheaton at 574; *Worcester v. Georgia,* 6 Peters at 552, 559–561; Story, *Commentaries on the Constitution* I: 136–137; *Cherokee Nation v. Georgia,* 5 Peters 1, at 27 (Johnson, concurring), 53 (Thompson, joined by Story, dissenting).

8. *Worcester v. Georgia,* 6 Peters at 559; *Goodell v. Jackson,* 20 Johnson's Repts. at 710, 717. Thus, according to Chancellor Kent, New York's extension of its criminal law to the Indians in order to put a stop to their "irregular and foul executions" was analogous to the United States' punishment of foreigners caught in carrying on the African slave trade.

indulgence to those principles of humanity and justice" which it behooved them to follow in dealing with "a helpless people depending on [the whites'] magnanimity and justice for the preservation of their existence."[9] With the accents of some earlier leaders, Marshall strove to remind his fellows that self-interest must be not only served but tempered. Unfortunately, those who most needed the lesson heard it not at all.

What Manner of Men?

Whatever the arena—forest, council fire, state or national legislature, cabinet, court of law—the confrontation of reds and whites raised problems that tested, even as they displayed, human strengths, limits, and differences. In fact, these strengths and limits and differences are the alpha and omega of the problem. We start from them and return to them.

The Indians, however they may have been or seemed to be to the whites first encountering them on the St. Lawrence, at Jamestown, or in Plymouth, neither were nor appeared to be the same in the late eighteenth century. The interaction of European goods and Indian skills had altered both white markets and Indian ways of living. Some features most popularly associated with aboriginal life—lack of fixed abode, neglect of agriculture, and disdain for labor—were heightened, or in some cases perhaps raised to a significantly different magnitude, by the new dependence on trade goods. Whether one can properly speak of a deterioration in Indian character amounting to an absurd aping of white ways is more problematic. In white opinion, at any rate, a deterioration had occurred. By the late eighteenth century, the Puritan's heathen was viewed mainly as an enemy, an object of fear and loathing. By the early nineteenth century, contempt and indifference best characterize the prevailing white opinions. No doubt

---

9. *Cherokee Nation* v. *Georgia,* 5 Peters at 57, 55 (Thompson and Story, dissenting), 16–17; *Johnson* v. *M'Intosh,* 8 Wheaton at 596. Marshall clearly meant that Indian nations, not individual Indians, resemble wards. He was neither authorizing nor justifying meddlesome projects to remold Indian character by taking individuals in hand, cutting their hair, separating children from their families, and the like. See also Marshall's oblique censure in *Worcester* v. *Georgia* of "high sounding expressions denoting superiority," 6 Peters at 554–555. Marshall to Story, 29 October 1828, Massachusetts Historical Society, *Proceedings,* 2d ser., 14 (1900–1901):337–338.

John C. Calhoun was correct in declaring that helplessness had succeeded independence; it was, indeed, a spectacle from which white beneficiaries averted their eyes and shielded their thoughts.[10] And yet, in one respect, Indian independence never faltered. For all their lusting after the white's kettles and knives and rifles and rum, for all their clownish infatuation with trinkets and notions, the Indians for the most part had little or no use for the Europeans' economics, politics, or god.

So extraordinary a resistance could not go unmarked. In accounting for Indian behavior by referring to some perversity, or an immutable racial character, or an unfortunate upbringing, succeeding commentators have told us something of their own cast of mind as well as that of the Indians. In 1798 Benjamin Lincoln foresaw a continuing Indian retreat to the north, "the last resort of a people, who, having sacrificed every consideration to their love of ease, were now compelled, by the effects of their obstinacy and disobedience," to remain, what Lincoln presumed them all to be, savage hunters. The root of this seemingly sinful pride lay in certain opinions—manners, customs, mores—entertained by the Indians and persisted in despite all countervailing argument and experience.[11] Less clear, but no less consequential, was the source of those opinions. Did they, as Joseph Story maintained, arise out of a peculiar nature, outfitted with singular vices and singular virtues? The Indians might then be presenting a sublime spectacle awesome to others and disastrous for themselves, but beyond anyone's control. More sanguine were those who found the source of Indian opinions (and Indian resistance) in that second nature, custom. Armed with the confidence that habit could replace habit, these reformers sought, as a first step, to overcome "the habits

10. Compare the description of Algonquian life at the outset of Puritan colonization in Alden T. Vaughan, *New England Frontier: Puritans and Indians, 1620–1675,* 30–34, 37–40, 43–50, with the changes noted by observers in Canada in the course .of the seventeenth century, as summarized in Harold A. Innis, *The Fur Trade in Canada,* 15–21. John C. Calhoun to Speaker Henry Clay, 5 December 1818, in Robert L. Meriwether et al., eds., *The Papers of John C. Calhoun* III:342. See Alexis de Tocqueville, *Journey to America,* 198–201.

11. Benjamin Lincoln, "Observations on the Indians of North-America," Massachusetts Historical Society, *Collections,* 1st ser., 5 (1798):11–12. The sovereign importance of opinion among the Indians has been noted again and again. See, among others, Thomas Jefferson, *Notes on the State of Virginia,* 93; Alexis de Tocqueville, *Democracy in America,* 293 (I, pt. ii, chap. 10); Edmund S. Morgan, "The American Indian: Incorrigible Individualist," in *The Mirror of the Indian,* 5–19; Dale Van Every, *Disinherited: The Lost Birthright of the American Indian,* 65–68.

of [the Indians'] bodies, prejudices of their minds, ignorance, pride, and the influence of interested and crafty individuals among them who feel themselves something in the present order of things and fear to become nothing in any other." Disregarding Jefferson's satirical byplay in this passage in his Second Inaugural Address, we may note in it the very premise underlying earlier and subsequent efforts at "civilizing" and "Christianizing" the Indians as well as most projects for "preserving" them. The tyranny of Indian habits, prejudices, ignorance, and pride had to be overthrown, ultimately (one may suppose) by reason and knowledge, more immediately by other passions, other habits. If it were true that "avarice and fear [were] the predominant passions that govern an Indian," a judicious mixture of the two might move them from their bad, old ways. Even those who viewed the Indians, as a whole, as essentially hunters and a barbarous people, as the least provident, frugal, and industrious branch of the human family (and the most resentful, passionate, and unprincipled), brooked the possibility of the Indians' acquiring new habits.[12]

Much of the whites' troubles with the Indians in North America may be traced to those Indian manners and opinions that might, with some justice, be called aristocratic. Tocqueville saw this. If the impoverished and ignorant Indians were free and equal—like the whites who were displacing them—they also showed striking affinities to a pre- or antidemocratic way of life. In their reserve and courtesy, pride in pretended nobility, and scorn for toil, the Indians reminded Tocqueville of medieval aristocracy. The red man needed only "to become a conqueror to complete the resemblance." But the circle of analogy, if it were to be closed at all, would be in the opposite

12. Story, "Centennial Discourse," 78–79; Thomas Jefferson, Second Inaugural Address, 4 March 1805, in James D. Richardson, ed., *A Compilation of the Messages and Papers of the Presidents, 1789–1897* I:380; Andrew Jackson to James Monroe, 4 March 1817, in John S. Bassett, ed., *The Correspondence of Andrew Jackson* II:281. See the report on Indian affairs by Gov. Lewis Cass and Gen. William Clark, 9 February 1829, published by the 20th Cong., 2d sess., as S. Doc. 72, 110–111; and [Lewis Cass], "Removal of the Indians," *North American Review* 30 (1830):64, 73. In the last-mentioned article Cass went on to argue (75): "The *fulcrum* is wanting, upon which the lever must be placed. They are contented as they are; not contented merely, but clinging with a death-grasp to their own institutions. This feeling, inculcated in youth, strengthened in manhood, and nourished in age, renders them inaccessible to argument or remonstrance." And yet, by page 109, Cass could envision the debarbarization of the Indians in their ethnic enclave west of the Arkansas Territory. It is due Cass to mention that he also viewed as possible the further removal of the Indians or their total disappearance. None of these possibilities seemed terribly urgent or, for that matter, terrible.

direction. Feudal lord and Indian chief each displayed an indifference to those concerns that commerce made central for itself. Each disdained what Adam Smith called the "pedlar principle of turning a penny wherever a penny was to be got"; yet what commerce required was precisely that "exact attention to small savings and small gains." Each, in turn, was overpowered by people for whom the attractions of prosperity were lively and present, people who did not suffer from a fatal ignorance of the value of wealth. As it turned out, the Indian's dream of fierce independence faded into the aristocrat's nightmare of wrongs unrequited.[13]

The white frontier population was in some respects even less manageable than the Indians. John Jay, writing to Jefferson in the twilight of the Confederation, complained of the mismanagement of Indian affairs. As his argument unfolds, however, the problem appears less a red than a white problem:

> Indians have been murdered by our People in cold Blood and no satisfaction given, nor are they pleased with the avidity with which we seek to acquire their Lands. Would it not be wiser gradually to extend our Settlements, as want of Room should make it necessary, than to pitch our Tents through the Wilderness in a great Variety of Places, far distant from each other, and from those Advantages of Education, Civilization, Law and Government which compact Settlements and Neighbourhood afford? Shall we not fill the Wilderness with white Savages, and will they not become more formidable to us than the tawny ones who now inhabit it?

Thoughtful men like Edmund Burke had earlier remarked the danger of settlers becoming "hordes of English Tartars" and had sought to avert the barbarization of the whites by making sure that the pack train of civil institutions was not far behind the advance party. The sound rule that "the ruling power should never be wholly out of sight" was, perhaps of necessity, only very imperfectly followed. There was much in the wilderness situation that set those pioneers apart, filling them with thoughts of particularity and feelings of a separate, because neglected, destiny. The moral consequences of such thoughts and feelings are varied, but for present purposes it is enough

13. Tocqueville, *Democracy in America*, 22, 294, 303 (I, i, 1, ii, 10); Adam Smith, *An Inquiry into the Nature and Causes of the Wealth of Nations*, 364, 391. See also Morgan, "The American Indian," 16.

to consider the dictum that the only good Indian is a dead Indian. A plain fact needs plain statement, and this George Ellis has supplied: "The white man made a logical syllogism which connected his right to improve the soil with his way of treating the Indians; namely, he satisfied himself that the savages were a part of the vermin and wild beasts which he was justified in removing, and compelled to remove, before the territory would serve its use."[14]

This dead-Indian rule of thumb was one of the massive political facts of frontier life. It was quickly recognized for what it was, a measure of the extent to which whites and reds had come to resemble each other. The reduction of one's enemy to the status of mere prey, in a situation of "unrestrained conduct" "by a parcel of Banditti," was more than enough to give some pause. Neither tenderness toward the Indians nor snobbery toward the settlers will fully account for a genuine seaboard concern over the brutalization of the whites. There may have been an attempt at evenhandedness in speaking of "scenes of craft, boldness, and ferocity, on the part of the savages, and of heroic and desperate defence by the semi-barbarous men, women, and children, who were the objects of these attacks." But it was surely no impartiality. The thrust of the concern is with one's own, with a growing population that had "imbibed much of [the Indians'] character."[15] Yet from the standpoint of national policy, the great problem of internal colonization was not the bloody episodes provoked by a half-wild white vanguard living on the fringes of society and of the

14. John Jay to Thomas Jefferson, 14 December 1786, in Julian P. Boyd et al., eds., *The Papers of Thomas Jefferson* X:599; Edmund Burke, "Speech on Moving His Resolutions for Conciliation with the Colonies," 22 March 1775, in *The Works of the Right Honourable Edmund Burke* I:473; George E. Ellis, *The Red Man and the White Man in North America*, 234. See also Jennings C. Wise, *The Red Man in the New World Drama*, 252–253; Henry Adams, *History of the United States during the Administrations of Thomas Jefferson and James Madison* VI:72. On the assimilation of men to "things noxious," see John Locke, *Two Treatises of Government*, bk. II, § 8.

15. George Washington to James Duane, 7 September 1783, in John C. Fitzpatrick, ed., *The Writings of George Washington* XXVII:133, 136–137; William Wirt, *Sketches of the Life and Character of Patrick Henry*, 239n, 240. See also Arthur St. Clair to Gov. John Penn, 29 May 1774, in William H. Smith, ed., *The St. Clair Papers: The Life and Public Services of Arthur St. Clair* I:301; Timothy Pickering to Rufus King, 4 June 1785, in Charles R. King, ed., *The Life and Correspondence of Rufus King* I:106; Henry Knox to Edward Telfair, 11 July 1792, in Walter Lowrie et al., eds., *American State Papers . . . : Class II, Indian Affairs* I:256, hereafter cited as *Am.St.P.:Ind.*; Timothy Pickering to Anthony Wayne, 29 June 1795, in Richard C. Knopf, ed., *Anthony Wayne: A Name in Arms*, 432.

law. The problem lay rather in the ordinary agrarian settler, the land speculator, the trader, all of whom operated within the system of state government and law and used that system to provoke encounters between reds and whites. Especially was this true after the Indians began to appear helpless and despicable.

It is in this context that the character of the white national leaders takes on special interest and importance. They knew well enough what they wanted. All of them assumed that the destiny of the North American continent was to serve as an arena for their triumphant selves. For most of them that triumph was justified by the superior use whites could make of the land and its resources. For some, however, it was a worrisome triumph; the comforting justification was complicated by some elementary moral misgivings. At their finest, white leaders disclose a pause, a half-step, as they reflect on the vast differences between themselves and the Indians. Considerations of honor and prudence led to the same conclusion: The United States could afford something like magnanimity in small matters. This concern with the moral aspects of the inevitable victory over ignorance, weakness, and barbarism is well expressed by General Lincoln, a man little given to cheap sentimentality:

I have not been altogether pleased with the conversation upon the subject of Indian affairs. The ideas entertained by our forefathers, that God was miraculously interposing his authority in their favour in transplanting them here and in driving out *the heathen* before them, seems to have gained a general reception. I think it is true of bodies of men, as well as of individuals, that the moment they consider themselves the peculiar favourites of Heaven they become vain in their imaginations, and though I will not say that they appear in the uncomely garb of their own righteousness, yet I will venture to affirm that it would be fortunate for mankind if in all instances it should clearly appear that they were clothed with the mantle of justice, mercy, and humility, which are the brightest ornaments of human nature. When I hear persons say that there is not any faith to be kept with savages, that they are not entitled to that justice, and that nothing is to be done with them but to spread fire and sword over the face of their country and to slay them wherever they can be found, I shudder at the sentiment. I, however, think the time will come when they will be either civilized or extinct.

You will observe that I have not made any observations on the right the natives have to the soil. I believe, however, that in all instances where they have not transferred their right it remains compleat. Although I think the savages will retire before light and truth, and make way for its becoming universal, yet to hasten this by unrighteous measures would be as improper as it would be to remove by unlawfull acts the present generation, because it is evident that God in his providence will remove them & make way for another.[16]

The correspondence and reports of President Washington and of his secretaries of war, Henry Knox and Timothy Pickering, yield further evidence of this moral concern. Plagued by an awareness of the incompetence of the central government to effect its will in managing and controlling encounters between reds and whites, these leaders groped for ways of securing the desired end at a lower cost in honor, lives, and cash. These early papers tell again and again of mutual provocations and outrages beyond the reach of law or force, of young warriors and malignant whites chafing under the restraints of an uneasy peace, and of jealousies and prejudices preventing the enactment of effective laws.[17] Washington despaired of "any thing short of a Chinese wall, or a line of troops" being able to keep land jobbers and squatters out of Indian country. What laws there were rang hollow, for neither indictments nor convictions were forthcoming where whites were the transgressors. The limits of law enforcement were clear enough. With a protasis such as this—"If too many of the inhabitants of your government have not been concerned in the outrages in question"—the instructions to a territorial governor told him what he hardly needed to be told, that exemplary punishment of white criminals was not expected of him. The ultimate confession of defeat lay in the government's refusal in 1795 to require any longer by treaty that the Indians deliver up murderers to white authorities for punishment "because experience has too long shown, that regardless of our stipulations *we cannot punish our own*. It is a maxim

---

16. Benjamin Lincoln to Jeremy Belknap, 21 January 1792, Massachusetts Historical Society, *Collections*, 6th ser., 4 (1891):516–517. See Committee Report, 28 May 1784, in Worthington C. Ford et al., eds., *Journals of the Continental Congress, 1774–1789* XXVII:455, hereafter cited as *Jnls. Cont. Cong.*; Knox to Washington, 7 July 1789, *Am.St.P.:Ind.* I:53; Van Every, *Disinherited*, 83; Reginald Horsman, *Expansion and American Indian Policy, 1783–1812*, 171.

17. See, for example, Henry Knox to George Washington, 26 December 1791, *Am.St.P.:Ind.* I:198; George Washington to Henry Knox, 5 August 1792, in Fitzpatrick, ed., *Writings of Washington* XXXII:108; George Washington to Edmund Pendleton, 22 January 1795, ibid. XXXIV:99–100; Timothy Pickering to Capt. William Eaton, 26 November 1795, in Louis B. Wright and Julia H. Macleod, "William Eaton, Timothy Pickering, and Indian Policy," *Huntington Library Quarterly* 9 (1946):395.

with the frontier people not to hang a White Man who murders an Indian. We ought to make no engagement that we have not a moral certainty of fulfilling."[18] Such confessions, however, were not for public consumption. No government could afford openly to abdicate its claim to define and punish criminality. Yet the fact is that no government—from the British attempts to enforce the Proclamation Line of 1763 to John Quincy Adams's efforts to secure the voluntary removal of the Creeks and Cherokees—had the means or even the fortitude to keep whites from subverting government policy.

The problem seemed clear enough: in Knox's words, "the deep rooted prejudices, and malignity of heart, and conduct, reciprocally entertained and practised on all occasions by the Whites and Savages will ever prevent their being good neighbours." The available options were few and stark: "Either one or the other party must remove to a greater distance, or Government must keep them both in awe by a strong hand, and compel them to be moderate and just." Whether the Continental Congress, to whom this counsel was addressed, was of a mind to heed it is beside the point. That government was already deliquescing. What is very much to the point is that in this and in subsequent reports for the new government, Knox displayed candor and intelligence in analyzing Indian affairs and balancing military, political, diplomatic, and moral considerations. A passage from his final report as secretary of war shows him at his best:

> The desires of too many frontier white people, to seize, by force or fraud, upon the neighboring Indian lands, has been, and still continues to be, an unceasing cause of jealousy and hatred on the part of the Indians; and it would appear, upon a calm investigation, that, until the Indians can be quieted upon this point, and rely with confidence upon the protection of their lands by the United States, no well grounded hope of tranquillity can be entertained.
>
> The encroachment of white people is incessantly watched, and in unguarded moments, they are murdered by the Indians. Revenge is sought, and the innocent frontier people are too frequently involved as victims in the cruel contest. This appears to be a principal cause of Indian wars. That there are exceptions will not be denied. The passion

18. George Washington to Timothy Pickering, 1 July 1796, in Fitzpatrick, ed., *Writings of Washington* XXXV:112; Henry Knox to William Blount, 26 August 1793, in Clarence E. Carter, ed., *The Territorial Papers of the United States* IV:299; Timothy Pickering to Anthony Wayne, 8 April 1795, in Knopf, ed., *Wayne*, 403.

of a young savage for war and fame, is too mighty to be restrained by the feeble advice of the old men. An adequate police seems to be wanting, either to prevent or punish the depradations of the unruly. It would afford a conscious pleasure, could the assertion be made on our parts, that we have considered the murder of Indians the same as the murders of whites, and have punished them accordingly. This, however, is not the case. . . .

It seems that our own experience would demonstrate the propriety of endeavoring to preserve a pacific conduct, in preference to a hostile one, with the Indian tribes. The United States can get nothing by an Indian war; but they risk men, money, and reputation. As we are more powerful, and more enlightened than they are, there is a responsibility of national character, that we should treat them with kindness, and even liberality. It is a melancholy reflection, that our modes of population have been more destructive to the Indian natives than the conduct of the conquerors of Mexico and Peru. The evidence of this is the utter extirpation of nearly all the Indians in most populous parts of the Union. A future historian may mark the causes of this destruction of the human race in sable colors.[19]

The announced intention of the Washington administration was to establish peace between whites and reds "on such pure principles of justice and moderation, as will enforce the approbation of the dispassionate and enlightened part of mankind." Earlier conduct toward the Indians had brought reproach on the United States. This was to be "obliterated" and the national character adorned by a new line of conduct designed to win and deserve the Indians' confidence. Over the next decades, public hopes and limited funds came to be placed in the appointment of government agents to the Indians, the licensing of white traders, the supply of desired articles through government stores, instruction in agricultural and domestic arts, and above all, the regulation of westward migration. At best it would be an experiment. But the alternative to conciliation was persistence in "corrosive measures," and these promised the extirpation of the Indians from the eastern half of the United States within twenty-five or thirty years. In such measures

19. Henry Knox to Continental Congress, 10 July 1787, in Carter, ed., *Territorial Papers* II:31; Henry Knox to George Washington, 29 December 1794, *Am.St.P.:Ind.* I:544. See also Knox's communications to Washington of 15 June and 7 July 1789, 4 January 1790, 22 January and 26 December 1791, ibid. I:13–14, 53–54, 61, 112–113, 198–199.

Knox could see "not a single particle of benefit . . . either in a pecuniary or moral view; but instead thereof, a black cloud of injustice and inhumanity will impend over our national character."[20]

Although Knox's preoccupation with national honor shows itself in report after report, his deference to "the verdict of mankind" was neither total nor uncritical. He knew that "men are ever ready to espouse the cause of those who appear to be oppressed provided their interference may cost them nothing." He also knew that even the more disinterested among America's critics were not necessarily informed or dispassionate, being perhaps too quick to see the Indians as victims. Yet as "the opinion of the world" might frown on white Americans digging in their heels and refusing to treat with the reds as equal high contracting powers, a concession on this point could safely be made. Knox viewed it as a concession "to the modes and customs of the indians in the disposal of their lands, without the least injury to the national dignity." It was, in short, not an utterly naive and starry-eyed man who saw in the refounding of the government in 1789 a new chance to make an honorable record with respect to the Indians. In a situation "requiring a noble, liberal, and disinterested administration of Indian affairs," there were opportunities as well as burdens. However contemptible, weak, and ignorant the Indian neighbors might be, "a nation solicitous of establishing its character on the broad basis of justice" would do well to refrain from playing the bully.[21]

It is to the enduring credit of the new national government that its leading figures concerned with Indian affairs chose to regard themselves as charged with a delicate moral responsibility. Both Indians and frontiersmen had in some sense to be governed, but this was no mere exercise of the police power. For though the triumph of the whites over the reds was seen as destined—and clearly the government of the United States acted as though commissioned to fulfill that destiny—something more than naked force was needed. It is entirely fair to argue that the administration had many inducements to moderation—the appalling state of its armed forces, the poverty of its

20. Henry Knox to William Blount, 22 April 1792, in Carter, ed., *Territorial Papers* IV:138, 141; Henry Knox to James Seagrove (agent to the Creek Nation), 11 August 1792, *Am.St.P.:Ind.* I:257.
21. Henry Knox to Continental Congress, 20 July 1787, *Jnls. Cont. Cong.* XXXIII:389; Henry Knox to Continental Congress, 2 May 1788, ibid. XXXIV:125; Knox to Washington, 7 July, 15 June 1789, *Am.St.P.:Ind.* I:53, 13–14.

treasury, the continuing British presence in the old Northwest showing a new solicitude for the Indians, and the diminishing eastern
interest in Indian removal. Yet it is well to remember that inducements to immoderation—the claims of one's own population for land
and even more elementally for protection, the disunion temper that
was nourished by western disappointments and fears, and the contempt reserved for a race thought inferior—also were great. In these
crosscurrents of principle and expediency there were leaders who
chose to believe that there was a national reputation to be won or lost
in the conflict with the Indians.

How "the good intentions of the public [were] frequently embarrassed with perplexing considerations" is a sufficiently told tale.[22]
But how white leaders struggled with their own hopes and fears, how
and how well or poorly they tried to bring facts and wishes into some
ordered relation, these are matters that bear retelling. The moral
history of early national Indian policy can be traced in the attempt of
those leaders to discriminate between a noble and a mean administration of Indian affairs. Yet the quality and significance of that attempt
have to be judged too. Wherein, we must ask, did the best men differ
from the worst? We must look to beliefs no less than to deeds.

Conquering Opinions, Conquering Acts

The incompatibility of white and red ways of life was accepted as
fact by most whites, just as it was by most Indians. Equally strong
was the expectation that the Indians were a long way from a resting
place, "for civilization and cultivation will make rapid strides, and
progress fast towards them." One need hardly add that this was more
than prognosis; it was a program for action. It might even seem to
require apology for documenting so obvious a fact; the continued
westward expansion of the whites and the continued dispossession of
the reds were matters taken for granted. Indeed, the removal of the
Indians from the immediate vicinity of the new settlers was, from the
whites' standpoint, only a temporary solution.[23]

22. Knox to Washington, 29 December 1794, *Am.St.P.:Ind.* I:543.
23. Lincoln, "Observations," Massachusetts Historical Society, *Collections,* 1st
ser., 5 (1798):11–12 (see also the text at n. 11 above); Washington to Duane, 7
September 1783, in Fitzpatrick, ed., *Writings of Washington* XXVII:139–140;
Thomas Jefferson to Henry Dearborn, 12 August 1802, in Carter, ed., *Territorial*

The first and abiding necessity, then, as the whites saw it, was to secure the next tier of westward settlement. It was a fixed doctrine among eastern political leaders that the humane way, the politic way, of so doing was to induce the Indians to vacate on their own. Happily, the very approach of white settlements heightened the Indians' need and inclination to move on—as long, that is, as they chose to live by the chase. The least that could be said for this policy of voluntary removal was that no alternative promised as much for as little expense, trouble, and risk.[24]

It is likely that Washington's thought and imagery closely paralleled prevailing enlightened views when he observed that

> policy and economy point very strongly to the expediency of being upon good terms with the Indians, and the propriety of purchasing their Lands in preference to attempting to drive them by force of arms out of their Country; which as we have already experienced is like driving the Wild Beasts of the Forest which will return [a]s soon as the pursuit is at an end and fall perhaps on those that are left there; when the gradual extension of our Settlements will as certainly cause the Savage as the Wolf to retire; both being beasts of prey tho' they differ in shape.

This ought not to be read as a demotion of the Indians from the ranks of mankind. Though their modes of livelihood put them among the predators, in their concern for their lands "the Indians appear to act a natural part for men in their situation." With that in mind, the government was advised to follow a policy of peace.[25]

Proximate white settlements, far from raising the price of Indian lands, would depress their value to the Indians and the price asked of the whites. But just as surely, a continuation of existing trends would

Papers VII:68; Thomas Jefferson to John C. Breckenridge, 12 August 1803, in Paul Leicester Ford, ed., *The Works of Thomas Jefferson* X:6n–7n. The incongruity of public measures, given the obviousness of this fact, is presented well in the report of Secretary of War James Barbour to the House of Representatives, *Preservation and Civilization of the Indians* (3 February 1826), 19th Cong., 1st sess., H. Doc. 102, 6–7, cited hereafter as Barbour, *Preservation*. See also Jacob Burnet, *Notes on the Early Settlement of the North-Western Territory*, 388–389.

24. See the excellent analysis by George Mason of the ways "this safe and easy Plan" was undone by avarice and impatience, and even by the "dangerous, whimsical (I had almost said childish) Project" of an unnamed Jefferson to publicly lay off the whole Indian country into prospective states long in advance of the line of actual white settlement; George Mason to James Monroe, 9 February 1792, in Robert A. Rutland, ed., *The Papers of George Mason, 1725–1792* III:1257–1259.

25. Washington to Duane, 7 September 1783, in Fitzpatrick, ed., *Writings of Washington* XXVII:140 (see also 133, 136).

mean that "in a short period, the idea of an Indian on this side the Mississippi will only be found in the page of the historian." For Knox, in 1789, this was still a painful consideration; like some after him, he believed that, if assimilation were to be the price of Indian survival, whites had a duty to help bring about that change. Though such projects for the adoption of white ways by the Indians continued to receive modest financial support and much lip service, white leaders did not lose sight of the main objective, "a furtherance of our final consolidation."26

The encouragement of Indian economic dependence and overwhelming private debt was advocated by Jefferson on the grounds that "there is perhaps no method more irresistable of obtaining lands." Other methods, perhaps no less irresistible, could be ruled out as unnecessary or worse. Jefferson rightly condemned the proposal to subject the Indians, without their consent, to the white men's laws: "A little patience and a little money are so rapidly producing their voluntary removal across the Mississippi, that I hope this immorality will not be permitted to stain our history."27 Jefferson did not explain the basis of his moral discrimination.

If the whites' first concern was Indian dispossession, the second was its corollary, Indian dependence. How whites viewed that dependence differed over time. Justice forbade the pursuit of self-interest to the extent of injuring "any neighboring community, however contemptible and weak it might be, either with respect to its manners or power." The special vulnerability of "the ignorant Indians" imposed a special responsibility on whites for some nicety in dealing with them. The early view was that the Indians enjoyed the right of the land, to disregard which "would be a gross violation of the fundamental laws of nature." It seemed incontestable that the Indians possessed "the natural rights of man."28 Having granted that much,

26. Committee Report, 9 August 1787, *Jnls. Cont. Cong.* XXXIII:479; Knox to Washington, 7 July 1789, *Am.St.P.:Ind.* I:53. See Horsman, *Expansion and American Indian Policy*, 172–173.

27. Thomas Jefferson to Gov. William Henry Harrison, 27 February 1803, in Carter, ed., *Territorial Papers* VII:91; Jefferson to Dearborn, 12 August 1802, ibid., 69–70; Thomas Jefferson to Albert Gallatin, 24 November 1818, in Ford, ed., *Works of Jefferson* XII:104–105.

28. Knox to Washington, 15 June 1789, 4 January 1790, *Am.St.P.:Ind.* I:13, 61. See also George Washington to Senate, 7 August 1789, ibid., 12; Knox to Washington, 29 December 1794, ibid., 544. By this understanding, the whites, in the form of the government of the United States, enjoyed only a right of preemption—a right that excluded other white nations and individuals but left undisturbed the natives' right to keep their land forever.

white statesmen saw the problem as calling less for wanton force than for management. Agents to the Indians might well despair of succeeding, so great were the apparent differences between "civilized and savage modes of life." But this, Knox hastened to assure them, was a false conclusion. The differences, awesome as they were, should be traced to "education and habits," not to any presumed "distinct primary qualities" of the various races. The agents' knowledge of human nature would be tested severely in "the art of managing the hopes and fears of an uncivilized race of men."[29]

Whether this management of the dependent Indians would lead to their conciliation with the whites (and with the fact of white hegemony) or rather to their extirpation still was an open question. Either way, policy suggested "commerce as a more effectual, economical, and humane instrument" than arms for governing the natives. And either way, to use Calhoun's plain talk, "our views of their interest, and not their own, ought to govern them." Indians were independent in name only; blinking at that fact could only further confuse policy and protract their agonies.[30] Removal and separation, with some form of self-government, seemed to be the future of most Indians; for the remaining few, the way lay open for amalgamation with the whites and their ultimate disappearance as objects of fear and hate— and as Indians. Yet even this modest proposal of Secretary of War James Barbour in 1826 appeared less feasible as pressures rose to remove "those unfortunate children of nature." Those pressures had been building up for a long time and now, as the crisis neared, expressed themselves in an openly proclaimed decision to deflate the prideful Indians. Their pretensions to being independent nations and sovereigns over vast territories had to be discarded as outgrown make-believe. Instead, they were to be considered as the subjects they really were.[31] A short and willful step led to the conclusion, a few

29. Henry Knox to Leonard Shaw (temporary agent to the Cherokee Nation), 17 February 1792, ibid., 247; Henry Knox to Col. Thomas Procter (on a mission to the Miami and Wabash Indians), 11 March 1791, ibid., 146.

30. Thomas Jefferson, Fourth Annual Message, 8 November 1804, in Richardson, ed., *Messages* I:371–372; Calhoun to Clay, 5 December 1818, in Meriwether et al., eds., *Papers of Calhoun* III:350–351. See also Calhoun's other reports on Indian affairs addressed to Henry Clay, 15 January 1820, and to James Monroe, 8 February 1822, ibid. IV:576–577, VI:681–682.

31. Barbour, *Preservation*, 9–11. The quoted phrase is from John Quincy Adams, Fourth Annual Message, 2 December 1828, in Richardson, ed., *Messages* II:416. See Jackson to Monroe, 4 March 1817, in Bassett, ed., *Correspondence of Jackson* II:279; James Monroe, Second Inaugural Address, 5 March 1821, in Richardson, ed., *Mes-*

years later, that "the Indians had no rights, by virtue of their ancient possession, either of soil or sovereignty." If the white men chose to pay the Indians something for their wild lands, it was largely because they found it more convenient to pay than to fight. The Indians were indeed now full-fledged dependents.[32]

These white opinions—the expectation of Indian removal and the belief in Indian dependence—coexisted uneasily in some minds with an audacious and complex belief that the Indians could be "civilized." Among those entertaining this project, the general opinion was that Indian habits and prejudices were the major obstacles to be overcome. Though success was in no way assured, neither was it impossible. The project itself "would require the highest knowledge of the human character, and a steady perseverance in a wise system for a number of years." A series of "rational experiments" might gradually win over the natives to civilization and its contentments. If these worked, the Indians would be saved—from barbarism and certain extirpation—and the whites' national character adorned. In more senses than one, it was right to speak of a "conversion of our aboriginal neighbors."[33]

Yet how might such changes in character and opinion best be effected and sustained? Most reliance was placed on the introduction of simple cottage industry and husbandry and above all "a love for exclusive property." In their preoccupation with the necessity and

---

sages II:92. Modern scholarship holds that "tribe" was a white invention, a convenient handle for dealing with Indians. Small bands or villages owned territory, but it suited the whites to invest nationality-tribes with attributes of sovereignty they had mostly never claimed; see A. L. Kroeber, "Nature of the Land-Holding Group," *Ethnohistory* 2 (1955):303–304, 313.

32. John Bell, *Removal of Indians* (24 February 1830), 21st Cong., 1st sess., H. Rept. 227, 5–6. Tocqueville deserves the final word on this report: "Reading this report, written, moreover, by an able man [Rep. John Bell of Tennessee], one is astonished at the facility and ease with which, from the very first words, the author disposes of arguments founded on natural right and reason, which he calls abstract and theoretical principles. The more I think about it, the more I feel that the only difference between civilized and uncivilized man with regard to justice is this: the former contests the justice of rights, the latter simply violates them"; *Democracy in America*, 312 n. 29 (I, ii, 10).

33. Knox to Washington, 7 July 1789, *Am.St.P.:Ind.* I:53; George Washington, Third Annual Address, 25 October 1791, in Richardson, ed., *Messages* I:104–105; James Madison, First Inaugural Address, 4 March 1809, ibid., 468. On the connection between proselytizing and cultural change, see Robert F. Berkhofer, Jr., *Salvation and the Savage: An Analysis of Protestant Missions and American Indian Response, 1787–1862*, 126–133.

glory of private property, in their insistence that the Indians adopt white notions of individual rights to own, improve, and sell land, white leaders disclosed something of their own souls. To be sure, the ferocity of the natives' manners had to be softened preparatory to their "enjoyment of a higher degree of happiness," and that softening would best be accomplished by their adoption of the useful arts and the habits of industry. But that large first step required that whites prove to Indians the value of those arts and habits "experimentally by facilitating the attainment of articles considered to be of comfort and convenience in civilized life." It is remarkable that whites—with little or no supporting evidence—actually believed that Indian dependence on trading goods could be developed to the point where love of comfort would overpower their love of ease. Although Indian leaders had surely had ample opportunity during the preceding century or two to observe that in many cases they fed, lodged, and were clad worse than a day laborer among the whites, they had not been moved to emulation. The limited success in converting the Cherokee to white ways was exceptional; the white response to that success was, to say the least, counterproductive. Nonetheless, it could be maintained in 1826 that, "although the difficulty of inducing him to labor, is duly appreciated, yet, when its benefits are once realized in the individuality of its productions, and by increasing his comforts, the hope can scarcely be deemed desperate which places him under the same influence as the white man."[34]

On this matter white leaders generally agreed: there was a model human nature that the Indians ought to, and could be brought to, approximate. Prescriptions differed and continue to differ about how to secure this change, but there was something like consensus that the Indians' possession of vast territory stood in the way of their "Americanization." In 1817 Jackson still saw in the circumscribing of the bounds of Indian landholdings and in the "placing near them an industrious and virtuous population" the short route to assimilation. It is more than suspicion that such good-neighborly influences were found more easily in speeches than on the frontier. Calhoun spoke in severer accents of governing the Indians "by a proper combination of force and persuasion, of punishments and rewards"—though in this

34. Knox to Washington, 7 July 1789, *Am.St.P.:Ind.* I:53; Henry Dearborn to William Lyman (temporary agent for Indian affairs in the Northwest and Indiana territories), 14 July 1801, in Carter, ed., *Territorial Papers* VII:26–27; Barbour, *Preservation*, 11.

he differed not at all from Jackson. "Our laws and manners ought to supersede their present savage manners and customs." That was the price to be paid for remaining in the white men's vicinity—that, and compressing Indian settlements "within reasonable bounds." If the "civilization" of the Indians was the main object in view, changing the mode of land tenure was considered fully as important as reducing the amount of land being held. As Monroe unhesitatingly put it, civilization required dissolving whatever bonds made a community of Indians and in their stead giving "a new character to every individual."[35] With such a program, two white demands converged. Not only would whites not tolerate the withholding of millions of acres from white use, but they would not tolerate the existence of substantial, separate, autonomous alien communities within the settled areas of the United States.

Though it was fully expected that the conversion of the Indians to agriculture would produce a coincidence of white and Indian interests, a misgiving lingered on. Plans to "civilize" large groups of self-identifying Indians carried the risk that an agricultural Indian nation, especially if holding its land individually, would frustrate whites eager to exercise the United States' right of preemption. A "civilized tribe" might never move or sell and yet still visibly remain (and consider themselves) Indians. Perhaps the measure of ultimate success would be the total absorption of the red by the white community. From time to time intermarriage commended itself to some white leaders as a means of both pacification and assimilation. For Patrick Henry, John Marshall, and Thomas Jefferson, interest and humanity alike suggested the need to overcome white prejudices against such marriages.[36] What they thought impossible with respect to blacks was seen as highly desirable with respect to Indians. It is not

35. Jackson to Monroe, 4 March 1817, in Bassett, ed., *Correspondence of Jackson* II:280; Calhoun to Clay, 5 December 1818, in Meriwether et al., eds., *Papers of Calhoun* III:350; James Monroe, Second Annual Message, 16 November 1818, in Richardson, ed., *Messages* II:46.

36. On Henry's plan to subsidize mixed marriages and to pay a bonus for each baby of such unions, see Wirt, *Sketches of Henry*, 240–242; and Gilbert Imlay, *A Topographical Description of the Western Territory of North America*, 246–247. For Marshall, see the citation in William W. Henry, *Patrick Henry: Life, Speeches and Correspondence* II:219. For Jefferson's views of intermixing and becoming one people, see Thomas Jefferson to Benjamin Hawkins, 18 February 1803, in Ford, ed., *Works of Jefferson* IX:447–448, and Thomas Jefferson to Baron von Humboldt, 6 December 1813, ibid. XI:353.

clear to what degree this difference was due to a political judgment reflecting the relative difficulty of absorbing three-quarters of a million as against one hundred thousand, or to a moral assessment of character and potentialities, or to their recognition of the singular passions and prejudices engendered in whites when considering blacks. In any event, the black slave who took over the whites' language, religion, and work, was to remain beyond the pale—or be returned to Africa—while the red native, who rejected all these out of hand, was to be assimilated—or removed beyond the frontier.

In a late revival of these plans, Secretary of War William H. Crawford suggested governmental encouragement of intermarriage as a last desperate effort to get Indians to adopt "ideas of separate property, as well in things real as personal."[37] The remolding of Indian opinions might entail altering Indian germ plasm. Once again, though, practical political considerations proved decisive for the whites, however the Indians may have regarded such proposals. The eagerness to be rid of the Indians and to inherit their lands overpowered any generalized sentiment to incorporate them into a white world. Removal became the first order of business. Civilization, at best a very difficult undertaking, might more handily be pursued elsewhere, beyond the reach of hostile whites. Amalgamation slid from being a pious wish to a dubious proposition. In 1826 Secretary of War Barbour, reviewing national Indian policy down to his time, saw a "spirit of benevolence" overwhelmed by a "master passion," namely, "that as yet unabated desire, to bereave [the Indians] of their lands." The growing belief that the Indians could not or would not or should not be civilized took on the character of a providential fact by the time of the crisis over removal of the southern tribes. "They know and feel, that there is for them still one remove farther, not distant, nor unseen. It is to the general burial-ground of their race."[38]

---

37. In a fine double-edged display of nativism, Crawford went on to argue: "This cannot fail to preserve the race, with the modifications necessary to the enjoyment of civil liberty and social happiness. It is believed, that the principles of humanity, in this instance, are in harmonious concert with the true interests of the nation. It will redound more to the national honor to incorporate, by a humane and benevolent policy, the natives of our forests in the great American family of freemen, than to receive, with open arms, the fugitives of the old world, whether their flight has been the effect of their crimes or their virtues"; William H. Crawford to Senate, 13 March 1816, *Debates and Proceedings in the Congress of the United States* 29:199.

38. Barbour, *Preservation*, 5–6; Story, "Centennial Discourse," 79.

Whites could bear up bravely in facing such a prospect, not, they said, because they were unfeeling and hardhearted, but because the result was just. Its justice lay, quite simply, in the moral superiority of the white American's use of the territory. John Quincy Adams gave clear and eloquent expression to this view in a manner that served the interests of filial piety and Indian removal. The "lordly savage" might scorn civilization and its ways, but his claims to hold and to use could not reach beyond whatever he had made his own by mixing his labor in it. Any grander claims were at once preposterous and impious:

> Shall he doom an immense region of the globe to perpetual desolation, and to hear the howlings of the tiger and the wolf, silence forever the voice of human gladness? Shall the fields and the vallies which a benefi-cent God has framed to teem with the life of innumerable multitudes, be condemned to everlasting barrenness? Shall the mighty rivers poured out by the hands of nature, as channels of communication between numerous nations, roll their waters in sullen silence, and eternal soli-tude to the deep? Have hundreds of commodious harbors, a thousand leagues of coast, and a boundless ocean been spread in front of this land, and shall every purpose of utility to which they could apply, be prohibited by the tenant of the woods? No, generous philanthropists! Heaven has not been thus inconsistent in the works of its hands![39]

It was sobering and comforting to think that Nature and Nature's God had so dictated. Whatever moralists might say, the triumph of white civilization seemed also an act of genuine philanthropy. The Indians appeared less possessors than mere occupiers, and North America on the eve of colonization "an empty continent." From this providential view of things, the Indians could enjoy only a short tenancy in a land of whose natural wealth and commercial pos-sibilities they were so heedless. "They were there, in some sense, *only waiting.*"[40]

---

39. John Quincy Adams, *An Oration, Delivered at Plymouth, December 22, 1802, At the Anniversary Commemoration of the First Landing of Our Ancestors at That Place*, 24. For the antecedents of this view, see Vaughan, *New England Frontier*, 111–112; Emmerich de Vattel, *Le droit des gens*, bk. I, § 209. Immanuel Kant, on the other hand, found it "easy to see through all this flimsy veil of injustice, which just amounts to the Jesuitism of making a good End justify any Means"; *The Philosophy of Law*, 93–94.
40. Tocqueville, *Democracy in America*, 24, 258 (I, i, 1, ii, 9).

White Thoughts for Red

The genuine difficulties that perplexed the whites' handling of Indian affairs are nowhere better seen than in the writings and speeches of Thomas Jefferson. Of all the leading men of his time, it was he who made the most sustained effort at understanding the Indians and the whites' relation to them. His lifelong theoretical interests in Indian origins, languages, racial traits, and culture set him apart from those whose thoughts barely ran beyond the tactics and strategy of white triumph. From the standpoint of a consistent believer in the principle of natural rights, the whites' forthcoming victory raised fundamental problems. Even if one wished to view that end as inevitable and right, one could not assume it to be so. Some explanations were in order, both to oneself and to others.

For all his admiration of various facets of Indian character, Jefferson saw the Indians basically as barbarians, savages. The Indians were, to be sure, America's own, and that fact alone required that they be defended against the calumnies of a Buffon or others intent on disparaging all things American. To vindicate the honor of "the Man of America" meant that the aboriginal no less than the transplanted, or emigrant, American had to be shown as at least the equal, in natural endowments, of the European. The Indians were held up by Jefferson as the very model of a society without law, "insomuch that were it made a question, whether no law, as among the savage Americans, or too much law, as among the civilized Europeans, submits man to the greatest evil, one who has seen both conditions of existence would pronounce it to be the last." Nonetheless, Indian character was no model for others, nor was Indian society the world's best hope. The palm would, indeed, be awarded the Man of America, but not to the savage American.[41]

Clearly, the Indians' "moral sense of right and wrong, which . . . in every man makes a part of his nature," had been much affected by the circumstances of their situation. "That a change in the relations in which a man is placed should change his ideas of moral right and wrong, is neither new, nor peculiar to the colour of the blacks." Indian barbarism is expressed in lawlessness, in a failure "to respect

41. Jefferson, *Notes on Virginia*, 58–65, 273 n. 83. On Jefferson's differing treatment of reds and blacks, see ibid., 140, and the interpretation of Winthrop D. Jordan, *White over Black: American Attitudes toward the Negro, 1550–1812*, 477–481, 89–91.

those rights in others which we value in ourselves." When the Declaration of Independence speaks of "the merciless Indian Savages,
whose known rule of warfare, is an undistinguished destruction of all
ages, sexes and conditions," it implies that savagery consists precisely
(though not exclusively) in an ignoring of those real differences that it
is a mark of civilized folk to see. The failure to distinguish among
humans is a barbarian trait.[42]

The Indians' barbarism was not something fixed or ineradicable in
their nature. Indeed, Jefferson persisted in the belief that "the ultimate point of rest & happiness for them is to let our settlements and
theirs meet and blend together, to intermix, and become one people."
But the Indians, he thought, were not yet ready to hear such shocking
proposals, and so he was satisfied to confide this conceit in a private
communication of his "personal dispositions and opinions" to his
superintendent of Indians in the South. Then, in a statement that
fairly quivers with cross-purposes, he went on: "Of course, you will
keep it for your own reflection; but, convinced of its soundness, I feel
it consistent with pure morality to lead them towards it, to familiarize
them to the idea that it is for their interest to cede lands at times to the
US, and for us thus to procure gratifications to our citizens, from time
to time, by new acquisitions of land." Similar instructions, equally
unofficial and private though even more candid and urgent, went to
the governor of the Indiana Territory. In addition to perpetual peace,
affectionate attachment, justice, and liberality, U.S. policy aimed at
helping the Indians move from hunting to farming, spinning, and
weaving.

> When they withdraw themselves to the culture of a small piece of land,
> they will percieve how useless to them are their extensive forests, and
> will be willing to pare them off from time to time in exchange for
> necessaries for their farms & families. To promote this disposition to
> exchange lands, which they have to spare & we want, for necessaries,
> which we have to spare & they want, we shall push our trading houses,
> and be glad to see the good & influential individuals among them run in
> debt, because we observe that when these debts get beyond what the

42. Jefferson, *Notes on Virginia*, 93, 142, 60; Boyd et al., eds., *Papers of Jefferson*
I:431. For a different interpretation of Jefferson's views of the Indian, in the context of
a comprehensive and perceptive account of his political thought, see Harvey C. Mansfield, Jr., "Thomas Jefferson," in *American Political Thought: The Philosophic Dimension of American Statesmanship*, ed. Morton J. Frisch and Richard G. Stevens,
23–50.

individuals can pay, they become willing to lop th[em off] by a cession of lands.

What the Indians needed to know was that their forests were of less and less use to them. What they did not need to know was the likely result of such a trend. "[In] their interests & their tranquility it is best they should see only the present [page] of their history."[43]

Because he believed in the ultimate assimilation of the red race by the white, Jefferson held fast to the notion that there was no fundamental conflict between the two. "We, like you, are Americans, born in the same land, and having the same interests." Much, however, turned on the Indians' seeing this "coincidence of interests," and that, as he put it in the *Notes on Virginia,* required nothing less than that "a people who lived principally on the spontaneous productions of nature" be awakened to the advantages of commerce, intensive farming, and household manufacture. Therein lay the way of Indian salvation. "We desire above all things, brother, to instruct you in whatever we know ourselves. We wish [you to learn] all our arts and to make you wise and wealthy." With this early, fraternal advice, Jefferson presumed the Indians to be a "free nation," cognizant of their right to punish those who injured them and free to accept or reject counsel.[44]

Although Jefferson knew that appearances could be deceiving,[45] he also knew that they were important. Accordingly, he could speak with genuine conviction of the desirability of obliterating "from the Indian mind an impression deeply made in it that we are constantly forming designs on their lands." Such impressions served the interests

43. Jefferson to Hawkins, 18 February 1803, in Ford, ed., *Works of Jefferson* IX:446–448; Jefferson to Harrison, 27 February 1803, in Carter, ed., *Territorial Papers* VII:90–92. "No one would have felt more astonishment than Jefferson had some friend told him that this policy, which he believed to be virtuous, was a conspiracy to induce trustees to betray their trusts; and that in morals it was as improper as though it were not virtuously intended. Shocked as he would have been at such a method of obtaining the neighboring estate of any Virginia family, he not only suggested but vigorously carried out the system toward the Indians"; H. Adams, *History of the United States* VI:75.

44. Speech to Jean Baptiste Ducoigne (a Kaskaskia chief), June 1781, in Boyd et al., eds., *Papers of Jefferson* VI:60–61, 63; Jefferson to Hawkins, 18 February 1803, in Ford, ed., *Works of Jefferson* IX:447; Jefferson, *Notes on Virginia,* 96.

45. Speaking of the many colonial records showing that whites had purchased, not conquered, Indian lands, he wrote and then crossed out in his manuscript: "It is true that these purchases were sometimes made with the price in one hand and the sword in the other"; Jefferson, *Notes on Virginia,* 281 n. 4.

of neither whites nor reds. By the end of his presidency, Jefferson discovered the rhetoric that would allow him to state the truths he had judged too shocking for Indians' ears in 1803. Agriculture and assimilation constituted the "brilliant aspect" held up to his Indian "children." By beginning with private landholdings, they would go on to form political and ultimately blood ties with the whites. It was up to the reds if they wished to recapitulate white phylogeny "by adopting the course which from the small beginning you describe has made us a great nation." The whites might propose, but it was for the Indians to dispose of their lands, of their fate: "We will never be angry with others for exercising their own rights according to what they think their own interests." But it was for the Indians also to know that the whites too would be exercising their own rights according to their own interests. On this matter, compromise was neither possible nor desirable.⁴⁶

Looking back in 1813 on government relations with the Indians, Jefferson saw the course of events more simply than he had as president. Perhaps he owed his old friend Humboldt something better than the following lopsided account of American benevolence frustrated by English perfidy, for this simple explanation strips the acts of the Americans of their moral ambiguity and the thoughts of the American leaders of self-awareness:

> You know, my friend, the benevolent plan we were pursuing here for the happiness of the aboriginal inhabitants in our vicinities. . . . On the commencement of our present war, we pressed on them the observance of peace and neutrality, but the interested and unprincipled policy of England has defeated all our labors for the salvation of these unfortunate people. They have seduced the greater part of the tribes within our neighborhood, to take up the hatchet against us, and the cruel massacres they have committed on the women and children of our frontiers taken by surprise, will oblige us now to pursue them to extermination,

46. Thomas Jefferson to Senate, 15 January 1808, in Richardson, ed., *Messages* I:434; Thomas Jefferson to Capt. Hendrick, the Delawares, Mohicans, and Munries, 21 December 1808, in Andrew A. Lipscomb and Albert E. Bergh, eds., *The Writings of Thomas Jefferson* XVI:451–453; Thomas Jefferson to the Chiefs of the Ottawas, Chippewas, Powtewatamies, Wyandots, and Senecas of Sandusky, 22 April 1808, ibid., 429. See also Horsman, *Expansion and American Indian Policy*, 108. I hardly mean to suggest that these gentle speeches were the only or even the predominant message to the Indians. With some broad hints to guide them, line officers were left to work things out as best they could. See the discussion in Dorothy B. Goebel, *William Henry Harrison: A Political Biography*, 93–105, 126–127.

or drive them to new seats beyond our reach. . . . The confirmed brutalization, if not the extermination of this race in America, is therefore
to form an additional chapter in the English history of the same colored
man in Asia, and of the brethren of their own color in Ireland, and
wherever else Anglo-mercantile cupidity can find a two-penny interest
in deluging the earth with human blood. But let us turn from the
loathsome contemplation of the degrading effects of commercial
avarice.[47]

This will not do. If, for example, Jefferson and his deputy Harrison
in their Indian policy "decided to disregard [a precedent] in order to
act on the rule better suited to their purposes," they knew they were
doing so and why. In plain fact, national policy from the beginning
assumed that reds and whites could not peacefully follow their separate ways of life in the same neighborhood. A necessary implication
was that Indian ways must become invisible. But what of the Indians
themselves? Must they too disappear? Henry Adams put the dilemma
in concluding that "nothing could be more embarrassing to Jefferson
than to see the Indians follow his advice; for however well-disposed
he might be, he could not want the Indians to become civilized,
educated, or competent to protect themselves—yet he was powerless
to protect them."[48]

Judgments from Afar

Given these shared beliefs concerning Indian removal and dependence, given these common expectations that Indians could not be
allowed to pursue their traditional ways in the vicinity of the whites,
is it still possible to distinguish among white leaders? I believe so,
although no simple litmus test is at hand. Words, surely, must be
given some weight. An open denial of the moral aspects of the problem bespeaks something worse than candor in a statesman, whereas
an avowal of such a moral concern—however discounted by opportunities overlooked or rejected—bespeaks something better than
mere cant. Actions, too, say much, but not everything. We may still
recognize the difference between sending smiths and tools to the

47. Jefferson to Humboldt, 6 December 1813, in Ford, ed., *Works of Jefferson*
XI:353–354.
48. H. Adams, *History of the United States* VI:79, 81.

Indians and sending them rotten provisions and sinking ships for their removal. Circumstances, above all, must be given their due. War with the Indians was never a pretty picture, but Wayne's campaign in the Ohio country in 1794 must be viewed in a quite different light from the war against the Seminoles forty years later. Acts that were defensible or necessary at one time or place lost that character when circumstances altered. Then too, only a predisposition to blanket condemnation or praise overlooks differences among the Indians themselves; the Cherokees were not Mandans, and whites unable to see and act on the difference deserve to be blamed.

In general, not all that might have been done by whites was done. Not all that was done was done well. Virtually every conceivable good intention would have been frustrated by the competition of claims between reds and whites. The best, no less than the worst, of the white leaders acted within fairly narrow political limits. The best, however, tended to use whatever leeway they thought they had to mitigate the harshness of white triumph. They saw the disparity between whites and Indians as both burden and opportunity. The worst permitted their contempt for Indian ways to harden their hearts in the face of needless suffering. Their impatience with Indian recalcitrance grew as the Indians became ever more vulnerable. The best aspired to magnanimity; the worst were only mean-spirited.

Jefferson, the man of affairs, like Knox and Washington before him and Calhoun and Barbour after him, sought a policy that would replace frontier acts of desperation with national acts of decency. In part, that policy was subverted by the lawless, the criminally avaricious, the Indian haters. But the policy itself was doomed, for it presupposed—necessarily and, more often than not, explicitly—the remolding of Indian character after a white image.

Tocqueville was not alone in believing that exposure to the whites had, on the whole, made the Indians "more disorderly and less civilized than they had been before." Though by his time whites had it in their power to extirpate the Indians, they could affect their characters only somewhat and, at that, more in the direction of barbarism than of civilization. Indian tastes and habits worked against the very prerequisites of white civilization. For the Indians to have changed their ways, for them to have sought (and succeeded in adopting) a foreign people's wisdom, they would have had to exchange places as conqueror and conquered. The barbarian conquest of Rome and the Mongol invasion of China each involved a kind of parity between force and intelligence. "But when the side that has the physical force has intellectual superiority too, it is rare for the conquered to become civilized; they either withdraw or are destroyed. For this reason one can say that, generally speaking, savages go forth in arms to seek enlightenment but do not accept it as a gift."[49]

White Americans found little or nothing to admire in the Indian world; their behavior toward them underlined that fact. With a people as proud as the Indians—perhaps with any people—there was a tribute that had first to be paid to self-respect. In its absence, prevailing Indian notions of manliness pointed to haughty rejection, to futile gestures, finally to the stupor of drink or death. It was as though the enduring, if self-defeating, sign of Indian vitality was the persistent "nay" to white terms.

Those terms remained relatively constant throughout this period, despite some changes of emphasis over time. There do not appear to have been any significant party differences on the essentials of the national government's Indian policy. Nor was there any debate over the fundamental principles informing that policy. It seems not to have mattered who held the reins of power—Knox, Jefferson, Calhoun, John Quincy Adams, Jackson. The same notions of national interest prevailed. Those notions were intimately connected with, in fact derived from, the Lockean point of view. Man's right and duty to improve on nature's gifts, property's origin in labor and its subsequent regulation by civil society, the role of government in protecting and fostering the different and unequal faculties of acquiring property—all these were accepted by the whites as the bases of civilized life. If the Indians chose to join the ranks of the civilized, they were welcome to do so (at least among the enlightened). Becoming Lockean men, however, would be the nonnegotiable condition of their remaining in the neighborhood of the whites. But although the Indians ought not, and perhaps could not, be forced to become Lockeans, it was vital that they understand that the whites would continue to view their relations with the Indians in Lockean terms. If the Indians learned nothing else from the whites, they would learn that.

The bitterest lesson of all, though, came with the forcible removal of the "civilized" tribes. John Quincy Adams could rightly condemn Jackson and Georgia for triumphing in a manner disgraceful to national character and reputation. The traditional policy, "from Wash-

49. Tocqueville, *Democracy in America*, 293, 301, 304 (I, ii, 10).

ington to myself," had been the civilization and preservation of the Indians through their assimilation to white ways. Whatever success that old policy had among the Creeks and Cherokees was now turned into a source of their misfortune. In effect, removal was an assertion that assimilation to white ways was not a sufficient condition for the toleration of Indian neighbors, perhaps even an assertion that there were no sufficient conditions. The new course, which culminated in the Second Seminole War and which Adams called "this abomination," "this sickening mass of putrefaction," rendered vain any further resistance in court or in Congress. Andrew Jackson had made his decision, and he would indeed enforce it.[50]

It was only the very rare white who could sense the profound strangeness of white ways. If one reflected on those ways, as John Marshall did, as Henry Thoreau did, one could see how easy would be the white American's triumph over the red American's body, and how uncertain would be the reworking of the red American's soul.

> The white man comes, pale as the dawn, with a load of thought, with a slumbering intelligence as a fire raked up, knowing well what he knows, not guessing but calculating; strong in community, yielding obedience to authority; of experienced race; of wonderful, wonderful common sense; dull but capable, slow but persevering, severe but just, of little humor but genuine; a laboring man, despising game and sport; building a house that endures, a framed house.[51]

The Indian would not or could not live in that house. To do that he would have had to bring himself to say to his earthly master, "Lord, I love the habitation of thy house, and the place where thy glory dwelleth." The Indian never did find that a compelling thought.

---

50. C. F. Adams, ed., *Memoirs of John Quincy Adams* X:491–492 (30 June 1841). See Mary Elizabeth Young, *Redskins, Ruffleshirts, and Rednecks: Indian Allotments in Alabama and Mississippi, 1830–1860*, 96–98, 191–193.
51. Henry D. Thoreau, *A Week on the Concord and Merrimack Rivers*, 52–53.

5

The Complexion of
Tocqueville's American

O F THE ninety-three chapters in Alexis de Tocqueville's *Democracy in America*, none can compare with that concluding the first volume. It takes up by itself almost a seventh of the entire work. It is the only chapter in which Tocqueville says he departs from his preoccupation with things democratic to consider things simply American. If the chapter is indeed a kind of appendix to the work and even tangential to its great theme, it is nonetheless fascinating. Entitled "Some Considerations Concerning the Present State and Probable Future of the Three Races That Inhabit the Territory of the United States," this chapter never fails to provoke and disturb those who read it. It is not only Americans or people interested in America who find it especially engrossing and disquieting. To be sure, Tocqueville uses the occasion to bring together some scattered observations on peculiarly American things for which he has not yet found a convenient place in the work. But although the chapter is rooted in the particulars of American historical accident, physical circumstance, and human choice, it is not limited by that grounding. Rather, it is at once a tying up of loose ends and a summing up of the volume as a whole. Beginning with the three races inhabiting Jacksonian America, Tocqueville goes on to draw out implications of worldwide significance.[1] For example, in wondering whether the European or (as he

1. A note of caution: In using words such as "race," "barbarian," and "savage," which may strike many as problematic at best and odious at worst, I am only following Tocqueville's usage with a view to displaying his analysis as faithfully as I can. If

once calls him) "man par excellence" does not stand in a relation of dominance over "men of other races [as] man is to the animals" (292), Tocqueville suggests some large generalizations about present and future colonialism. And in illustrating, without quite saying, that the Anglo-Americans are to the French in North America as the Europeans in general are to the Indians (306 n. 19), he makes some large generalizations about the world rivalry among colonial powers and its likely outcome. Yet, for all that, what interests us most is Tocqueville's consideration of the three races that inhabit *this* territory. In viewing them, we view our American past, our present, and (as far as we can tell) our democratic future. None of that can be a matter of indifference to us.

In grappling with a chapter of some eighty pages, we do well to bear its organization in mind clearly from the very outset. There is, first, an introduction that sets the problem—the contrasting destinies of different races thrown by chance into the same vicinity; second, "The Present State and the Probable Future of the Indian Tribes Inhabiting the Territory of the Union"; third, "The Position of the Black Race in the United States; Dangers Entailed for the Whites by Its Presence"; fourth, no parallel section on the state or situation of the whites, but rather one section each on (a) the chances of the Union's survival, (b) the chances of the survival of republican institutions, and (c) an analysis of the causes of the Americans' commercial greatness; fifth, a conclusion in which the traveler, leaving the vast city and going up on a nearby hill, takes in the entire scene and for the first time "grasps its shape" (374).

Tocqueville's main concern is with the interaction of these races on the North American continent, but that of course already presupposes some clear view of the several races taken by themselves. So before turning to his analysis of their contact and mutual involvement, we must extract or reconstruct his characterization of each.

---

some are inclined to say after all this that Tocqueville is a racist, I would deny it in either the present-day loose meaning of the term or the nineteenth-century strict meaning. Were this an essay on Tocqueville and race, I would attempt to prove my assertion, but in the present context I refer interested readers to his letters to Count Arthur de Gobineau, dated 17 November 1853 and 24 January 1857, in Alexis de Tocqueville, *Oeuvres complètes,* ed. J.-P. Mayer, IX, *Correspondance d'Alexis de Tocqueville et d'Arthur de Gobineau,* ed. Maurice Degros, 201–203, 276–278. Where not otherwise indicated, parenthetical page references in the text are to Alexis de Tocqueville, *Democracy in America,* I, pt. ii, chap. 10.

Very briefly, then, and not in Tocqueville's order but in the order of their arrival in North America, we have these:

First, the Indians: For Tocqueville these are savages. They are human beings, to be sure, but imperfect, undeveloped ones. It would not be misleading to view them as children, for in their generally short-range view of their situation and their dangers, they display what Tocqueville calls a "childish carelessness of the morrow." Exceptional individuals among them, "men of genius," could not overpower the prevalent Indian addiction to a life of idleness, adventure, and hunting. In preferring that life to one of "constant and regular" agricultural labor, the Indians are not just exhibiting their "national habit" (301); that exciting, somewhat vagrant life has a fascination for all or most people by nature—at least when compared to hoeing and weeding. This natural preference is reinforced by a peculiarly Indian trait; the Indians regard labor not only as an evil but as a disgrace, something a self-respecting man would shun. According to Tocqueville, this combination of laziness and pride has rendered the Indians impervious to European ways and conspires to keep them savage and semibarbarous, for without the rootedness of cultivators a people is in no position for civilization to take hold of it. In the American context, this fateful disability turns out to be fatal.[2]

Next on the North American scene were the Europeans. Tocqueville does discriminate somewhat among the Indians, distinguishing the Cherokees and Creeks, for example, from Indians who have rejected white ways out of hand, and distinguishing the Indians whom the Spanish encountered from those farther north. This discrimination, however, is as nothing compared to his depiction of the differences among European conquerors and settlers, particularly the Spanish, French, and English. Yet even here his tendency is to treat the differences, interesting though they are, as only of transient importance. Ultimately all must succumb to the Anglo-Americans, becoming victims of assimilation or a disastrous competition or cultural hegemony. The scattered minority of Frenchmen in the old Northwest simply fade away; the compact community of Quebeckers are

2. Yet, as Tocqueville himself witnesses, no less fatal has been the adoption by some Indians of the whites' farming, government, and letters. For where previously barbarians needed only to be nudged by the whites to follow the westward-fleeing game, now the prospect that civilized, agricultural Indians might *never* move provokes greater fears and fiercer efforts.

brought to heel; the Mexicans belatedly claiming their own find "strangers quietly settled in [their] heritage" (375). Even the southern Anglo-American, so distinctive a type in 1831, is marked for subordination to the northerner with his winning ways and, finally, for "fusion . . . into one national character. So the civilization of the North appears destined to be the norm to which all the rest must one day conform" (353).

What manner of men, then, are these northern Anglo-Americans? As Tocqueville presents them, they are best described as versatile, restless, and quick to help themselves. They are impatient with those conventional "thou shalts" and "thou shalt nots" that prescribe how a craft or a profession is to be conducted. Indeed, they treat such limiting axioms and prejudices with indifference or even contempt. Filled with a sense of their uniqueness and limitless possibilities, these whites rush on, goaded by greed, giddy with a kind of gambling-table fever. "Choose any American at random," Tocqueville asserts, "and he should be a man of burning desires, enterprising, adventurous, and above all, an innovator" (370).

Last to arrive in North America was the black race. Their contrast with the whites in this account is singular. Although Tocqueville's whites have many natures that tend to fuse into one, it is not clear whether Tocqueville's Negroes have any nature at all, at least in America. Tocqueville's blacks are what they have become: slaves and descendants of slaves, visible, incapable of suppressing the memories and hence the effects of their oppression and humiliation. Their rule of life is, perforce, submission. As slaves they submit to even the irrational demands of their degraders; as freedmen they submit to the irrational demands of their own wants and desires. Trained never to resist, they cannot say no, even when their self-interest rightly requires it of them.

If in the light of these brief sketches we were to ask, What is the complexion of Tocqueville's American?, the first and obvious answer would be "white." The work as a whole would appear to confirm that answer. The second volume of *Democracy in America* especially is devoted to an elaborate examination of the effects of democracy on the Americans' thinking, feeling, and acting; and in all these respects it is in fact the thinking, feeling, and acting of the whites that are being described. One might go further. Just as in America Tocqueville saw "more than America" but even "the shape of democracy itself"

[177]

(12, Introd.), so may one say that in the white Anglo-American Tocqueville saw more than the Yankee but even the quintessential democrat himself.

Yet this simple answer suffers from just that—its very simplicity.
The whites of 1831 are not the whites of Massachusetts Bay Colony
but rather what those whites have become. Similarly, those "two
unlucky races," the reds and the blacks, are what they are in 1831
because of what has happened to them during the two or more centuries since their "chance" involvement with the whites. We can at
least conceive of this possibility: that although each of the three races
"follows a separate destiny" (292), each has marked the other and has
done so in a way that shows another hue of the American democrat.

Fateful Encounters

To explore that possibility, let us begin again, looking once more at
the three races, but with our attention focused on the effects of their
encounter. Let this romantic sketch of a woodland scene serve as the
point of departure:

> I remember that, passing through the forests that still cover the state
> of Alabama, I came one day to the log cabin of a pioneer. I did not wish
> to enter the American's dwelling, but went to rest a little beside a spring
> not far off in the forest. While I was there, an Indian woman came up
> (we were in the neighborhood of the Creek territory); she was holding
> by the hand a little girl of five or six who was of the white race and who,
> I supposed, must be the pioneer's daughter. A Negro woman followed
> her. There was a sort of barbarous luxury in the Indian woman's dress;
> metal rings hung from her nostrils and ears; there were little glass beads
> in the hair that fell freely over her shoulders, and I saw that she was not
> married, for she was still wearing the bead necklace which it is the
> custom of virgins to lay down on the nuptial couch; the Negro was
> dressed in European clothes almost in shreds.
>
> All three came and sat down by the edge of the spring, and the young
> savage, taking the child in her arms, lavished upon her such fond ca-
> resses as mothers give; the Negro, too, sought, by a thousand innocent
> wiles, to attract the little Creole's attention. The latter showed by her
> slightest movements a sense of superiority which contrasted strangely
> with her weakness and her age, as if she received the attentions of her
> companions with a sort of condescension.
>
> Crouched down in front of her mistress, anticipating her every desire,

the Negro woman seemed equally divided between almost maternal affection and servile fear, whereas even in the effusions of her tenderness, the savage woman looked free, proud, and almost fierce.

I had come close and was contemplating the sight in silence; no doubt my curiosity annoyed the Indian woman, for she got up abruptly, pushed the child away from her, almost roughly, and giving me an angry look, plunged into the forest. (294–295)

Tocqueville stages this little scene to dramatize his central point—the way conventions can and do overwhelm nature. Far from being isolated actors, this trio do their thinking, feeling, and acting within a field of social forces—European prejudices and laws directed against Indians and Negroes, Indian prejudices directed against European ways. (The Negroes, according to this account, are excluded rather than excluding, acted on rather than acting.) Red and black seem to have nothing to do with one another, perhaps recognizing in the other someone equally powerless and irrelevant. All responses run to and from the white, dominant even in the form of a little Creole girl. Not only does convention here sunder those whose common nature would draw together as members of the family of man, but power finally shapes convention and renders red and black separate but equal subordinates. The bulk of Tocqueville's chapter is devoted to exploring how these conventions have affected the interactions of the three races and even altered their natures.

That Indian character previously described is seen as persistent yet subject to change. Their pride, which Tocqueville calls their "pretended nobility" (294), completely fills the Indians' thoughts and imaginings. Viewing themselves as second to none, they cherish their tribal freedom to move or act as they please, neither seeking nor requiring any others' leave. Their communal order and loyalties, sustained largely by habit and tradition, foster in the Indians a collective pride, independence, and love of freedom that lead them to reject and resist white ways and white power. From that vantage point, the white American's offer—limitless opportunity for self-advancement—is as alluring as an appeal to self-betrayal can be. The white finger points to a shimmering goal on the horizon; the Indian sees at his feet a permanent place in the very lowest rank of white society, a rank at once degraded and monotonous, a life sentence to ignoble and hard labor.

Thus the Indians resist assimilation and taming; they resist (irony of ironies) being "Americanized"; they resist, even if the price be death and dissolution. Tocqueville leaves no doubt in our minds that such indeed is the price the Indians will pay for this unequal and unfortunate meeting of a half-barbarous people with "the most civilized nation in the world, and . . . the greediest" (305). As the Europeans move westward, the Indians' modes of life and means of livelihood are disrupted and corrupted. Tocqueville insists on our seeing that the Indians of his time are "more disorderly and less civilized than they had been before," that European expansion has "condemned them to a wandering vagabond life" (293), that the sole source of their possible enlightenment is also the first cause of their barbarization.

Nowhere does the force of "European tyranny" display its power more profoundly, more imperiously, than in its effects on Indian opinions and mores. These it saps and destroys by weakening the Indians' feeling for their country, dispersing their families, obscuring their traditions, and breaking their chain of memories (293, 305 n. 18). Such effects are no strangers to us; we twentieth-century Americans recognize them as prevalent among the men and women who came to America as immigrants and took their turn in the melting pot. But it is one thing to leave one's homeland in order to go to America; the Europeans who did so were, after all, looking for more than a change of scenery. It is yet another thing to have "America" come to you. The European immigrants may have had much they wished to forget; the Indians, on the other hand, cherished hardly anything more than their ancestral ties. In losing those, they thought they had lost any reason for living. With his last words on the subject, Tocqueville damns the quiet way the Americans have brought about the ruination of the Indians, using language that can hardly be surpassed: "It is impossible to destroy men with more respect to the laws of humanity" (312).

If Tocqueville's Indians are isolated in their own country, a country that has been stolen or bought from under them, Tocqueville's Negroes have no country at all. Sold by one society and repudiated by the other, they remain suspended, rootless, one is tempted to say denatured. The tyranny of modern slavery has left the latter-day American descendant of the Africans without "even the memory of his homeland; he no longer understands the language his fathers spoke; he has abjured their religion and forgotten their mores." In these respects, someone might argue, the black is not unlike most sixth-generation Americans. But, of course, the transferred and transformed white has found a new homeland in America, while the trans-

ferred and transformed black can find only a semblance of a homeland (if even that) at "his master's hearth," and nowhere else. Yet
such is the peculiarity of men—Tocqueville does not know whether
to call this a blessing of God or His final curse—that they develop "a
sort of depraved taste for the cause of their afflictions." As though
mindless of the cause of his wretchedness, the slave finds special "joy
and pride in a servile imitation of his oppressors" (292). This ought
not to be mistaken for the way servants ape the pretensions of their
masters. For Tocqueville's Negro is a human being utterly transformed by the experience of tyrannical rule; soul and intelligence are
alike degraded. Ceasing in any sense to be his own man, he ends up
being no man at all. With deep irony, Tocqueville can speak of the
slave peacefully enjoying "all the privileges of his humiliation" (293),
the privileges, we might say, enjoyed by livestock who have no responsibilities and hence no need for thought.

Tocqueville's picture seems overwrought. At least it is not immediately obvious why the blacks' imitation of their white oppressors
should be damned as "servile" while the reds' spurning of white ways
should seem somehow grandly suicidal. Is it self-evidently mindless for
the Negro to attempt "to insinuate himself into a society that repulses
him" and to adopt as his own the tastes and opinions of his oppressors?
(294) Has the black nothing to learn from the European? Tocqueville's
answers seem to be yes and no. Through a strange reversal, the migration of American Negroes to Liberia shows another side of slavery:
"Barbarians have in servitude acquired the enlightenment of civilization and learned through slavery the art of being free" (330). This
anticipates the argument Booker T. Washington was to make at the
turn of the century, asserting the extraordinary benefits gained by
those like himself, slaves or the descendants of slaves, on going through
"the school of American slavery."[3] But whereas Washington sees in
this a black people's gradual triumph over degradation, a triumph that
would *entitle* them to a full share in America, the land of their birth,
Tocqueville sees no such prospect. Rather, he sees in the black's
adoption of the white's opinions a self-defeating self-contempt. To the
extent that the black believes what he has been told about his in-
feriority, he would if he could "gladly repudiate himself entirely"
(294). By virtue of this enslavement to the white man's opinion of him,

3. See Herbert J. Storing, "The School of Slavery: A Reconsideration of Booker T.
Washington," in *100 Years of Emancipation*, ed. Robert A. Goldwin, 47–79.

he effectively cuts off the means by which he might prove that opinion a lie. Whites and blacks, then, both appear to be enslaved to an opinion that degrades the blacks, confirms the whites' low opinion, and reconfirms the blacks' degradation (314 n. 32). Tocqueville pointedly contrasts the chains and shackles of ancient slavery with the "spiritualized despotism and violence" of American Negro chattel slavery, where the attempt is to prevent the slave from even wishing to break his bonds (332). The attempt does not, however, make for easy nights. Given half a glimpse of freedom, the slaves rebel against their masters; the demands of human nature assert themselves against even powerful convention and grinding condition. There is, then, good reason for that silent terror Tocqueville sees all about him in the South; the "nightmare constantly haunting the American imagination" is no mere figment (329).

Tocqueville's whites require a more complicated analysis. To understand them as they are, we must first look back to what they all once were; we must return to Tocqueville's "point of departure." For all their differences, the early English settlers of the seventeenth century shared a common language and background. They had received a distinctive political education in the institutions of local government of Tudor and Stuart England. They had been schooled by the religious controversies of those times and their minds given an austere and argumentative cast. And then, too, those early settlers shared the common equality of immigrants; it is, by and large, not the satisfied who uproot themselves in order to make a new life on the far side of the ocean.

This common background, according to Tocqueville, accounts in great measure for the character of democracy in America; but the differences among the early settlers were to prove no less consequential. The first settlers of Virginia were gold seekers, devoid of any nobler thought than gain. The artisans and farm workers who followed them, though less tumultuous, were not above "the level of the English lower classes." It was upon this population, later augmented by some rich landowners, that slavery was "destined to exert [its] immense influence" (28–29, I, i, 2). For Tocqueville, slavery was *the* basic fact that converted English character into that stock figure of the Old South. Floating down the Ohio River, Tocqueville sees on the left bank an American who "scorns not only work itself but also enterprises in which work is necessary to success" (319). The very presence of slavery diverts the white man's thoughts from commerce and encourages instead those tastes and prejudices that we associate with an aristocracy. If the slaveowner expends energy, it is less likely to be for money grubbing than for hunting or war. Though he loves his pleasures, he is in a sense above concerning himself with such matters. The "domestic dictatorship" over which he presides takes care of those things for him and goes far toward making him "a haughty, hasty, irascible man, ardent in his desires and impatient of obstacles," a man who feels free to indulge his imaginings and pursue his dreams of "greatness, luxury, renown, excitement, enjoyment, and, above all, idleness" (344). The Southern white, we might say, is almost as much marked by the presence of the black as the African is shaped by his contact with the white.

Very different, indeed, were the first settlers of New England—not solitary adventurers, but families; neither rich nor poor, men of education who "tore themselves away from home comforts in obedience to a purely intellectual craving," daring to do what they did out of hope for "the triumph of *an idea*" (30, I, i, 2). Once off by themselves in their own desolate corner of the world, these settlers could put into practice their peculiar democratic and republican theories. "Legally the state was a monarchy, but each locality was already a lively republic," peopled by those who (in the language Tocqueville quotes from Nathaniel Morton) "knew that they were pilgrims and strangers here below, and looked not much on these [worldly] things, but lifted up their eyes to heaven, their dearest country, where God has prepared for them a city" (37, 31, I, i, 2). Out of the loins of those Puritans come forth Yankees, but not by virtue of some unfathomable mystery. Tocqueville's Puritan seeks his way to heaven through this world and its work; this peculiar, volatile compound of religious and secular motives fuels him with astonishing energy and drive. Tocqueville's Yankee seeks his way to earthly freedom and prosperity, but within the bounds of a fixed and even severe (albeit constricted) morality. If there be any miracle at all in this transformation, it is rather in what Puritan and Yankee share—"a marvelous combination" of seemingly heterogeneous elements, "the *spirit of religion* and the *spirit of freedom*" (40, I, i, 2). Gradually, church and state forms diverge; gradually (I am inclined to believe), the popular principles of their institutions sap their otherworldly convictions. Meanwhile, their capacity for singleminded exertions is left not only intact but extended by the peculiar circumstances of their nonslave society.

Looking over to the right bank of the Ohio River, then, Tocqueville sees a man very different from the southerner. The Jacksonian descendant of the New England settler is dedicated to, and preoccupied with, material well-being: "There is something wonderful in his resourcefulness and a sort of heroism in his greed for gain." Where his forebear was tormented by a longing for salvation, the Yankee is "tormented by a longing for wealth" (319). Lacking slaves who must obey without a murmur, the northerner comes soon enough to learn the arts by which he might gain the favors of others. Since he cannot *command* compliance, he develops patience and perseverance in dealing with other free men. Since he cannot *assume* a superior position in society, he concentrates his mind on those "trivial details of life" that will secure him against poverty (344–345). Just as the inequality of a slave society makes it possible for a few to let their dreams and thoughts range freely, idly, and even grandly, so does the equality of a nonslave society narrow the mind, suffocate the imagination, and direct people's energies in practical ways to help themselves.

A New Model

It is toward this model of a Yankee that Tocqueville believes all of the Americans are moving. Nay, more: it is toward this model of an Anglo-American that Tocqueville believes all of mankind are moving. Consider briefly his reasons for each of these expectations. The assimilation of the Americans into the Yankee turns on the continual and increasing mingling of the various kinds of Americans. This mingling is promoted by the success of the Union, which has over time "mellowed a mass of provincial prejudices" and helped men to think of themselves as fellow citizens. The mingling is furthered by the channels of communication and commerce by which the parts of the Union come to know and need one another. "There is no French province," Tocqueville asserts, "where the inhabitants know each other as well as do the thirteen million men spread over the extent of the United States." In these respects Tocqueville's expectations resemble those of Publius in *The Federalist*. But Tocqueville goes farther and sees in the restlessness and insatiable desires of the Americans yet another factor working toward the homogenization of the people. As northerners spread throughout the country, "they bring with them their beliefs, opinions, and mores" (353)—and their comparative advantage. In John Jay's image, "young swarms" from "the *Northern*

Hive" are often "tempted to gather honey in the more blooming fields and milder air of their luxurious and more delicate neighbors." In a manner of speaking, then, the North colonizes the South.[4]

What of the assimilation of all of mankind into the Anglo-American? That looks like a tall order indeed. Here it makes sense to view some of the characteristics of Tocqueville's Americans less as American than as democratic. Viewed from that perspective, his expectations do not seem quite so bizarre. Consider, for example, the restlessness and insatiable desires that set the Yankee peddler or Yankee pioneer in motion. If such traits and preoccupations typify the democrat, the one who has been emancipated from the restrictions and axioms of an earlier theological-political order, *and* if (as Tocqueville argues throughout both volumes of this work) the whole movement of Europe or of Christendom or of mankind is toward democracy— if, that is to say, democracy is "a providential fact" (5–6, Introd.)— then *some* version of the Anglo-American might be expected to predominate in Europe and perhaps everywhere. Given these assumptions, the commercial republicanism of the Americans would help dissolve parochial prejudices among nations much as it has within the United States. Similarly, most people, freed of the restraints and preoccupations that typify predemocratic society, would be inclined to turn their thoughts to the material and the tangible. Whether their cupidity, once emancipated, would be as extraordinary as that of the Americans, Tocqueville does not predict. And whether those new democrats, once emancipated, would gain or preserve the exceptional self-confidence that Tocqueville sees as rendering the Americans so kinetic depends much on those new democrats being schooled in self-government.

The following, however, seems not to be a matter of doubt for Tocqueville: When a people so filled with democratic self-confidence as the northern whites come in contact with a people governed by other passions and prejudices, those Yankees will dissolve or destroy all they touch. In this way one might view the confrontation of the

---

4. This colonization has mixed results, for the northern Anglo-American's ways themselves feel the force of those old imperatives of slavery and race. Tocqueville asserts truly that "slavery, amid the democratic liberty and enlightenment of our age, is not an institution that can last" (333). Yet when slavery fell it was not through the force of the carpetbagger's example having won over the southern Anglo-American, but through the terrible force of northern arms. Jay's characterization appears in Jacob E. Cooke, ed., *The Federalist*, No. 5, 26.

Anglo-Americans with the French in North America and with the Spanish in Latin America, the confrontation of the Anglo-Americans with the Indians, and the confrontation of the northerners with the southerners as variations on the same theme. Of course southern whites, too, confront Indians in Georgia and Spanish-Mexicans in Texas—and with equally overwhelming effect. But where those victories assure the expansion of slavery and all that that entails, the theme of the Yankees' confrontations is nothing other than the theme of Tocqueville's entire work: the confrontation of democracy with aristocracy; the ardent, even zealous, pursuers of commercial republicanism against those who reject it as unworthy; the prophets of self-help and boosterism against the idle dreamers of glory; those whom self-confidence has energized against those whom pride has immobilized.

But where does Tocqueville's black race fit in this analysis? Their vice is hardly that of the Indians: not pride, but self-contempt; not haughty rejection, but servile imitation. Perhaps Tocqueville would say that the black in North America suffers from being too democratic, or benightedly democratic—something like the *son* of the democrat immortalized in Book IX of Plato's *Republic*. It is clear, at any rate, that although he needs all the help he can get, the freedman cannot rely on the help of the one who has humiliated him, even in taking the first steps toward self-governance.[5] If he is not to relapse into barbarism, he must achieve by himself some measure of self-interest rightly understood. In this respect he differs not at all from any newly democratic people, any people newly charged with responsibility for itself.

As for the whites, filled with their own busy thoughts—have they anything to learn from the "two unlucky races" with whom they share this continent? The question invites a longer view, one that takes the perspective afforded by the second volume of *Democracy in America*, one that recognizes (as my cool account has not) the awful sadness that suffuses much of this long chapter. In presenting his considerations on the present state and probable future of the three races, Tocqueville is able to illumine both America and the democratic order for which it stands. His account encourages us to draw parallels between the whites' triumph and the democrats' triumph. In each case the manner of the triumph raises doubts, entails risks, and displays limitations. In each case triumph is accompanied by a tragic fate from which even victors are not exempt.

5. See Tocqueville's "Report on Abolition," 23 July 1839, in Seymour Drescher, ed., *Tocqueville and Beaumont on Social Reform*, 115, 117.

The reds and the aristocrats alike are doomed by movements Tocqueville wishes us to view as divinely fated (347, 376–377). There may in fact be no place in the new order for the immovable red or the irreconcilable aristocrat, hopeless anachronisms in an age on the make. Yet it is clear that the Anglo-American democrats need to be reminded of things not dreamt of in their philosophy. Those doomed figures confront the democrats as alternative human possibilities, fast fading in an age of calculation and leveling. Thus, when Tocqueville urges the aristocrats (who are within the reach of his voice) not to make a hopeless stand against the inevitable, this is not the expression of a conservationist desiring to save the few remaining members of an endangered species; rather, the best of the aristocrats are better alive than dead, better lending to democracy the qualities and capacities it needs if it is to be educated and corrected. "Indeed, one may say that it depends on us whether in the end republics will be established everywhere, or everywhere abolished" (lxxxviii, Pref.).

The tragic fate of the blacks in America likewise suggests more universal parallels. Tocqueville stresses what an aberration modern slavery is. Condemned alike by Christian teaching and democratic principle and even by the whites' own economic interests, Negro chattel slavery is utterly out of place in the brave new democratic world. That peculiar institution cannot last, and yet its effects seem ineradicable. In the course of exploring this terrible paradox, Tocqueville delivers a profound critique of democracy itself. For it is that very democracy that cannot tolerate the injustice of slavery which likewise stands in the way of peaceable emancipation and the ultimate harmony of free blacks and whites within a democratic nation. At issue is, not only whether "the white and black races will ever be brought anywhere to live on a footing of equality," not only whether the race prejudice and fear on the one hand and the race hatred and denaturing experience of slavery on the other can be overcome, but even more profoundly, whether it is possible for "a whole people to rise, as it were, above itself" (327, 354).[6] Stripped of its singular features, then, the problem of the status of the blacks in America is

---

6. "If the English in the Antilles had governed themselves, one can be sure that they would not have granted the act of emancipation which was imposed by the motherland" (327 n. 47). It is precisely because the imperial authorities at home have no great stake in the institution that they can afford to act on larger principles of justice and the national interest and impose a solution. Tocqueville himself acted on this understanding when leading the fight for the abolition of slavery in the French colonies.

but a particular version of Tocqueville's universal problem—the relation between equality and liberty.

If this is so, then his analysis of the blacks may properly be examined for larger lessons, and especially if he is correct in emphasizing (toward the end of the entire work) the "sort of despotism democratic nations have to fear" (665, II, iv, 6). In those final chapters Tocqueville holds before us the prospect or possibility of a power altogether different from any that has existed up to now, a power for which such old-fashioned terms as "despotism" and "tyranny" no longer fit. This new despotism would resemble ancient despotism as little as modern slavery resembles ancient slavery. We are warranted, then, in exploring the parallels and intersections between servile democracy and slavery itself.

Democracy's Darker Hues

Ancient slavery was the unexceptionable case in a world premised on the inequality of men. That inequality in no way presumed a simple homogeneity or equality within a given race or people. It was based, rather, on the natural inequality of souls. Some, it was held, were fit to be self-governing and free; others, it was held, were fit only to be ruled. By convention, Greeks might be fit to rule barbarians; but by nature, matters were more complicated. As Tocqueville remarks, the ancient slave was often superior to his master in education and civilization. His enslavement was cruel, but it was limited to the body. His emancipation, once achieved, was total, for the freedman might be indistinguishable from the freeborn citizen.

Different indeed is modern slavery. It is the exceptional case in a world premised on the equality of men. This equality rejects outright the political conclusions drawn by the ancients. If servitude is to be justified at all in modern times, it must rest on some visible distinction. Furthermore, if slavery is to succeed in a world premised on the equality of men, the enslaved must be demoted from the ranks of mankind. As a result, we see in American Negro chattel slavery a despotism that "most fatally" combines "the insubstantial and ephemeral fact of servitude" with "the physical and permanent fact" of racial difference. "Memories of slavery disgrace the race, and race perpetuates memories of slavery" (314). The relatively simple assimilation of freedmen to the citizen body that marked ancient slavery seems out of the question here. This modern slavery, moreover, is a despotism that does not stop at binding the Negro's body; it reaches for the soul as well. Tocqueville finds this modern "spiritualized despotism" altogether singular and singularly cruel (332). This calls to mind the characterization made behind closed doors by an American slaveowner speaking to slaveowners: "We have seen the mere distinction of colour made in the most enlightened period of time, a ground of the most oppressive dominion ever exercised by man over man."[7]

The trouble with slavery may be more than that it does not fit in a modern democratic world. Tocqueville certainly makes much of that point. But he also compels us to wonder how there could have been such a radical reversal, such a massive deviation from the providential plan of steadily growing democratization. Our wonder turns to bewilderment or dismay when we begin to recognize the ways modern slavery does indeed fit in a modern democratic world, does indeed fit all too well. When Senator Stephen A. Douglas faced the question of whether slavery ought to be permitted to expand into the western territories of the United States, he treated it as a matter to be "voted up" or "voted down" by the people. He professed not to care which way the vote went, but was happy to abide by whatever the popular sovereign decreed. "In the United States," Tocqueville says, "as in all countries where the people reign, the majority rules in the name of the people" (159, I, ii, 1). If popular sovereignty is a principle of democracy, majority rule is the mode in which that sovereignty necessarily expresses itself. But the extreme form of majority rule is what Tocqueville calls "tyranny of the majority," and the extreme form of tyranny of the majority is the enslavement of a part of the population by a greater part.

All this is not to assert that, for Tocqueville, popular sovereignty necessarily leads to enslavement, but only that it may. That enslavement, let me hasten to add, is by no means identical with Negro slavery, though we may discern in the one some of the features of the other. If, after pondering over Tocqueville's description of the position of the black race in the United States, one turns back to his earlier discussion of "the power exercised by the majority in America over thought," one cannot help being struck by the parallels. "Formerly

7. James Madison, 6 June 1787, in Max Farrand, ed., *The Records of the Federal Convention of 1787* I:135.

tyranny used the clumsy weapons of chains and hangmen; nowadays even despotism, though it seemed to have nothing more to learn, has been perfected by civilization." "Under the absolute government of a single man, despotism, to reach the soul, clumsily struck at the body, and the soul, escaping from such blows, rose gloriously above it; but in democratic republics that is not at all how tyranny behaves; it leaves the body alone and goes straight for the soul." This conversion of despotism into something immaterial or spiritual is no accidental feature of democracy; only "its good use" can be said to be an accident. The same force that denatures the black man and attempts to stop him from even wishing to break his bonds is at work on the white man: "The majority has such absolute and irresistible sway that one must in a sense renounce one's rights as a citizen and, so to say, one's status as a man when one wants to diverge from the path it has marked out" (234–238, I, ii, 7). Tocqueville sees more than a little of the complexion of the black American in the complexion of the white American.

Nor is this—popular sovereignty—the only source of despotic rule. The social egalitarianism that is the very soul of democracy poses yet another and even greater threat. This is what Tocqueville comes to see during his "five years of meditation" (665, II, iv, 6). Usually, when we speak of equality we have in mind the equality of free people, but that, of course, is not the only possible kind of equality. Consider this:

> At the time when Christianity appeared on earth, Providence, which no doubt was preparing the world for its reception, had united a great part of mankind, like an immense flock, under the scepter of the Caesars. The men composing this multitude were of many different sorts, but they all had this in common, that they obeyed the same laws, and each of them was so small and weak compared to the greatness of the emperor that they all seemed equal in comparison to him. (411, II, i, 5)

It is sobering to compare this situation of Imperial Rome to the analogues that emerge from the pages of *Democracy in America*. Tocqueville argues extensively and persuasively that equality is likely to promote a mistaken sense of self-sufficiency that leads to a dangerous isolation of man from man. This condition, which he calls individualism, renders men fearfully vulnerable and withdrawn into themselves. If he touches others, the once and future democrat feels nothing. "He exists in and for himself, and though he still may have a family, one can at least say that he has not got a fatherland. Over this kind of men stands an immense, protective power which is alone responsible for securing their enjoyment and watching over their fate." With this, Tocqueville launches into a powerfully moving portrait of an absolute paternalism, one directed not at helping human beings grow up but at keeping them in a "perpetual childhood." Eager to supply them with their daily ration of Soma, this new despotism is ready to relieve men "entirely . . . from the trouble of thinking and all the cares of living." Taking each citizen "in turn in its powerful grasp and shap[ing] him to its will," this new despotism proceeds to reduce each nation in the end to "no more than a flock of timid and hardworking animals" (666–667, II, iv, 6).

In this awful scene we can recognize, if we will, the features of the red American and the black American, each cut off from forebears and contemporaries, immobilized by the preoccupations of a perpetual childhood. We can recognize, if we will, the features of the black American, who has been rendered unfit to stand on his own by a despotic rule that afflicts his mind even more than his body. "Desires," Tocqueville asserts, "are masters against whom one must fight" (293). In his ready submission to his desires, the black freedman shows the mark of one who is not prepared for freedom. So too may the degraded white democrat—but with this difference. The emancipated black democrats are disabled by their old masters from struggle against their new masters, and so they perpetuate their own bondage. The white democrats (Tocqueville has European examples firmly in mind) willingly give up the struggle against their desires and so give themselves up to bondage—a bondage at least as fearsome, vastly more gentle, and hence probably more final. In each case, giving up the fight leads to the greatest possible harm.

I view Tocqueville's "American chapter" as, among other things, a cautionary lesson. That lesson is meant to help us see what he takes to be a democratic disease and to help us accept the remedies he proposes. Among those remedies and countermeasures is the encouragement of democratic self-rule, itself a potential source of tyranny. But that is no reason (in Tocqueville's eyes) for rejecting men's "strongest remaining guarantee against themselves" (499, II, ii, 8) and the only hope he sees for their remaining free.

PART THREE

THE REVOLUTIONARY

DESIGN RECONSIDERED

6

Commerce and Character

The hope of glory, and the ambition of princes, are not subject to
arithmetical calculation.

Benjamin Franklin

In democracies nothing has brighter luster than commerce.

Alexis de Tocqueville

BETWEEN THEM, Adam Smith and Alexis de Tocqueville have provided us with a detailed, fully realized portrait of the new man of
commerce. Their psychological analysis—both of the universal type
and of its American democratic exemplar—is by now familiar and
persuasive. We no longer startle at the strange blend of limitless
aspiration, quasi-heroic effort, and sensible calculation that characterizes their model man of the future. And, of course, we rarely
wonder at how much domestic tranquillity owes to the influence of
commerce on tastes, thoughts, and manners. In the eighteenth century, however, when this model of civil behavior was being formu-
lated, all this stood in need of explication and argument. A case had
to be made, and then won. The advocates—men as diverse as Montesquieu and John Adams, Adam Smith and Benjamin Franklin,
David Hume and Benjamin Rush—were united at least in this: They
saw in commercial republicanism a more sensible and realizable alternative to earlier notions of civic virtue and a more just alternative to
the theological-political regime that had so long ruled Europe and its
colonial periphery. However much these advocates differed—in their
philosophic insight, in their perception of the implications of their

proposal for the organization of economic life, even in the degree of their acceptance of the very commercial republic they were promoting—for all this, they may be considered a band of brethren in arms.[1]

The language of campaign and contention is no empty figure, for in many respects the commercial republic is defined best by what it rejects: constraints and preoccupations based on visions of perfection beyond the reach of all or most; disdain for the common, useful, and mundane; judgments founded more on an individual's inherited status than on acts and demonstrated qualities. These were characteristics of an order or orders that the advocates of the commercial republic might still (in a limited way) admire but could not recommend. They saw fit, rather, to promote a new ordering of political, economic, and social life. Further, they perceived in the Anglo-American people and setting both the matter and the fitting occasion for their great project's success.

It is not my intention here to trace the philosophic reasoning that led these men to reject the foundations of the older orders; that would lead us back to Locke and Spinoza, to Hobbes and Descartes, to Bacon and Machiavelli. Consider, rather, the public speech by which eighteenth-century thinkers—European and American—sought to persuade their contemporaries to adopt maxims, conclusions, and rules of action so much at odds with the certitudes of the day before yesterday. They had first to show their audience that the old preoccupations entailed unacceptable costs and consequences. Then—a much larger task—they had to propose a new model of political and social life, sketch its leading features in some detail, develop a case for preferring it, and defend it as sufficient to cope with the shortcomings of the existing order. In all these undertakings the advocates of the commercial republic show themselves to have been uncommon men, exceptionally clear- and sharpsighted moderns who knew what they were rejecting and why.

---

1. In proposing to treat the advocates of commercial republicanism as a conscious collectivity, I run the risk of asserting what cannot be proved for the sake of emphasizing what tends to be neglected. It was their shared commitment to ordered liberty and their desire to promote it by emancipating mankind from many of the modes of thought of the past that led those thinkers to commend the commercial republic in the first place. What was a republic might, in this sense, be ascertained better by regarding the sphere of liberty rather than the formal organization of a state. Thus, for Montesquieu, England was a republic masquerading as a monarchy; for Smith, the trading world as a whole was a mercantile republic.

Prideful Pretensions Detected

The old order was preoccupied with intangible goods to an extent we now hardly ever see. The king had his glory, the nobles their honor, the Christians their salvation, the citizens of pagan antiquity their ambition to outdo others in serving the public good. However much they vied for a fine field, a good herd, a large purse, it was not by these alone that they would make their mark. So at least they said. Latter-day observers might be inclined to discount these pretensions but could not dismiss them out of hand. Like Tocqueville, they might doubt "whether men were better in times of aristocracy than at other times," and they might ponder why those earlier men "talked continually about the beauties of virtue" while studying its utility "only in secret."[2] The sense of shame or pride that kept that study secret was itself a revealing social fact. To such thinkers as Montesquieu, Hume, and Smith, those earlier pretensions evinced a state of mind in some respects admirable, in other respects astonishing, in most respects consequential, but at bottom absurd. A good part of the political program of these commercial republicans was getting others to judge likewise.

Eighteenth-century men had to be brought to see how fanciful those noncommercial notions were. To the commercial republicans, aristocratic imagination and pretension were not totally devoid of social value. Honor could be specious and yet politically useful; pride could engender politesse and delicacy of taste, graces that make life easy. The weightier truth, however, was that concern with these fancies skewed public policy and public budgets, sacrificing the real needs of the people to the petty desires of their governors. As Montesquieu put it, these "imaginary needs are what the passions and foibles of those who govern ask for: the charm of an extraordinary project, the sick desire for a vain glory, and a certain impotence of mind against fantasies."[3]

It was not only the few who labored under such delusions. An entire populace might be so taken up with its peculiar vision of what was most important as almost to cease being recognizably human. As little as Rousseau could imagine a nation of true Christians could

2. Alexis de Tocqueville, *Democracy in America*, 497 (II, pt. ii, chap. 8).
3. Charles Louis de Secondat, Baron de Montesquieu, *De l'esprit des lois*, bk. III, chap. 7, bk. IV, chap. 2, bk. XIII, chap. 1.

Hume imagine a nation of latter-day Spartans consumed with a passion for the public good. Though the "positive and circumstantial" testimony of history kept Hume from dismissing the original Spartan regime as "a mere philosophical whim or fiction," it did not compel him to say much, if anything, good about "a people addicted to arms, who fight for honour and revenge more than pay, and are unacquainted with gain and industry, as well as pleasure."[4] If people would only recognize what is genuinely human, they would see these distorting preoccupations for the grotesques they truly were.

Disabusing the many was no small task. Those whom Smith pleased to call "the great mob of mankind" were the awestruck admirers of wealth and greatness, of success, however well or ill deserved. Such popular presumption in favor of the powerful had its good side, too, making more bearable the obedience that the weak dared not withhold. But that was hardly the whole story, according to Smith, for people came to perceive heroic magnanimity where there was only "extravagant rashness and folly"; "the splendour of prosperity" kept them from seeing "the blackness of . . . avidity and injustice" in the acts of those in high places. Smith pointed to an escape from these conventional delusions. We have within us, he maintained, a means of distinguishing the admirable from the meretricious, the genuine from the fanciful—a means of more truly assessing both our own worth and "the real merit" of others. How, he asked, would a particular act appear to an "impartial spectator," the vicarious conscience of mankind within everyone's breast? From this uncommon vantage of common humanity, we could see what "the most successful warriors, the greatest statesmen and legislators, the eloquent founders and leaders of the most numerous and most successful sects and parties" rarely were able to see—how much of their success and splendor was owing to their excessive presumption and self-admiration. If such excess was useful and necessary for the instigators to undertake what "a more sober mind would never have thought of," and for the rest of mankind to acquiesce and follow them, it was, nonetheless, excess bordering on insane vanity. Hardly anything Smith taught was more subversive of the old order than his cool deflation of the proud man's "self-sufficiency and absurd conceit of

---

4. Jean-Jacques Rousseau, *Du contrat social,* bk. IV, chap. 8; "Of Commerce," in David Hume, *Essays Moral, Political and Literary,* 264–266, 268–269.

his own superiority."5 He did not seek to have his readers deny or sneer at the real differences between men but rather to discount the claims of all who presumed on those differences, real or imagined.

These presumptuous men imposed terrible costs on the whole of society—political costs that were insupportable, economic costs that were irrational. Hume believed that to some extent ambitious pretensions were self-correcting; enormous monarchies overextend themselves, condemned to repeat the chain of causes and effects that led to the ruin of Rome. In this way "human nature checks itself in its airy elevation." But another kind of preoccupation with intangible goods was less surely or easily deflected. Though Hume found no counterpart in modern times to the factional rage of ancient oligarchs and democrats, another type unknown to the pagans still persisted. It was the effect of what Hume called "parties from principle, especially abstract speculative principle." That men should divide over distinct interests was intelligible, over affection for persons and families only somewhat less so. But that they should divide, with mad and fatal consequence, in "controversy about an article of faith, which is utterly absurd and unintelligible, is not a difference in sentiment, but in a few phrases and expressions, which one party accepts of without understanding them, and the other refuses in the same manner"— that they should so divide was even more absurd than the behavior of those Moroccans who waged civil war "merely on account of their complexion." For a variety of reasons Christianity had fostered a persecuting spirit "more furious and enraged than the most cruel factions that ever arose from interest and ambition."6 On this point Hume and the commercial republicans generally could agree with the ancients: fanaticism prompted by principle was incompatible with civility, reason, and government.

The economic costs of pursuing imaginary preoccupations might be less bloody than the political costs, but they were no less real; for proof consider the colonies in the New World. The frugal, simple, yet

5. Adam Smith, *The Theory of Moral Sentiments*, 127, 235, 405–409, 416, 420–421. See also D. D. Raphael, "The Impartial Spectator," in Andrew S. Skinner and Thomas Wilson, eds., *Essays on Adam Smith*, 86–94; Arthur O. Lovejoy, *Reflections on Human Nature*, 247–264; and Joseph Cropsey, *Polity and Economy: An Interpretation of the Principles of Adam Smith*, 18–19.

6. "Of the Balance of Power," in Hume, *Essays*, 347–348; "Of the Populousness of Ancient Nations," ibid., 405; "Of Parties in General," ibid., 57–61; "Of the Coalition of Parties," ibid., 484–485.

decent civil and ecclesiastical establishments of the English colonies were, for Smith, "an ever-memorable example at how small an expence three millions of people may not only be governed, but well governed." They also were an indictment of contrasting pretensions and practices, most notably in the Spanish and Portuguese colonies, where both rich and poor suffered the oppressive consequences. A plundering horde of mendicant friars "most carefully" taught the poor "that it is a duty to give, and a very great sin to refuse them their charity"; this licensed, consecrated beggary "is a most grievous tax upon the poor people." The rich, too, were ill instructed. The elaborate ceremonials in those colonies habituated the rich to vanity and expense, thereby perpetuating "the ruinous taxes of private luxury and extravagance."[7] Though vanity (as with the French) might be productive of refinement, tastefulness, and luxury, as well as industry, pride (as with the Spanish) generally produced nothing but laziness, poverty, and ruin.[8] Aristocratic pride, in particular, was singled out by the commercial republicans for censure. Whatever slight sense feudal institutions might once have made, they had become atavisms, sustained by bizarre notions of honor and shame. Family pride, absorption with honor and glory, habitual indulgence of one's fancy for ornament and elegance—all these unfitted one to perceive, let alone tend to, one's "real interest." "Nothing," Smith asserted, "could be more completely absurd" than adhering to a system of entails and, by extension, to the system of thought that made entails seem sensible. Clearly, no mode of thought was less likely to render someone inclined and able to pay "an exact attention to small savings and small gains."[9] In recommending an alternative mode, the commercial republicans thought they were returning to simple reason.

7. Adam Smith, *An Inquiry into the Nature and Causes of the Wealth of Nations,* 541, 742. See Cropsey, *Polity and Economy,* 33–34, on the luxury of benevolence.

8. The distinction between these forms of self-esteem is critical for Montesquieu's analysis, but the reader is left to define them for himself (*Esprit des lois,* bk. XIX, chaps. 9–11, bk. XX, chap. 22). Lovejoy's attempt to impose terminological order on eighteenth-century discussions of the passions (*Reflections on Human Nature,* 87–117) was in the end frustrated by his many authors' "exceedingly variable and confused" usage (p. 129). Here I follow Smith in treating vanity as an individual's ostentatious display undertaken in the hope that others will regard him as more splendid than he really is at the moment, and pride as the self-satisfied and severely independent behavior of one sincerely convinced of his own superiority (*Theory of Moral Sentiments,* 410–421). See the cogent analysis of Smith's doctrine concerning pride in Cropsey, *Polity and Economy,* 49–53.

9. Smith, *Wealth of Nations,* 362–364.

Utility Resplendent

The recommended alternative was what we today call the market model, what Smith called "the natural system of perfect liberty and justice." This way of eliminating a kind of unreason did not presuppose that human beings in general would use their reason more. Far from seconding the proud aspirations of Reason to grasp the whole of society and to direct its complex workings in detail, the commercial republicans counseled humility. They thought human behavior was adequately accounted for by dwelling on the wants by which all are driven—wants that are largely, though not exclusively, physical; wants that are part and parcel of the self-regarding passions; wants that cannot in most cases be satisfied. Butchers and bakers, prelates and professors—all could be understood in more or less the same way. Once the similitude of our passions was recognized (however much the objects of those passions differed in individual cases), our common neediness and vulnerability became apparent. This Hobbesian truth was axiomatic for the commercial republicans. Their reason told them that a surer guide to sane behavior could be found in the operations of a nonrational mechanism, the aggregate of small, anonymous calculations of things immediately known and felt by all. It was more reasonable to rely on the impersonal concourse of buyers and sellers than on the older standard of reasoned governance for proper hints and directions precisely because the market could better reckon with the ordinary passions of ordinary folk. Indeed, where the ancient polity, Christianity, and the feudal aristocracy, each in its own fashion, sought to conceal, deny, or thwart most of the common passions for private gratification and physical comfort, the commercial republic built on those passions. Seen in this light, the market, and the state that secured its preconditions, were impersonal arenas where people could sort out their wants and tend to them.[10] The openness of these institutions to attempts at satisfying all kinds of wants would especially commend them to all kinds of men.

In seeking satisfaction under the new dispensation, an individual needed to be at once warm and cool, impassioned and calculating, driven yet sober. Eschewing brilliance and grandeur, the new-model

10. Ibid., 572, 14, 717; Smith, *Theory of Moral Sentiments,* 487–494, 417; "Of the Dignity or Meanness of Human Nature," in Hume, *Essays,* 87–88; Thomas Hobbes, *Leviathan; or the Matter, Forme and Power of a Commonwealth Ecclesiasticall and Civil,* 6, 98, 138–139.

man of prudence followed a way of life designed to secure for himself a small but continual profit. As Smith noted, he avoided whatever "might too often interfere with the regularity of his temperance, might interrupt the steadiness of his industry, or break in upon the strictness of his frugality." He deferred present ease for greater enjoyment later; he did his duty, but beyond that he minded his own business. He was, in short, a private man whose behavior "commands a certain cold esteem but seems not entitled to any very ardent love or admiration."[11] Notwithstanding these reservations, preoccupation with incremental gains made sense to Smith the political economist. The energies set in motion would bring forth an array of small comforts and conveniences beyond the reach or imagining of serf or savage, relieving miseries once thought fated. As people looked more to their economic interest, that interest would loom larger in their eyes and thoughts. Other concerns would matter less—sometimes because the accumulation of wealth was seen as the key to satisfying all desires, sometimes because a conflicting noneconomic interest (family feeling, attachment to a landed estate) was seen as only sentimental, illusory. It was but a short step from this awakening to the adoption of what Tocqueville called "standards of prudent and conscious mediocrity," the adjustment of production and of products to satisfy ordinary folk's demands for the gratification of their wants. In the end "there is no sovereign will or national prejudice that can fight for long against cheapness."[12]

The implications of all this for how and what people think were not lost on Montesquieu and Smith. But it remained for Tocqueville—with a commercial, if barely industrialized, Jacksonian America before him—to make the full depiction. Wherever he turned, he saw people calculating and weighing and computing. Everything had more or less utility and hence could be hefted and judged with a trader's savvy. Because knowledge was seen to be a source of power, because knowledge paid, people sought it. The market mentality shrugged off that "inconsiderate contempt for practice" typical of aristocratic ages; the *use* to which the discoveries of the mind could be put became the leading question. Tocqueville traced the modern predilection for generalizations to a "lively yet indolent" democratic

11. Smith, *Theory of Moral Sentiments*, 350–353. See also Montesquieu, *Esprit des lois*, bk. XX, chap. 4.

12. Tocqueville, *Democracy in America*, 45–46, 372, 433–434, 591 (I, i, 3; ii, 10; II, i, 11; iii, 17).

ambition: generalizations yielded large returns for very small investments of thought. Among commercial republicans, even religion was brought down to earth: "in the very midst of their zeal one generally sees something so quiet, so methodical, so calculated that it would seem that the head rather than the heart leads them to the foot of the altar." Where the central concern was with utility, there could be little room for the play of the imagination, for poetry; people not only spoke prose but thought prose, all the days of their lives.[13]

Quiet and prosaic though such people might be, they could be passionate, energetic, and willing to run risks. Just as Montesquieu saw these qualities in England, his model commercial republic, so Tocqueville saw them in America, his model commercial republic. Again and again he remarked on "the soaring spirit of enterprise," a product in part of peculiarly American conditions, to be sure, but at a deeper level a natural consequence of the freedom to indulge in "a kind of decent materialism." Restlessness goaded these people on, and the prospect of happiness, like the horizon, beckoned and receded before them. Life itself became a thrilling gamble as greed and ever-changing desires elicited efforts of heroic proportions from unheroic men and women for unheroic objectives.[14]

No sketch of the commercial republic should neglect to stress that, as a model both for a national polity and for the entire trading world, it tended to ignore or transcend the conventional divisions within and among nations. Its eighteenth-century proponents could realistically urge men to consider their larger interdependence without expecting (or even desiring) the neglect of national interest and identity, for commerce, properly understood and reasonably conducted, would serve both man and citizen. Commerce inclined people to consider one another primarily as demanders and suppliers, to consider the world as constituting "but a single state, of which all the [particular] societies are members."[15] Commerce was preeminently traffic in movables, things that have little if any identification with a particular state of the kind real property necessarily has. In what Adam Smith

---

13. Ibid., 405, 424–425, 428–429, 501, 573, 585 (II, i, 3, 9, 10; ii, 9; iii, 11, 15).

14. Montesquieu, *Esprit des lois*, bk. XIX, chap. 27, bk. XX, chap. 4; Tocqueville, *Democracy in America*, 148, 225, 260–262, 319, 504–505, 633, 707 n. X (I, i, 8; ii, 6, 9, 10; II, ii, 11; iii, 24). See also Marvin Meyers, *The Jacksonian Persuasion: Politics and Belief*, 31–41.

15. Montesquieu, *Esprit des lois*, bk. XX, chap. 23. See the interpretation of this attenuation of parochial passions in J. G. A. Pocock, *The Machiavellian Moment: Florentine Political Thought and the Atlantic Republican Tradition*, 492–493.

called "the great mercantile republic," by which he meant all pro-
ducers and traders of movables, the owners and employers of capital
stock were properly citizens of the world and "not necessarily attached to any particular country."[16] What began as a simple recognition of our separate and common needs would end in a complex,
ever-changing interdependence. Even as each labored intently to satisfy his own wants, people would become commercial cousins, cool
fellow citizens of a universal republic.

A More Human Alternative

This was the world—part vision, part fact—that these eighteenth-
century advocates pronounced good. If others were to judge likewise,
they had to understand why the commercial republicans preferred the
market regime; they had to see that, better than any of its predecessors and alternatives, this regime suited human nature because, more
than any of its predecessors and alternatives, it could be realized
taking men as they are.

The contrast with and opposition to the Christian and Greek
worlds could hardly have been greater. In Montesquieu's analysis it
was the Christian Schoolmen, not the commercial practices they condemned, that deserved the label "criminal." In condemning something "naturally permitted or necessary," the doctrinaire and unworldly Scholastics set in train a series of misfortunes, most immediately for the Jews, more generally for Europe. Gradually, however,
princes learned to be more politic; experience taught them that toleration paid. "Happy is it for men to be in a situation in which, while
their passions inspire in them the thought of being wicked, it is,
nevertheless, to their interest not to be." The calculation prompted by
nature or necessity overpowered the passion prompted by religion
and corrected the enthusiastic excesses of those professing it.

For Montesquieu, the reliance of Greek thinkers on virtue as the
support of popular government displayed an equal disregard for how
human beings are. Political thinkers of his own time, in contrast,

---

16. Smith, *Wealth of Nations*, 412, 800; see also 345–346, 395, 858, 880. The
point is nicely illustrated by the political neutrality or indifference of late eighteenth-
century Nantucket whalemen. See the editorial discussion and Jefferson's echoing of
Smith's characterization of merchants in Julian P. Boyd et al., eds., *The Papers of
Thomas Jefferson* XIV:220–221.

"speak to us only of manufacture, commerce, finance, opulence, and even of luxury." This was not a change that Montesquieu regretted. According to the commercial republicans, the ancient polity rested on a distortion of almost every quality of human nature. Nowhere was this seen more clearly than in the case of Sparta. The Spartan's heroic virtue and his indifference to his own well-being were almost perfectly antithetical to the cast of the commercial republican. John Adams's characterization could serve as the verdict of all the commercial republicans: "Separated from the rest of mankind, [the Spartans] lived together, destitute of all business, pleasure, and amusement, but war and politics, pride and ambition; . . . as if fighting and intriguing, and not life and happiness, were the end of man and society. . . . Human nature perished under this frigid system of national and family pride."[17] This attack on Sparta (an extreme case if ever there was one) may be seen as a rejection of that primary reliance on virtue placed not only by the ancients but by later people who drew their inspiration from classical models. Commercial republicans could reject the ancient premises even while admiring some ancient accomplishments.[18] In so doing, some may have been unaware or perplexed, and others torn between zealous wishes and sober doubts, but the foremost of them were, for these purposes, concerned less with the rare excellence of a rare individual than with what might ordinarily be expected of the generality.

Sparta, and the ancient world generally, accomplished astonishing feats, astonishing because they defied "the more natural and usual course of things." For Hume and his fellows, Sparta was a "prodigy," less a model than a freak. The ancient policy of preferring the greatness of the state to the happiness of the subject was "violent"; recurrence to that policy in modern times was "almost impossible." But beyond that, what sense did such a policy make? The sovereign who heeded Hume's counsel would know that "it is his best policy to comply with the common bent of mankind, and give it all the improvements of which it is susceptible. Now, according to the most

17. Montesquieu, *Esprit des lois*, bk. XXI, chap. 20, bk. III, chap. 3; Charles Francis Adams, ed., *The Works of John Adams* IV:554.

18. See the pithy analysis in Gerald Stourzh, *Alexander Hamilton and the Idea of Republican Government*, 63–75; and the extensive documentation in Pocock, *Machiavellian Moment*, chaps. 14–15. Pocock's contention that "the founders of Federalism were not fully aware of the extent to which their thinking involved an abandonment of the paradigm of virtue" (p. 525) stirs a question that cannot be answered while dealing with aggregates.

natural course of things, industry, and arts, and trade, increase the power of the sovereign, as well as the happiness of the subjects." Far from being tempted to deal harshly with his subject to compel him to produce a surplus, the modern sovereign would take care to "furnish him with manufactures and commodities, [so that] he will do it of himself." The sovereign would take to heart Hume's lesson that "our passions are the only causes of labour"; he would appreciate and use the mighty engine of covetousness. And let it even be granted that the ancient policy of infusing each citizen-soldier with a passion for the public good might not be *utterly* futile, for it is at least conceivable that a community might be converted temporarily into a camp of lean and dedicated citizens. "But as these principles [of ancient citizenship] are too disinterested, and too difficult to support, it is requisite to govern men by other passions, and animate them with a spirit of avarice and industry, art and luxury."[19] With less pain—and less nobility—commercial republican principles could lead to a strong, secure polity.

American commercial republicans did not promote this new policy with quite the breezy equanimity of Hume. The groping, hesitation, and even anguish catalogued by Gordon Wood amply document that fact. But neither did the leading Americans reject Hume's premises. In the long run, perhaps, the corruption of the republic was inevitable. Precautions might be taken to postpone that day, but the foundations were not themselves in question.[20] Again, we find in Tocqueville a distillation of what most Americans were not yet able or willing to state for themselves. The generalized expression of the commercial republican view of man and of human association was what Tocqueville called "the doctrine of self-interest properly understood," the fusing of public interest and private profit to the point where "a sort of selfishness makes [the individual] care for the state." The result was a kind of patriotism in no way to be confused with the ardent love of the ancient citizen for his city; it was less a public passion than a private conviction, a conviction arising out of private passions. Each individual would come to recognize his need for involvement with others; he might even learn to temper his selfishness. Whatever

19. "Of Commerce," in Hume, *Essays*, 262–269.
20. Gordon S. Wood, *The Creation of the American Republic, 1776–1787;* Gerald Stourzh, "Die tugendhafte Republik—Montesquieus Begriff der 'vertu' und die Anfaenge der Vereinigten Staaten von Amerika," in *Oesterreich und Europa,* ed. Heinrich Fichtenau and Hermann Peichl, 260–262.

else might be said of this frame of mind, there was no denying that it sustained and was sustained by commercial activity. Even as commerce reminded people of their common needs and made them more like one another and more aware of that likeness, the doctrine of self-interest properly understood taught them simply and plainly to give the dictates of "nature and necessity" their due. Human nature stood stripped of the pretensions that had kept earlier generations from satisfying their natural wants.[21]

Mild Ambitions and Wild Ones

Though some might well prefer the commercial republic because it better suited human beings as they are, they had to look still further. Were the political ills that had beset mankind from time out of mind less likely under the new dispensation? To what extent would the commercial republic ameliorate the self-induced miseries of political life? Its eighteenth-century proponents had high but not excessive hopes that all would live in greater security as more of mankind adopted the market model. They believed that, on the whole, people would find it easier to be less cruel toward one another as they came to care more about their own safety and comfort.

Montesquieu clearly expected this to be the case in relations among the nations: "Commerce cures destructive prejudices"; it "polishes and softens barbaric morals." In making people more aware of both human variety and sameness, commerce made them less provincial and in a sense more humane: "The spirit of commerce unites nations." Driven by their mutual needs, trading partners entered into a symbiosis they could ill afford to wreck by war. They would learn how to subordinate disruptive political interests to those of commerce. Such nations, devoting themselves to a "commerce of economy," had, so to speak, a necessity to be faithful; since their object was gain, not conquest, they would be "pacific from principle."[22]

21. Tocqueville, *Democracy in America*, 85, 217, 481–482, 497–499, 524–525, 602 (I, i, 5; ii, 6; II, ii, 4, 8, 19; iii, 18). Compare Melvin Richter's interpretation in "The Uses of Theory: Tocqueville's Adaptation of Montesquieu," in *Essays in Theory and History: An Approach to the Social Sciences*, ed. Melvin Richter, 95–97.

22. Montesquieu, *Esprit des lois*, bk. XX, chaps. 1, 2, 7, 8. See Thomas L. Pangle, *Montesquieu's Philosophy of Liberalism: A Commentary on "The Spirit of the Laws,"* 203–209; "Of the Jealousy of Trade," in Hume, *Essays*, 338; and the discussion by Paul E. Chamley, "The Conflict between Montesquieu and Hume," in Skinner and Wilson, eds., *Essays on Adam Smith*, 303–304.

American variations on these themes were both more and less sober than the Montesquieuan original. Writing in the nonage of the American nation, Thomas Paine noted with seeming indifference that the preoccupation with commerce "diminishes the spirit both of patriotism and military defence." He could accept this diminution (once the times that tried men's souls were past) because "our plan is commerce," not "setting the world at defiance." For John Jay and Alexander Hamilton, however, a reliance on the presumed pacific genius of commercial republics would be "visionary." If anything, commerce, especially when conducted in the forward American manner, would create its own occasions for aggrandizement and warfare.[23] Thus, according to Hamilton, the proposition that the *people* of a commercial republic, under the influence of the new prevailing modes of thought, had to grow less martial would not, even if true, entail a belief in an end to war. It was more likely that where the business of the people was business, the economic objections to a citizen army would be "conclusive" and war would be left to the professionals. Generally, however, European and American commercial republicans believed that commerce gave promise of influencing international relations for the better. Like Benjamin Rush, they viewed commerce as "the means of uniting the different nations of the world together by the ties of mutual wants and obligations," as an instrument for "humanizing mankind."[24] Hamilton was the outstanding demurrer.

Even greater than these transnational benefits was the anticipated dividend in increased domestic security. For Hume, the simultaneous indulgence and tempering of the passions was almost a matter of course. People would continue to be instructed in "the advantages of human[e] maxims above rigour and severity." Relieved of the distortions imposed by ignorance and superstition, political life would come more and more to wear a human face. "Factions are then less inveterate, revolutions less tragical, authority less severe, and seditions less frequent." Free to pursue happiness as each individual saw it, people would be able to continue to rise above their ancestors'

23. Thomas Paine, "Common Sense," in Philip S. Foner, ed., *The Life and Major Writings of Thomas Paine*, 36, 20; Jacob E. Cooke, ed., *The Federalist*, No. 4, 19–20, No. 6, 31–32, No. 11, 66, hereafter cited as *Federalist*. See Stourzh, *Hamilton and the Idea of Republican Government*, 140–150.

24. *Federalist*, No. 24, 156–157, No. 25, 162, No. 29, 183–184; Benjamin Rush, "Of the Mode of Education Proper in a Republic," in Dagobert D. Runes, ed., *The Selected Writings of Benjamin Rush*, 94.

ferocity and brutishness. Furthermore, the development of commerce and industry drew "authority and consideration to that middling rank of men, who are the best and firmest basis of public liberty." Smith seconded Hume's observation, pronouncing this effect the most important of all those stemming from commerce and manufacturing. Where before mankind had "lived almost in a continual state of war with their neighbours, and of servile dependency upon their superiors," now they increasingly had "order and good government, and, with them, the liberty and security of individuals." The self-regarding actions of a part had led to the gradual elevation of the whole.[25]

The turmoils and revolutions of the seventeenth and eighteenth centuries demonstrated that the monopoly of public service enjoyed by the great could be broken. They also suggested how even the humblest man, by adopting and acting on commercial maxims, might serve himself and thereby the public good.[26] These lessons were not lost on a newly emancipated order of men, whose typical member (in Smith's sketch) was an impatient "man of spirit and ambition, who is depressed by his situation." For him and his kind, escape from the mediocrity of one's station was the first order of business.[27] In principle he would stick at nothing to accomplish this. "He even looks forward with satisfaction to the prospect of foreign war or civil dissension," the attendant confusion and bloodshed creating opportunities for him to cut a figure. In the old regime such a frustrated man would have been ridiculous and might have been dangerous, but in the commercial republic he came into his own—and without having to take to the barricades. For it was above all in the world of commerce and in the polity devoted to commerce that this new man enjoyed a comparative advantage over the conventional aristocrat, over "the man of rank and distinction." The latter "shudders with horror at the thought of any situation which demands the continual and long exertion of patience, industry, fortitude, and application of thought." For the new man, however, such humdrum exertions afforded the likeliest escape from detested obscurity and insignificance.

25. Pangle, *Montesquieu's Philosophy of Liberalism*, 114–117, 125–130, 147–150, 197–199; "Of Refinement in the Arts," in Hume, *Essays*, 280–281, 283–284; Smith, *Wealth of Nations*, 385.

26. Harvey C. Mansfield, Jr., "Party Government and the Settlement of 1688," *American Political Science Review* 58 (1964):933–946, esp. 936, 944–945.

27. See Harold C. Syrett et al., eds., *The Papers of Alexander Hamilton* I:4.

His prudence consisted of a blend of foresight and self-command with a view to private advantage. His road to fame and fortune was straight and narrow; he respected the conventions of society "with an almost religious scrupulosity," of which Smith deemed him a much better example than that frequently set by "men of much more splendid talents and virtues." His virtues, indeed, were closer to the virtues of "the inferior ranks of people" than to those of the great. They were emphatically private virtues. Needless to say, they would have been altogether unfashionable in the reign of Charles II.[28]

Where such burghers were preponderant, civil life took on a distinctive coloration. The private preoccupations, the quiet virtues, the insistent passions of commercial individuals became the core of an entire system of honor. When Tocqueville looked at the Americans more than half a century later, he thought he saw a people who carried the "patient, supple, and insinuating" habits of traders into political life. He was struck by their love of order, regard for conventional morality, distrust of genius, and preference for the practical over the theoretical. He offered what he thought a sufficient explanation: "Violent political passions have little hold on men whose whole thoughts are bent on the pursuit of well-being. Their excitement about small matters makes them calm about great ones."[29] It would not be hard to regard this broad characterization of American life as at best fanciful and tendentious. But any such quick dismissal probably says more about differing understandings of "great" and "small" than about the validity of Tocqueville's explanation.

Whatever else it was, this prosaic, politically cautious people was anything but sluggish. Its tastes and feelings were intense but well channeled. Thus the natural taste for comfort became an all-consuming passion, filling the imaginations and thoughts of all ranks of the people with middling expectations. "It is as hard for vices as for virtues to slip through the net of common standards." Tocqueville saw democratic ambition as "both eager and constant," but generally confined to "coveting small prizes within reach." Self-made men found it hard to shake off the prudent habits of a lifetime: "A mind cannot be gradually enlarged, like a house." Courage and heroism, too, were present, but again with a difference. Trade and navigation

---

28. Smith, *Theory of Moral Sentiments*, 52–53, 167, 188–191, 177–178.
29. Tocqueville, *Democracy in America*, 262–263, 612–613, 617 (I, ii, 9; II, iii, 21).

and colonization were with the Americans a surrogate for war. The ordeals they endured, the dangers they braved, the defeats they shrugged off were astonishing, not least because the coveted laurel was, more often than not, something comparable to being able to "sell tea a farthing cheaper than an English merchant can." From such a man of commerce, who treated all of life "like a game of chance, a time of revolution, or the day of a battle," much was to be expected and little feared.[30]

American experience confirmed Hamilton's observation that "the love of wealth [is] as domineering and enterprising a passion as that of power or glory." But it also showed that the effects of that passion could go beyond avaricious accumulation. John Adams maintained that "there is no people on earth so ambitious as the people of America." Whereas in other lands, he thought, "ambition and all its hopes are extinct," in America, where competition was free, where every office—even the highest—seemed within one's grasp, the ardor for distinction was stimulated and became general. In America "the lowest can aspire as freely as the highest." The farmer and tradesman pursued their dream of happiness as intensely as anyone. Most revealing, however, were the objects of those dreams. "The post of clerk, sergeant, corporal, and even drummer and fifer, is coveted as earnestly as the best gift of major-general." No one was so humble but a passion for distinction was aroused; no object so small but it excited somebody's emulation. In Adams's Arcadian vision the general emulation taking place in a properly constituted, balanced government "makes the common people brave and enterprizing" and, thanks to their ambition, "sober, industrious and frugal. You will find among them some elegance, perhaps, but more solidity; a little pleasure, but a great deal of business."[31] The commercial republicans could, in good conscience, recommend the unleashing of human ambition because they saw how, in the case of the Many (even including most of the traditional Few), that ambition would be tame. Political checks, powerfully supported by new social and economic aspirations, would keep men busy, wary, and safe.

What, though, of the problem posed by the others, those whom James Madison in *The Federalist* noted as "a few aspiring charac-

---

30. Ibid., 502–505, 598, 604–605, 368–370 (II, ii, 10–11; iii, 18, 19; I, ii, 10).
31. *Federalist*, No. 6, 32; John Adams to Josiah Quincy, 18 February 1811, in C. F. Adams, ed., *Works of John Adams* IX:633–634; "Thoughts on Government," in Robert J. Taylor et al., eds., *Papers of John Adams* IV:92.

ters"? A philosopher or statesman concerned with promoting and sustaining a commercial republic had to be mindful of the political threat likely to arise from such individuals. What, Hamilton asked, was to be done about men whose aspirations fell only sometimes within the ordinary system of rewards held out by a republic, men of "irregular ambition" intent on seizing or even creating chances for self-promotion?[32] To this challenge the commercial republicans responded with counsel and modest hopes, but with no sure solution. The limits of the market model were in sight.

John Adams's lifetime of rumination on this theme testifies to its importance—and its intractability. There was, he thought at age twenty-six, no "source of greater Evils, than the Tendency of great Parts and Genius, to imprudent sallies and a Wrong Biass." It was to "the giddy Rashness and Extravagance of the sublimest Minds" that man's bloody and tumultuous past was owed. Popular government, far from being immune, was more vulnerable to this danger than any other form. The proper course to follow was not "the general Method in Use among Persons in Power of treating such spirits." Experience indicated, rather, that "unskilfull and rough Usage" only succeeded in making genius more desperate and troublesome. Treated differently, "with a wise and delicate Management," such minds might be made into "ornaments and Blessings."[33]

Would an example of a beneficient management be Smith's proposal, in *The Wealth of Nations,* for dealing with the "ambitious and high-spirited men" of British America? Smith's premise was that free government could endure, and endure well, only if "the greater part of the leading men, the natural aristocracy of every country," had it within their power to gratify their sense of self-importance. He went on to make a suggestion that seemed to him obvious: Present those colonial worthies with "a new and more dazzling object of ambition"; raise their sights from "piddling for the little prizes" offered by "the paltry raffle of colony faction" to "the great prizes which sometimes come from the wheel of the great state lottery of British politics"; direct their hopes and abilities to the imperial seat of "the great scramble." Smith's was a more politic proposal than those brought forward by successive ministries and privy councils after 1763. But

---

32. *Federalist,* No. 57, 386, No. 59, 402, No. 72, 491–492.
33. L. H. Butterfield et al., eds., *Diary and Autobiography of John Adams* I:221–222.

was it enough? A wearier and less sanguine Adams might doubt that. Among men of spirit, whose private interest could be enlisted chiefly or only through noncommercial appeals, he knew that there were some few—the extreme and practically most important—who insisted on engrossing all the coin of pride. "This . . . is the tribe out of which proceed your patriots and heroes, and most of the great benefactors to mankind." As he confided to his old comrade Benjamin Rush, "there is in some souls a principle of absolute Levity that buoys them irresistably into the Clouds."[34] Just as prudential investments held little charm for the likes of these, so would honors shared with others not satisfy. The threat and the problem remained. Ultimately, the only safeguard against a dangerously overreaching ambition was what Hume called the "watchful *jealousy*" of the people.[35]

Consider this modestly elevated multitude on whom the shapers of the commercial republic placed their hopes. At the end, they soberly expected, ordinary farmers, mechanics, and tradesmen would remain just that—and voters as well—busy with their own affairs, forever preoccupied with the economic side of life and without more vaulting ambition. But that did not exhaust the matter. Though the ordinary work of society remained to be done by ordinary folk, the commercial republic promised these citizens literally a new birth of freedom and invested them with a new sense of self-esteem. For now, as these people collectively and for the first time assumed decisive political and social significance, they found their aspirations raised, their energies stirred and directed, their capacities enlarged.[36] They would

34. Smith, *Wealth of Nations*, 586–588, 898; C. F. Adams, ed., *Works of John Adams* VI:248–249; John Adams to Benjamin Rush, 12 April 1807, in Alexander Biddle, ed., *Old Family Letters: Copied from the Originals . . .*, ser. A, 130.

35. "Of the Liberty of the Press," in Hume, *Essays*, 10–11. This was a common theme in the period under discussion, and one on which many changes were rung. In a class apart, though, is the profound—and profoundly disquieting—discussion in Lincoln's "Young Men's Lyceum Address," 27 January 1838, in Roy P. Basler et al., eds., *The Collected Works of Abraham Lincoln* I:108–115. See the interpretations by Gerald Stourzh, "Alexander Hamilton: The Theory of Empire Building"; Stourzh, *Hamilton and the Idea of Republican Government*, 204–205; and Harry V. Jaffa, *Crisis of the House Divided: An Interpretation of the Issues in the Lincoln–Douglas Debates*, 182–232.

36. In reading the history of the life of "the youngest Son of the youngest Son for 5 Generations back" of an "obscure Family," they would learn how little ashamed he was of having no distinguished ancestry; they would have a vivid demonstration of "how little necessary all origin is to happiness, virtue, or greatness" (Leonard W. Labaree et al., eds., *The Autobiography of Benjamin Franklin*, 46, 50, 137). In the details of this individual's career they might easily glimpse their own career, "the

move forward with confidence, believing that "one Man of tolerable Abilities may work great Changes, and accomplish great Affairs among Mankind" if only he brought the proper method and diligence to his task. They would move forward with no apology to those who might view their concerns as "trifling Matters not worth minding or relating," because a "seemingly low" or trivial matter, when recurring frequently, gained "Weight and Consequence." They would act on the belief that "Human Felicity is produc'd not so much by great Pieces of good Fortune that seldom happen, as by little Advantages that occur every Day." Thus, in promoting their private affairs and tending to their public business, however slight or narrow, they could look forward to physical gratification, enhanced social standing, and the satisfaction of performing an acknowledged public service. Even their notions of what *is* their business grew; they would come to take a selfish interest in the public weal. This, then, was the electorate that, freed of the benighting miseries of the past, might yet be alert enough in their own interests to keep the threatening natural aristocracy in check. Given a properly contrived constitution, they might even employ that aristocracy's talents to advantage.[37]

The commercial republicans were cautiously hopeful that the emancipation promised by their new regime would not be self-destructive. Tocqueville, taking in the scene at a later date and from a different perspective, was somewhat less hopeful. Looking beyond the jarring wishes and fears of Jacksonian America, he thought he saw how a preoccupied electorate might turn into an indifferent crowd, how a "people passionately bent on physical pleasures" might come to regard the exercise of their political rights as "a tiresome inconvenience," a trivial distraction from "the serious business of life." He thought he saw how, with their anxieties fueled by a self-contradictory hedonism, such a people might readily hand over their liberties to whatever able and ambitious man promised them the untroubled enjoyment of their private pursuits. Alternatively, they might slide—quietly, mindlessly—into a bondage altogether new, where "not a person, or a class . . . , but society itself holds the end of the chain." Either way, they would lose their liberty and their very

---

manners and situation of *a rising* people" (ibid., 135). The last two quotations are from a letter by Benjamin Vaughan, 31 January 1783, which Franklin intended to insert in his autobiography.

37. Ibid., 163, 207.

character as human beings and citizens. It was in anticipation of this Tocquevillean nightmare that Rousseau inveighed against those who would rather hire a representative than spare the time to govern themselves, who would rather pay taxes than serve the community with their bodies. Absorbed in their ledgers and accounts, they stood to lose all. "The word 'finance,'" Rousseau wrote, "is slave language; it has no place in the city's lexicon."[38]

Assessing Benefits and Costs

Although the founding fathers of commercial republicanism were neither money grubbers nor philistines nor indifferent citizens, Rousseau's statement could not be farther from their conclusion. Ultimately, commerce commended itself to them because it promised a cure for destructive prejudices and irrational enthusiasms, many of them clerically inspired. Commerce was an engine that would assault and level the remaining outposts of pride in all its forms: family pride, aristocratic pride, pride that concealed from "mankind that they were children of the same father, and members of one great family," pride in "learning" (which Rush distinguished sharply from "useful knowledge"), pride in whatever led people to believe that they could rise above the workaday world. Commerce, like the plain teachings of the Gospels, like useful knowledge, would humble the mind, soften the heart, help bring "the ancient citizen to a level with the men of [only] yesterday," and assimilate all people everywhere to one another.[39] If, in a sense, commerce imposed a ceiling on the aspirations of some, it more significantly also supplied a floor on which most could stand. Commercial men would come at last to regard themselves and their societies as members of a single universal state, a brotherhood of demanders and suppliers.

That this triumph of commerce would entail significant human losses was a foregone conclusion for these commercial republicans. Nonetheless, they were prepared to accept those losses, even as they

38. Meyers, *Jacksonian Persuasion*, 4–23, 92–107; Tocqueville, *Democracy in America*, 503, 508–509, 511–512, 613, 667–668 (II, ii, 10, 13, 14; iii, 21; iv, 6); Rousseau, *Du contrat social*, bk. III, chap. 15.

39. Rush, "Of the Mode of Education," in Runes, ed., *Selected Writings of Rush*, 94; "Observations upon the Study of the Latin and Greek Languages," in Benjamin Rush, *Essays, Literary, Moral and Philosophical*, 43; "Leonidas" [Benjamin Rush], "The Subject of an American Navy," *Pennsylvania Gazette*, 31 July 1782.

sought ways to mitigate them. For Montesquieu, a regime dedicated to commerce partook less of a union of fellow citizens bound together by ties of friendship than of an alliance of contracting parties intent on maximizing their freedom of choice through a confederation of convenience. It was in this character of an alliance that individuals found themselves cut off from one another or, rather, linked to one another principally through a market mechanism. It was a world in which everything had its price—and, accordingly, its sellers and buyers. It is not surprising that the habits of close calculation and "exact justice" appropriate to one kind of activity were extended to all kinds, that political community was replaced by a marketplace of arm's-length transactions.[40]

Smith was even more explicit and detailed than Montesquieu in assessing "the disadvantages of a commercial spirit." He saw it as bringing about a narrowing and demeaning of souls, with the "heroic spirit" being "almost entirely extinguished." As in his discussion of the effects of the division of labor on "the great body of the people," Smith squarely faced the debasement implicit in his scheme of civilization. Whether his proposals for public education would forfend the predicted "mental mutilation," "gross ignorance and stupidity," and corruption of "all the nobler parts of the human character" is not my present question. I note here only that Smith recognized the need that civilized society had for civilized men and women, a kind that his society normally would not nurture.[41]

The American commercial republicans who struggled with this problem sought a solution in some passion or pride that might vie with the love of wealth. For them, America's dedication to commerce was both fitting and frightening. On the one hand, it would take commerce and all the energies it could command to exploit the opportunities offered by the new land.[42] Modern statesmen, such as

40. Montesquieu, *Esprit des lois*, bk. XIX, chap. 27, bk. XX, chap. 2; Aristotle, *Politics*, III.9.1280b6–11. See also Richard Jackson to Benjamin Franklin, 17 June 1755, in Leonard W. Labaree et al., eds., *The Papers of Benjamin Franklin* VI:81.
41. Edwin Cannan, ed., *Lectures on Justice, Police, Revenue and Arms, Delivered at the University of Glasgow by Adam Smith, Reported by a Student in 1763*, 259; Smith, *Wealth of Nations*, 734–740, 744–748. See Cropsey, *Polity and Economy*, 88–95.
42. "We occupy a new country. Our principal business should be to explore and apply its resources, all of which press us to enterprize and haste. Under these circumstances, to spend four or five years in learning two dead languages, is to turn our backs upon a gold mine, in order to amuse ourselves in catching butterflies"; "Observations upon the Study of the Latin and Greek Languages," in Rush, *Essays*, 39.

Hamilton, were mindful of how effectively commerce moved people: "By multiplying the means of gratification, by promoting the introduction and circulation of the precious metals, those darling objects of human avarice and enterprise, . . . [commercial prosperity] serves to vivify and invigorate the channels of industry, and to make them flow with greater activity and copiousness. The assiduous merchant, the laborious husbandman, the active mechanic, and the industrious manufacturer, all orders of men look forward with eager expectation and growing alacrity to this pleasing reward of their toils." Discerning statesmen, such as Adams, also understood how in certain European lands it was in the general interest for the nobility to affect "that kind of pride, which looks down on commerce and manufactures as degrading." Reinforced by "the pompous trumpery of ensigns, armorials, and escutcheons," "the proud frivolities of heraldry," aristocratic prejudice might retard "the whole nation from being entirely delivered up to the spirit of avarice." Though these particular pretensions could only be considered mischievous and ridiculous in America, the need for some countermeasures persisted.[43] For in this respect America was no exception; an unrestrained indulgence in the passion for wealth would lead only to "cowardice, and a selfish, unsocial meanness," "a sordid scramble for money." To save "our bedollared Country" from "the universal Gangrene of avarice," Adams suggested making republican use of the rivals of ambition and pride of birth, thereby employing "one prejudice to counteract another." All this befitted a man who knew something of himself and had hopes for his son. Individuals and indeed families might reasonably cherish qualities that set them apart and above—for example, a deserved reputation for public service in war and peace. In a commercial republic such pretensions would be manageable, even indispensable. The solution, however, remained an uneasy one, and Adams himself wavered between hope and despair for his country.[44]

Benjamin Rush's ambivalence toward commercialism is especially

43. *Federalist*, No. 12, 73–74; C. F. Adams, ed., *Works of John Adams* IV:395. See also John Adams to James Warren, 4 July 1786, in Worthington C. Ford, ed., *Warren–Adams Letters: Being Chiefly a Correspondence among John Adams, Samuel Adams, and James Warren* II:277.

44. C. F. Adams, ed., *Works of John Adams* VI:270–271; Adams to Rush, 20 June 1808, in Biddle, ed., *Old Family Letters*, ser. A, 186–187. See Mercy Warren, *History of the Rise, Progress and Termination of the American Revolution, Interspersed with Biographical, Political and Moral Observations* III:415; and Peter Shaw, *The Character of John Adams*, 198–199, 232–235, 241, 315–316.

revealing. Though he did not think commercial wealth was necessarily fatal to republican liberty, he hastened to add parenthetically, "provided that commerce is not in the souls of men." For commerce, "when pursued closely, sinks the man into a machine." And yet when considering the mode of education proper in a republic, he exalted commerce as right for America and for mankind. However much his taste as a private man was offended by a merchant class who "have little relish for the 'feast of reason and the flow of soul,'" as a public man Rush could only be pleased by the promotion and triumph of the commercial mode of thought. "I consider commerce in a much higher light [than as a means of promoting public prosperity] when I recommend the study of it in republican seminaries. I view it as the best security against the influence of hereditary monopolies of land, and therefore, the surest protection against aristocracy." In this perspective, the costs of commerce could be borne gladly.[45]

The American Terminus

In the beginning, Locke asserted, all the world was America. In the end, Tocqueville predicted, all the world would be American. To speak of America, then, was to speak of human fate, perhaps even of a divine decree. This country's rapid passage from a Lockean state of nature to a Tocquevillean democracy instructively telescoped the creation or emergence of the new man of commerce. The American democrat was the man of the future, an exemplar for humanity. He had adopted habits of mind and action that could not fail to be intelligible and attractive to most people everywhere. So, at any rate, Tocqueville thought, and in this he was not alone. In setting forth the American commercial republican as the new-model man, Tocqueville was simultaneously predicting and prescribing. In each case, however, he was beset by foreseeable certainties and by a sense that "the spirit of man walks through the night."[46] If we draw back from the margin of the providentially predestined circle and confine our spec-

---

45. L. H. Butterfield, ed., *Letters of Benjamin Rush* I:285, 85; "Of the Mode of Education," in Runes, ed., *Selected Writings of Rush*, 94. See also J. E. Crowley, *This Sheba, Self: The Conceptualization of Economic Life in Eighteenth-Century America*, 99, 152. (Rush was quoting from Pope's *Imitations of Horace: Satires*, bk. 2, sat. 1, line 127.)

46. Tocqueville, *Democracy in America*, 677 (II, iv, 8).

ulations to things we can see with our own eyes, the reasons for his prescription emerge clearly enough.

Consider the spectacle of a united people spreading relentlessly over the land, a people who for all their present or future diversities and divisions were made one and kept one by their social state and by their habits, manners, and opinions. Whatever the future might bring, "the great Anglo-American family" would remain kinsmen by virtue of their equality of social condition, their taste for physical well being, and their single-minded enterprise in seeking to gratify that taste. That much, at least, would remain both common and constant; "all else is doubtful, but that is sure." Lifting our gaze above the fortuitous and peculiarly American features of this scene, we can detect what Tocqueville deemed fundamental for all people and all places in the new world aborning. As "the great bond of humanity is drawn tighter," people would become more equal, more comfortable, and more alike in conforming to some middling standard. Much of what set people against people and country against country would loosen its grip; in a sense, all would become votaries at the same shrine. To this extent, the realm of freedom would be constricted. But though we are fated to live our lives as members of the new egalitarian cosmopolitan regime, we are not without choices, choices that tax to the limit our strength, our will, and our art. The province of statesmanship or of political science is preserved with Tocqueville's assurance (at the end of the second volume of *Democracy in America*) that it is up to us "whether equality is to lead to servitude or freedom, knowledge or barbarism, prosperity or wretchedness."[47] It is in the light of that choice that Tocqueville's recommendations are to be understood—a recommendation of the commercial republic and a recommendation of those means consistent with the regime that are most likely to foster freedom, knowledge, and prosperity.

There was much in the commercial republic that Tocqueville found distasteful—its discreet sensualism, the countinghouse character of its politics, the stifling of public spirit by the petty concerns of private life. But beyond the commercial republic, beyond "America," was the alternative—not Greece or Rome, not "China,"[48] but "Russia." The grand and awesome alternatives with which Tocqueville ended *De-*

47. Ibid., 376–378, 678–680, 649 (I, ii, 10; II, iv, 8, 3); cf. ibid., 55 (I, i, 5).
48. A code word for the limp, prosperous barbarism that a civilized people can impose on itself; ibid., 82 n. 50, 431, 512, 605–606 (I, i, 5; II, i, 10; ii, 14; iii, 19).

mocracy in America were prefigured (at the conclusion of the first volume) by the contrast between "Russia" and "America." He insisted that the servitude and centralization of the one were as compatible with egalitarianism as were the freedom and individualism of the other.[49] Indeed, that equality of condition Tocqueville would have us regard as a providential fact, a fated certainty, might more easily be manifest in servitude than in the kind of independence that crumbles into anarchy. If in one sense "Russia" is literally Russia, a harsh, barbarous despotism, an atavism totally apart from the modern egalitarian tendency, in another sense it may be Tocqueville's relevant cautionary example of the vast and terrible power that can be generated by uniformity and concentration. The saving grace of "America," then, and of the commercial republic for which it stands, is the way it "relies on personal interest and gives free scope to the unguided strength and common sense of individuals." "Trade makes men independent of one another and gives them a high idea of their personal importance; it leads them to want to manage their own affairs and teaches them how to succeed therein."[50] But for all its utility, even necessity, commerce may not be sufficient. For though commerce was part of Tocqueville's solution, it also was part of Tocqueville's problem. To counter the forces that press in on modern men and narrow their souls, Tocqueville looked to the commercial men's predisposition to liberty. Yet commerce may also predispose them to acquiesce in a new type of oppression—not the naked personal power of a Muscovite czar, but the gloved and masked impersonal power of a modern "sovereign, whatever its origin or constitution or name." Faced with an alternative that would degrade men into "a flock of timid and hard-working animals," Tocqueville searched for the highest grounds on which he could justify men's "strongest remaining guarantee against themselves."[51]

That search led him to "the doctrine of self-interest as preached in America." Most generally stated, people are more preoccupied with wants they feel than with needs they must reason about. And oddly enough, a system that frees people to try to satisfy their physical wants is more apt than any likely alternative to lead them to see their

49. Consider an analogous kind of equality of conditions that Tocqueville saw as having prevailed in the Roman empire at the time of Christianity's origin; ibid., 411 (II, i, 5).

50. Ibid., 643, 378–379, 612 (II, iv, 1; I, ii, 10; II, iii, 21).

51. Ibid., 666–668, 675, 499 (II, iv, 6, 7; ii, 8).

need for liberty—more apt, that is, if their egoism is enlightened, if each (as with the Americans) "has the sense to sacrifice some of his private interests to save the rest." But where a political system fails to instruct and encourage individuals in this calculated self-restraint and fails to show them that what is right may also be useful, there can be neither freedom nor public peace nor social stability. Where each (as with the Europeans) insists on keeping the lot for himself, he often ends up losing the lot. Tocqueville, like some predecessors of his, could praise and recommend the commercial republican way of life because it can go beyond accommodating itself to our weaknesses. It also invites us to "try to attain that form of greatness and of happiness which is proper to ourselves."[52] Tocqueville, like a successor of his, might well have called this the last, best hope of earth.

52. Ibid., 499, 679 (II, ii, 8; iv, 8).

WORKS CITED

Adams, Charles Francis, ed. *Memoirs of John Quincy Adams, Containing Portions of His Diary from 1795 to 1848.* 12 vols. Philadelphia, 1874–1877.
———. *The Works of John Adams, Second President of the United States, with a Life of the Author, Notes and Illustrations.* 10 vols. Boston, 1850–1856.
Adams, Henry. *History of the United States during the Administrations of Thomas Jefferson and James Madison.* 9 vols. New York, 1889–1892.
———. *John Randolph.* Boston, 1883.
Adams, John Quincy. *The Jubilee of the Constitution.* New York, 1839.
———. *An Oration, Delivered at Plymouth, December 22, 1802, At the Anniversary Commemoration of the First Landing of Our Ancestors at That Place.* Boston, 1802.
Addison, Alexander. *Reports of Cases in the County Courts of the Fifth Circuit . . . of Pennsylvania. And Charges to Grand Juries of those County Courts.* Washington, D.C., 1800.
Appleby, Joyce. "Republicanism in Old and New Contexts." *William and Mary Quarterly,* 3d ser., 43 (1986):20–34.
———. "The Social Origins of American Revolutionary Ideology." *Journal of American History* 64 (1977–1978): 935–958.
Archer, Peter. *The Queen's Courts.* Harmondsworth, England, 1956.
Aristotle. *Politics.*
Bailyn, Bernard. "The Central Themes of the American Revolution: An Interpretation." In *Essays on the American Revolution,* edited by Stephen G. Kurtz and James H. Hutson, 3–31. Chapel Hill, N.C., 1973.
———. *The Ideological Origins of the American Revolution.* Cambridge, Mass., 1967.

Works Cited

_____. *The Origins of American Politics*. New York, 1968.

_____. "Political Experience and Enlightenment Ideas in Eighteenth-Century America." *American Historical Review* 67 (1961–1962):339–351.

Banning, Lance. "Republican Ideology and the Triumph of the Constitution, 1789 to 1793." *William and Mary Quarterly*, 3d ser., 31 (1974):167–188.

Barbour, James. *Preservation and Civilization of the Indians*. U.S. Congress. House of Representatives. 19th Cong., 1st sess., 1826. H. Doc. 102. Serial 135.

Basler, Roy P., et al., eds. *The Collected Works of Abraham Lincoln*. 9 vols. New Brunswick, N.J., 1953–1955.

Bassett, John S., ed. *The Correspondence of Andrew Jackson*. 7 vols. Washington, D.C., 1926–1935.

Bell, John. *Removal of Indians*. U.S. Congress. House of Representatives. 21st Cong., 1st sess., 1830. H. Rept. 227. Serial 200.

Berkhofer, Robert F., Jr. *Salvation and the Savage: An Analysis of Protestant Missions and American Indian Response, 1787–1862*. Lexington, Ky., 1965.

Berthoff, Rowland. "Independence and Attachment, Virtue and Interest: From Republican Citizen to Free Enterpriser, 1787–1837." In *Uprooted Americans: Essays to Honor Oscar Handlin*, edited by Richard L. Bushman et al., 97–124. Boston, 1979.

Biddle, Alexander, ed. *Old Family Letters: Copied from the Originals for Alexander Biddle*. ser. A. Philadelphia, 1892.

Boyd, Julian P., et al., eds. *The Papers of Thomas Jefferson*. 21 vols. to date. Princeton, N.J., 1950– .

Brown, William Garrott. *The Life of Oliver Ellsworth*. New York, 1905.

Burke, Edmund. *The Works of the Right Honourable Edmund Burke*. 6 vols. Bohn's British Classics. London, 1854–1856.

Burnet, Jacob. *Notes on the Early Settlement of the North-Western Territory*. Cincinnati, Ohio, 1847.

Butterfield, L. H., ed. *Letters of Benjamin Rush*. 2 vols. Princeton, N.J., 1951.

Butterfield, L. H., et al., eds. *Adams Family Correspondence*. 4 vols. to date. Cambridge, Mass., 1963– .

_____. *Diary and Autobiography of John Adams*. 4 vols. Cambridge, Mass., 1961.

Cannan, Edwin, ed. *Lectures on Justice, Police, Revenue and Arms, Delivered at the University of Glasgow by Adam Smith, Reported by a Student in 1763*. Oxford, 1896.

Cappon, Lester J., ed. *The Adams–Jefferson Letters: The Complete Correspondence between Thomas Jefferson and Abigail and John Adams*. 2 vols. Chapel Hill, N.C., 1959.

Carter, Clarence E., ed. *The Territorial Papers of the United States*. 26 vols. Washington, D.C., 1934–1962.

[Cass, Lewis.] "Removal of the Indians." *North American Review* 30 (1830):62–121.

Cass, Lewis, and William Clark. *Report from the Secretary of War . . . on Indian Affairs*. U.S. Congress. Senate. 20th Cong., 2d sess., 1829. S. Doc. 72. Serial 181.

Clark, Walter, ed. *The State Records of North Carolina*, vol. XIII. Winston, N.C., 1896.

Cohen, Felix S. *The Legal Conscience: Selected Papers of Felix S. Cohen*. Edited by Lucy Kramer Cohen. New Haven, Conn., 1960.

Cooke, Jacob E., ed. *The Federalist*. Middletown, Conn., 1961.

Cropsey, Joseph. *Polity and Economy: An Interpretation of the Principles of Adam Smith*. The Hague, 1957.

Crowley, J. E. *This Sheba, Self: The Conceptualization of Economic Life in Eighteenth-Century America*. Johns Hopkins University Studies in Historical and Political Science, 92d ser., no. 2. Baltimore, 1974.

Debates and Proceedings in the Congress of the United States, 1789–1824. 42 vols. Washington, D.C., 1834–1856 (cited as *Annals of Congress*).

Devlin, Sir Patrick. *The Enforcement of Morals*. London, 1965.

Diggins, John Patrick. *The Lost Soul of American Politics: Virtue, Self-Interest, and the Foundations of Liberalism*. New York, 1984.

Drescher, Seymour, ed. *Tocqueville and Beaumont on Social Reform*. New York, 1968.

Eckenrode, Hamilton J. *Separation of Church and State in Virginia: A Study in the Development of the Revolution*. Special report of the Department of Archives and History, Virginia State Library. Richmond, Va., 1910.

Elliot, Jonathan, ed. *The Debates in the Several State Conventions on the Adoption of the Federal Constitution. . . .* 2d ed. 5 vols. Philadelphia, 1888.

Ellis, George E. *The Red Man and the White Man in North America*. Boston, 1882.

Ernst, Joseph. "Ideology and the Political Economy of Revolution." *Canadian Review of American Studies* 4 (1973):137–148.

Evans, Charles. *Report of the Trial of the Hon. Samuel Chase. . . .* Baltimore, 1805.

Farrand, Max, ed. *The Records of the Federal Convention of 1787*. Rev. ed. 4 vols. New Haven, Conn., 1937.

Field, Richard S. *The Provincial Courts of New Jersey, with Sketches of the Bench and Bar*. New Jersey Historical Society *Collections*, vol. III. New York, 1849.

Fitzpatrick, John C., ed. *The Writings of George Washington*. 39 vols. Washington, D.C., 1931–1944.

Works Cited

Flanders, Henry. *The Lives and Times of the Chief Justices of the Supreme Court of the United States.* Rev. ed. 2 vols. New York, 1875.

Fleet, Elizabeth, ed. "Madison's 'Detached Memoranda.'" *William and Mary Quarterly,* 3d ser., 3 (1946):534–568.

Foner, Philip S., ed. *The Life and Major Writings of Thomas Paine.* New York, 1961.

Foote, William Henry. *Sketches of Virginia, Historical and Biographical (First Series).* Philadelphia, 1850.

Force, Peter, comp. *American Archives: Consisting of a Collection of Authentick Records, State Papers, Debates, and Letters and Other Notices of Publick Affairs . . . ,* 4th ser. 6 vols. Washington, D.C., 1837–1846.

Ford, Paul Leicester, ed. *Pamphlets on the Constitution of the United States, Published during Its Discussion by the People, 1787–1788.* Brooklyn, 1888.

———. *The Works of Thomas Jefferson.* Federal ed. 12 vols. New York, 1904–1905.

Ford, Worthington Chauncey, ed. *Warren–Adams Letters: Being Chiefly a Correspondence among John Adams, Samuel Adams, and James Warren.* 2 vols. Massachusetts Historical Society *Collections,* vols. LXXII–LXXIII. Boston, 1917–1925.

Ford, Worthington C., et al., eds. *Journals of the Continental Congress, 1774–1789.* 34 vols. Washington, D.C., 1904–1937.

Frankfurter, Felix, and James M. Landis. *The Business of the Supreme Court.* New York, 1927.

Goebel, Dorothy B. *William Henry Harrison: A Political Biography.* Indianapolis, 1926.

Hand, Learned. *The Bill of Rights.* Cambridge, Mass., 1958.

Hazard, Samuel, ed. *Pennsylvania Archives,* 1st ser. 12 vols. Philadelphia, 1852–1856.

Henderson, H. James. *Party Politics in the Continental Congress.* New York, 1974.

Hening, William Waller, ed. *The Statutes at Large; Being a Collection of All the Laws of Virginia, from the First Session of the Legislature, in the Year 1619.* 13 vols. Richmond, 1809–1823.

Henry, William W. *Patrick Henry: Life, Speeches and Correspondence.* 3 vols. New York, 1891.

Hobbes, Thomas. *Leviathan; or the Matter, Forme and Power of a Commonwealth Ecclesiasticall and Civil.* Edited by Michael Oakeshott. Blackwell's Political Texts. Oxford, [n.d.].

Horsman, Reginald. *Expansion and American Indian Policy, 1783–1812.* East Lansing, Mich., 1967.

Howe, Daniel Walker. "European Sources of Political Ideas in Jeffersonian America." *Reviews in American History* 10, no. 4 (1982):28–44.

Hume, David. *Essays Moral, Political and Literary.* Oxford, 1963.

Hutson, James H. "Country, Court, and Constitution: Antifederalism and the Historians." *William and Mary Quarterly,* 3d ser., 38 (1981):337–368.

Imlay, Gilbert. *A Topographical Description of the Western Territory of North America.* London, 1792.

Innis, Harold A. *The Fur Trade in Canada.* Rev. ed. Toronto, 1956.

Jaffa, Harry V. *Crisis of the House Divided: An Interpretation of the Issues in the Lincoln–Douglas Debates.* Garden City, N.Y., 1959.

Jefferson, Thomas. *Notes on the State of Virginia.* Edited by William Peden. Chapel Hill, N.C., 1954.

———. *Reports of Cases Determined in the General Court of Virginia. From 1730, to 1740; and from 1768, to 1772.* Charlottesville, Va., 1829.

Johnston, Henry P., ed. *The Correspondence and Public Papers of John Jay.* 4 vols. New York, 1890–1893.

Jordan, Winthrop D. *White over Black: American Attitudes toward the Negro, 1550–1812.* Chapel Hill, N.C., 1968.

Kant, Immanuel. *The Philosophy of Law: An Exposition of the Fundamental Principles of Jurisprudence as the Science of Right.* Translated by W. Hastie. Edinburgh, 1887.

Keim, C. Ray. "Primogeniture and Entail in Colonial Virginia." *William and Mary Quarterly,* 3d ser., 25 (1968):545–586.

Kent, James. *Commentaries on American Law.* 1st ed. 4 vols. New York, 1826–1830.

King, Charles R., ed. *The Life and Correspondence of Rufus King.* 6 vols. New York, 1894–1900.

Knopf, Richard C. *Anthony Wayne: A Name in Arms.* Pittsburgh, 1960.

Kroeber, A. L. "Nature of the Land-Holding Group." *Ethnohistory* 2 (1955):303–314.

Labaree, Leonard W., et al., eds. *The Autobiography of Benjamin Franklin.* New Haven, Conn. 1964.

———. *The Papers of Benjamin Franklin.* 24 vols. to date. New Haven, Conn., 1959–

Lemisch, Jesse. "Bailyn Besieged in His Bunker." *Radical History Review* 3 (1976):72–83.

Lincoln, Benjamin. "Letter to Jeremy Belknap, 21 January 1792." In Massachusetts Historical Society *Collections,* 6th ser., 4 (1891):512–517.

———. "Observations on the Indians of North-America." Massachusetts Historical Society *Collections,* 1st ser., 5 (1798):6–12.

Lingley, Charles Ramsdell. *The Transition in Virginia from Colony to Commonwealth.* New York, 1910.

Lipscomb, Andrew A., and Albert E. Bergh, eds. *The Writings of Thomas Jefferson.* 20 vols. Washington, D.C., 1905.

Locke, John. *Two Treatises of Government.* 1689.

Lovejoy, Arthur O. *Reflections on Human Nature.* Baltimore, 1961.

Lowrie, Walter, et al., eds. *American State Papers . . . : Class II, Indian Affairs.* 2 vols. Washington, D.C., 1832–1834.

McCloskey, Robert Green, ed. *The Works of James Wilson.* 2 vols. Cambridge, Mass., 1967.

McRee, Griffith J., ed. *Life and Correspondence of James Iredell.* 2 vols. New York, 1857–1858.

Main, Jackson Turner. *The Antifederalists: Critics of the Constitution, 1781–1788.* Chicago, 1964.

———. "Government by the People: The American Revolution and the Democratization of the Legislatures." *William and Mary Quarterly,* 3d ser., 23 (1966):391–407.

Mansfield, Harvey C., Jr. "Party Government and the Settlement of 1688." *American Political Science Review* 58 (1964):933–946.

———. "Thomas Jefferson." In *American Political Thought: The Philosophic Dimension of American Statesmanship,* edited by Morton J. Frisch and Richard G. Stevens, 23–50. New York, 1971.

———, ed. *Selected Letters of Edmund Burke.* Chicago, 1984.

Marshall, John. "Letter to Joseph Story, 29 October 1828." In Massachusetts Historical Society *Proceedings,* 2d ser., 14 (1900–1901):337–338.

Meriwether, Robert L., et al., eds. *The Papers of John C. Calhoun.* 16 vols. to date. Columbia, S.C., 1959– .

Meyers, Marvin. *The Jacksonian Persuasion: Politics and Belief.* Stanford, Calif., 1957.

Monaghan, Frank. *John Jay.* New York, 1935.

Montesquieu, Charles Louis de Secondat, Baron de. *De l'esprit des lois.* 1748.

Morgan, Edmund S. "The American Indian: Incorrigible Individualist." In *The Mirror of the Indian: An Exhibition of Books and Other Source Materials . . . ,* 5–19. Providence, R.I., 1958.

Morpurgo, J. E. *Their Majesties' Royall Colledge: William and Mary in the Seventeenth and Eighteenth Centuries.* Williamsburg, Va., 1976.

Niles, Hezekiah, ed. *Principles and Acts of the Revolution in America.* New York, 1876.

Noonan, John T., Jr. *Persons and Masks of the Law: Cardozo, Holmes, Jefferson, and Wythe as Makers of the Masks.* New York, 1976.

Pangle, Thomas L. *Montesquieu's Philosophy of Liberalism: A Commentary on "The Spirit of the Laws."* Chicago, 1973.

Plato. *Laws.*

Pocock, J. G. A. *The Machiavellian Moment: Florentine Political Thought and the Atlantic Republican Tradition.* Princeton, N.J., 1975.

———. "*The Machiavellian Moment* Revisited: A Study in History and Ideology." *Journal of Modern History* 53 (1981):49–72.

———. "Political Ideas as Historical Events: Political Philosophers as Historical Actors." In *Political Theory and Political Education,* edited by Melvin Richter, 139–158. Princeton, N.J., 1980.

———. "1776: The Revolution against Parliament." In *Three British Revolutions: 1641, 1688, 1776,* edited by J. G. A. Pocock, 265–288. Princeton, N.J., 1980.

Pound, Roscoe. *The Formative Era of American Law.* Boston, 1938.

———. *Organization of Courts.* Boston, 1940.

Quincy, Josiah, Jr., comp. *Reports of Cases . . . of the Province of Massachusetts Bay, between 1761 and 1772.* Boston, 1865.

Randolph, Edmund. *History of Virginia.* Edited by Arthur H. Shaffer. Charlottesville, Va., 1970.

Register of Debates in Congress, 1824–1837. 14 vols. in 29. Washington, D.C., 1825–1837 (cited as *Congressional Debates*).

Richardson, James D., ed. *A Compilation of the Messages and Papers of the Presidents, 1789–1897.* 10 vols. Washington, D.C., 1896–1899.

Richter, Melvin. "The Uses of Theory: Tocqueville's Adaptation of Montesquieu." In *Essays in Theory and History: An Approach to the Social Sciences,* edited by Melvin Richter, 74–102. Cambridge, Mass., 1970.

Rousseau, Jean-Jacques. *Du contrat social.* 1762.

Runes, Dagobert D., ed. *The Selected Writings of Benjamin Rush.* New York, 1947.

Rush, Benjamin. *Essays, Literary, Moral and Philosophical.* 2d ed. Philadelphia, 1806.

[Rush, Benjamin.] "Leonidas." "The Subject of an American Navy." *Pennsylvania Gazette,* 31 July 1782.

Rutland, Robert A., ed. *The Papers of George Mason, 1725–1792.* 3 vols. Chapel Hill, N.C., 1970.

Schmitt, Gary J., and Robert H. Webking. "Revolutionaries, Antifederalists, and Federalists: Comments on Gordon Wood's Understanding of the American Founding." *Political Science Reviewer* 9 (1979):195–229.

Schouler, James. *Constitutional Studies, State and Federal.* New York, 1904.

Shalhope, Robert E. "Republicanism and Early American Historiography." *William and Mary Quarterly,* 3d ser., 39 (1982):334–356.

———. "Thomas Jefferson's Republicanism and Antebellum Southern Thought." *Journal of Southern History* 42 (1976):529–556.

Shaw, Peter. *The Character of John Adams.* Chapel Hill, N.C., 1976.

Skinner, Andrew S., and Thomas Wilson, eds. *Essays on Adam Smith.* Oxford, 1975.

Skinner, Quentin. "Hermeneutics and the Role of History." *New Literary History* 7 (1975):209–232.

———. "The Limits of Historical Explanations." *Philosophy* 41 (1966):199–215.

———. "Meaning and Understanding in the History of Ideas." *History and Theory* 8 (1969):3–53.

Works Cited

_____. "Motives, Intentions and the Interpretation of Texts." *New Literary History* 3 (1972):393–408.

_____. "Some Problems in the Analysis of Political Thought and Action." *Political Theory* 2 (1974):277–303.

Smith, Adam. *An Inquiry into the Nature and Causes of the Wealth of Nations.* Edited by Edwin Cannan. Modern Library. New York, 1937.

_____. *The Theory of Moral Sentiments.* Indianapolis, 1976.

Smith, William H., ed. *The St. Clair Papers: The Life and Public Services of Arthur St. Clair.* 2 vols. Cincinnati, Ohio, 1882.

Storing, Herbert J. "The School of Slavery: A Reconsideration of Booker T. Washington." In *100 Years of Emancipation,* edited by Robert A. Goldwin, 47–79. Chicago, 1964.

_____, ed. *The Complete Anti-Federalist.* 7 vols. Chicago, 1981.

Story, Joseph. *Commentaries on the Constitution of the United States.* 1st ed. 3 vols. Boston, 1833.

_____. *The Miscellaneous Writings, Literary, Critical, Juridical, and Political, of Joseph Story, LL.D., Now First Collected.* Boston, 1835.

Stourzh, Gerald. *Alexander Hamilton and the Idea of Republican Government.* Stanford, Calif., 1970.

_____. "Alexander Hamilton: The Theory of Empire Building." Paper presented at the annual meeting of the American Historical Association, New York, 30 December 1957.

_____. "Die tugendhafte Republik—Montesquieus Begriff der 'vertu' und die Anfaenge der Vereinigten Staaten von Amerika." In *Oesterreich und Europa,* edited by Heinrich Fichtenau and Hermann Peichl, 247–267. Graz, Austria, 1965.

Syrett, Harold C., et al., eds. *The Papers of Alexander Hamilton.* 26 vols. New York, 1961–1979.

Tarcov, Nathan. "Quentin Skinner's Method and Machiavelli's *Prince.*" *Ethics* 92 (1982):692–709.

Taylor, Robert J., et al., eds. *Papers of John Adams.* 6 vols. to date. Cambridge, Mass., 1977– .

Thom, William Taylor. *The Struggle for Religious Freedom in Virginia: The Baptists.* Johns Hopkins University Studies in Historical and Political Science, 18th ser., nos. 10–12. Baltimore, 1900.

Thoreau, Henry D. *A Week on the Concord and Merrimack Rivers.* Boston, 1961.

Tocqueville, Alexis de. *Democracy in America.* Translated by George Lawrence. New York, 1966.

_____. *Journey to America.* Translated by George Lawrence. New Haven, Conn., 1959.

_____. *Oeuvres complètes.* Edited by J.-P. Mayer. 10 vols. in 16 pts. to date. Paris, 1951– . Vol. IX, *Correspondance d'Alexis de Tocqueville et d'Arthur de Gobineau,* edited by Maurice Degros, 1959.

Tucker, St. George, ed. *Blackstone's Commentaries: With Notes of Reference, to the Constitution and Laws, of the Federal Government of the United States; and of the Commonwealth of Virginia.* 5 vols. Philadelphia, 1803.

Van Every, Dale. *Disinherited: The Lost Birthright of the American Indian.* New York, 1966.

Van Santvoord, George. *Sketches of the Lives and Judicial Services of the Chief-Justices of the Supreme Court of the United States.* New York, 1854.

Vattel, Emmerich de. *Le droit des gens.* 1758.

Vaughan, Alden T. *New England Frontier: Puritans and Indians, 1620–1675.* Boston, 1965.

Warren, Charles. "New Light on the History of the Federal Judiciary Act of 1789." *Harvard Law Review* 37 (1923):49–132.

———. *The Supreme Court in United States History.* 3 vols. Boston, 1923.

Warren, Mercy. *History of the Rise, Progress and Termination of the American Revolution, Interspersed with Biographical, Political and Moral Observations.* 3 vols. Boston, 1804.

Webster, William Clarence. "A Comparative Study of the State Constitutions of the American Revolution." American Academy of Political and Social Science *Annals* 9 (1897):380–420.

Wharton, Francis. *State Trials of the United States during the Administrations of Washington and Adams.* Philadelphia, 1849.

Wheeler, Russell. "The Extrajudicial Activities of the Early Supreme Court." In *1973 The Supreme Court Review,* edited by Philip B. Kurland, 123–158. Chicago, 1973.

White, Leonard D. *The Federalists.* New York, 1948.

———. *The Jeffersonians.* New York, 1951.

Williamson, Chilton. *American Suffrage: From Property to Democracy, 1760–1860.* Princeton, N.J., 1960.

Wilson, Douglas L. "Sowerby Revisited: The Unfinished Catalogue of Thomas Jefferson's Library." *William and Mary Quarterly,* 3d ser., 41 (1984):615–628.

Wirt, William. *The Letters of the British Spy.* Reprint ed. Chapel Hill, N.C., 1970.

———. *Sketches of the Life and Character of Patrick Henry.* 3d ed. Philadelphia, 1818.

Wise, Jennings C. *The Red Man in the New World Drama.* Washington, D.C., 1931.

Wood, Gordon S. "Conspiracy and the Paranoid Style: Causality and Deceit in the Eighteenth Century." *William and Mary Quarterly,* 3d ser., 39 (1982):401–441.

———. *The Creation of the American Republic, 1776–1787.* Chapel Hill, N.C., 1969.

Works Cited

———. "The Democratization of Mind in the American Revolution." In *The Moral Foundations of the American Republic,* edited by Robert H. Horwitz, 102–128. Charlottesville, Va., 1977.

———. "Intellectual History and the Social Sciences." In *New Directions in American Intellectual History,* edited by John Higham and Paul K. Conkin, 27–41. Baltimore, 1979.

———. "Rhetoric and Reality in the American Revolution." *William and Mary Quarterly,* 3d ser., 23 (1966):3–32.

Wright, Louis B., and Julia H. Macleod. "William Eaton, Timothy Pickering, and Indian Policy." *Huntington Library Quarterly* 9 (1946):387–400.

Young, Mary Elizabeth. *Redskins, Ruffleshirts, and Rednecks: Indian Allotments in Alabama and Mississippi, 1830–1860.* Norman, Okla., 1961.

Younger, Richard D. *The People's Panel: The Grand Jury in the United States, 1634–1941.* Providence, R.I., 1963.

INDEX

Adams, Henry, 110n., 168n.43, 170
Adams, John
  on ambition, 21, 23, 25, 211–213, 217
  "Dissertation on the Canon and the
    Feudal Law," 22–24
  on education, 23–26
  historians' views, 6, 8, 18–20
  on pride, 29, 217
  republicanism of, 21–29, 33–34, 37–
    38
  on Sparta, 205
  on spirit of commerce, 27, 195, 217
  on vices, 21–23, 27–28
Adams, John Quincy, 66n.10, 134–135
  and Indian removal, 145n.6, 154, 160,
    165, 172–173
Addison, Alexander, 96n.9, 97
Addison, Joseph, 49
al-Farabi, Abu Nasr, 6
Ambition
  Hamilton on, 212
  John Adams on, 21, 23, 25, 211–213,
    217
  Madison on, 211–212
  Smith on, 209–212
  Tocqueville on, 210–211
America as example, 98–99, 185, 218–
  221
American Philosophical Society, 42
American Revolution, language of, 6–9,
  111
Anglican church, 61, 77, 83
Anglo-Americans, 176–177, 185–186,

196. *See also* Northerners, character
  of; Southerners, character of;
  Yankees
Anti-Federalists, 16–17, 101, 116,
  125n.47
Antilles, abolition in, 187n.
Appleby, Joyce, 13
Aratus, 131, 134
Aristocracy, 113n., 183
  feudal, 149–150, 200
  natural, 71, 79–80, 212, 214
Ashe, Samuel, 95–96

Bailyn, Bernard, 3, 6–9, 12–15
Banning, Lance, 8, 13, 16–17
Barbour, James, 160, 162, 164, 171
Bayard, James A., 145n.6
Beccaria, Cesare Bonesana, Marchese di,
  74
Bell, John, 161
Berthoff, Rowland, 7
Blacks, 163–164
  effects of slavery on, 166, 180–182,
    186, 188–189, 191
  See also Slavery
Blackstone, Sir William, 75
Boyd, Julian P., 67n.10, 74, 80n.
Boyle, Robert, 84
Braddock, Edward, 43, 57
British America, 32, 199–200, 212
Browne, John, 54
Buffon, Georges-Louis Le Clerc, Comte
  de, 51, 166

[233]

Index

Index

Library of Congress Cataloging-in-Publication Data

Lerner, Ralph.
  The thinking revolutionary.

  Bibliography: p.
  Includes index.
  1. Political science—United States—History. 2. United States—Politics and
government—1789–1815. I. Title.
JA84.U5L39 1987   973.4   87-5287
ISBN 0-8014-2007-5 (alk. paper)